JAN FOULKE'S
GUIDE TO DOLLS

JAN FOULKE'S GUIDE TO DOLLS

Photographs by Howard Foulke

A Definitive Identification and Price Guide

Bangzoom Publishers
(A Division of Bangzoom Software, Inc.)
14 Storrs Avenue
Braintree, MA 02184
www.bangzoom.com

Front Cover Photograph by Howard Foulke.
Cover – 18in (46cm) A 9 T *bébé*. For additional information, see page 183.
Kay Jensen Antique Dolls.
Title Page – 15in (38cm) Bing cloth pair of dolls, all original. For additional
information, see page 131. *Howard & Jan Foulke.*
Back Cover – 18in (46cm) Huret child, wood body. For additional information,
see page 45. *James D. Julia, Inc.*

The prices given within this book are intended as guides rather than arbitrarily set prices. They are recorded as accurately as possible, but in the case of errors – typographical, clerical or otherwise – the author and the publisher assume neither liability nor responsibility for any loss incurred by users of this book.

Jim Kelley – Publisher
Leatrice Sherry – Design Director
Sharen Forsyth – Operations Manager
Chuck Barnard – Sales and Service Manager

Library of Congress Control Number: 2006906322

Printed in the United States of America

10 9 8 7 6 5 4 3 2 1

Table of Contents

Table of Contents (continued)

About This Book

Welcome to the fun and exciting world of doll collecting! This is a hobby that grabs you and won't let you go. It is a thrilling chase for that one special doll which you just know is out there, waiting for you to find it. It is the satisfaction of studying and learning as much as possible about the history and characteristics of your favorite dolls. It is the contented feeling you get looking in your doll cabinet. It is the happiness of getting a doll to look "just so." It is a worldwide network of interesting people, all banded together by the love of dolls. It is the relief you feel to find out that there are other collectors out there like you, people who also love dolls. You are not alone. You are not the only one who arranges your calendar around doll events, conventions and shows. You are hooked on dolls, and you are in good company!

10in (25cm) French celluloid Asian baby, all original. For additional information, see page 66. *Howard & Jan Foulke.*

Dolls still give me a thrill, and I have been in the doll world for over 33 years, as author of 16 volumes of the *Blue Book of Dolls & Values*® and 10 other books on dolls and doll collecting. I am also a collector of antique dolls, primarily all-bisques, as well as a dealer with an active web site (www.janfoulke.com), internet sales through eBay, displays at several East Coast shows and at the United Federation of Doll Collectors national salesroom. I also appraise doll collections as well as individual dolls, and advise estates and collectors on the sales of their doll collections. My price guides and books have been filling the needs of doll lovers, collectors, dealers, appraisers and estate executors for over 30 years. This new price guide is another link in this long chain.

Whether you are new to dolls, or an old hand at them, this book was written for you. It can help you identify, learn more about, and appraise the dolls that you already own. And, it can guide you in choosing future additions to your collection by providing information and suggesting a range of prices to pay for thousands of dolls. It puts a great amount of knowledge, in a well-organized easy-to-use format, right at your fingertips. This guide will be helpful in building your doll collection, and best of all, you can take it with you when you go out "dolling" because it will fit right into your handbag.

For your convenience in locating a doll more quickly, this book is divided into two sections: *Antique & Vintage Dolls* and *Modern & Collectible Dolls*. Generally, the dolls in the *Antique Section* are the older dolls made from wood, wax, papier-mâché, china, bisque and cloth. Most of the dolls in the *Modern Section* are newer dolls made of composition, cloth, hard plastic and vinyl; although there is some unavoidable overlapping with companies, such as Louis Amberg and Georgene Averill, and it was a hard call to decide in which section to list them. Where certain dolls, such as *Raggedy Ann* and *Kewpie*, were made over very long time periods, the modern examples are included with the main entry in the *Antique Section* in order to keep the whole production history of a doll in one place. An

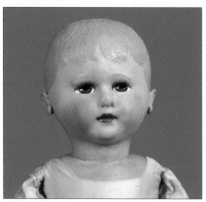

24in (61cm) Chase cloth doll. For additional information, see page 68 *Howard & Jan Foulke.*

extensive index of doll names and manufacturers and an index of mold numbers of bisque and china heads are included at the back of the book to help you find dolls more quickly. For your information, we have also included a *Bibliography* of suggested books for in-depth study and a *Glossary* of doll terms.

Within their sections, dolls are listed alphabetically by maker, material or trade name. For the most part, dolls are arranged in chronological order by date within a main entry, earlier dolls coming first. For each doll, we have included historical information, a physical description, a general comment, marks and labels, and the retail selling price. Photographs are shown for as many dolls as possible, but since every doll cannot be shown in one volume, you should consult other editions of my books for additional photographs of specific dolls or mold numbers. The sizes of the dolls used in the book are chosen at random, so you shouldn't assume that the dolls are made only in the sizes listed. If we do not list your doll's size, just use a little common sense to interpolate a price.

To arrive at a suggested retail price for each doll, I gathered prices from antique shops and shows, auctions, internet sales, doll shops and shows, dealers' web sites, advertisements in collectors' periodicals, lists from doll dealers and purchases and sales reported by both dealers and collectors. This information, along with our own valuations and judgments, was computed into the range of prices shown in this book. For some of the rarer antique and vintage dolls, there were very few price samples available, so we marked these accordingly.

The price range for a doll listed in this book is the retail value of the doll in the condition as noted in the description, if purchased from a dealer. Fine examples, especially those that are all original or boxed with original tags or never played with, can bring a premium of at least 50 percent more than the prices quoted. Sometimes one particular example will bring a very high price because of its visual appeal or "presence," but it's just not possible to factor this aspect into a price guide.

19in (48cm) *Bébé Schmitt* with cup and saucer neck, incised Bte SGDG. For additional information, see page 165. *Kay Jensen Antique Dolls.*

All prices given in this book for antique and vintage dolls are for those of good quality and condition, but showing some normal wear and aging. Dolls should be appropriately dressed in old clothing or new clothing made from old fabrics. They should have vintage human hair or mohair wigs or appropriate new wigs, no synthetics. Bisque or china heads should not be cracked, broken or repaired, but may have slight manufacturing imperfections, such as light speckling, surface lines, or darkened mold lines. Bodies may have repairs, but should be old and appropriate to the head. An antique doll with its original old dress, shoes and wig will generally be valued 25 to 50 percent higher than the quoted prices.

All prices given in this book for composition dolls are for those in overall good to excellent condition with original hair and clothing, unless noted otherwise. Composition may be slightly crazed, but should be colorful. Hard plastic and vinyl dolls must be perfect with hair in its original set, crisp original clothes, and no mildew or odor. A never-played-with doll in original box with labels will bring a premium price.

18in (46cm) 1850s china with long curls, so-called Sophia Smith. For additional information, see page 71.
Kay Jensen Antique Dolls.

Remember that we don't set these prices, we just report them. The prices are set by the marketplace. The harder a particular doll is to find, the higher its price will be. As long as the demand for certain antique and collectible dolls remains high, prices will hold or rise. When the demand goes down, prices fall. It is simply the old "supply and demand" axiom. This explains the higher prices of less common dolls, such as the early French *bébés*, rare German character children, early china head and papier-mâché dolls, and certain Madame Alexander dolls that were made in very small numbers. Dolls that are fairly common, such as the German dolly faces and character babies, vinyl Madame Alexander dolls and 1990s collectible Barbie dolls, are easier to find so sell for lower prices. Of course, there are a few types of rare dolls, such as rubber heads or American metal heads, which do not bring high prices because there is little demand for these types of dolls; very few collectors are looking for them.

When you use this book, please keep in mind that no price guide is the final word about a doll. It is only an aid to you in purchasing and evaluating a doll. It's your money, it's your collection, and it's your heart. So, ultimately, you are the only one who can decide what the doll is worth to you. Also, please remember that no book can take the place of actual field experience. Before you buy, do a lot of looking. Ask lots of questions. You will find most dealers and collectors are more than happy to talk about their dolls and would be pleased to share their information. If you are online, the internet provides a wonderful opportunity for interacting with other collectors in chat areas dedicated to doll collecting. And so, bring on the dolls!

Happy Dolling!
Jan Foulke
August 2006

3

Acknowledgements

Many heartfelt thanks go to the following friends, doll collectors, and dealers who allowed us to photograph their dolls or provided information for this book: Kay Jensen, Rosemary Kanizer, Gloria & Mike Duddlesten, James Julia, Connie & Jay Lowe, Connie Blain, Gidget Donnelly, Yvonne Baird, Mary Barnes Kelley, Richard Saxman, Diane Costa, Nancy Smith, Linda Kellerman, John Clendenien, Carole Stoessel Zvonar, Bart Boeckmans, Ruth Covington West, Pat Vaillancourt, Esther Schwartz, Elba Buehler, Jean Grout, Rosalie Whyle, Kathy & Terri's Dolls, Mary Jane's Dolls, Sidney Jeffrey, Kathy Kiefer, Rosemary Dent, Doodlebug Dolls, George & Kathleen Bassett, Norman & June Verro, Annelise Norhudi, and Nancy Miller at letsplaydolls.com.

Special thanks to Jim Kelley at Bangzoom Publishers who made it all possible, and his staff who put it together and made it look great!

Jan Foulke
August 2006

17in (43cm) American Character *Sweet Sue Walker*, all original. For additional information, see page 213.
Kathy & Terri's Dolls.

Collecting Dolls

Doll collecting is a fun hobby, and finding a special doll to add to your collection is the most exciting part, but making that final decision about whether it is the right doll and what to pay for it, can sometimes be rather daunting. So here are a few basic tips, which I've compiled, to help you know what to look for and how to get your money's worth.

My first tip is buy what you love. A doll collection is intensely personal, and it reflects you, your personality, and your likes and dislikes. Every time you look into your doll cabinet, or even walk by it, you should feel a thrill because what's in there makes you feel happy. Don't buy what someone else tells you that you ought to own or add to your collection. Buy what you personally like and enjoy. Probably the thing which most draws you to a specific doll is the face. The appeal of the face is most important to collectors. As you look over shelves and rows of dolls, those which make you smile are the ones with the best face for you. You should pick a doll with your heart, but you shouldn't buy with your heart alone. You also need to consider some other aspects of the doll.

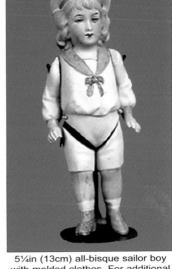

5¼in (13cm) all-bisque sailor boy with molded clothes. For additional information, see page 23. *Howard & Jan Foulke.*

Mark

Look at the mark, as it identifies the doll. Most antique bisque, and some papier-mâché, cloth and china heads, are marked or labeled, as are composition and hard plastic dolls. A marked doll is great because the mark gives you confidence as well as information. It might tell you the maker, trade name, country of origin, style or mold number, and maybe the patent date. Doll marks may be on the back of the head, stamped on the body, on a label sewn into the clothes, or on a hangtag on the doll's wrist. Of course, some dolls are unmarked, but after you have seen quite a few dolls, you begin to notice the individual characteristics that will help you determine whether an antique doll is French or German, whether it is common or unusual, whether it is of fine or average quality. You will also become adept at judging the doll's age. The same is true for composition and hard plastic dolls.

Quality

Always buy the best example of a certain doll that you can find and afford. This always pays in the long run if you ever decide to sell it. Of course, you are buying because you love it, but tastes do change, and someday you may decide that you want to specialize in an entirely different type of doll. With bisque and china heads, there can be a big difference in quality, depending upon the depth of the molding, eye cuts, painting of the features, and detail of the eyes. The molding detail is especially important to examine when purchasing dolls with molded hair, where curls and comb marks are delineated. It is also important in character dolls to show details of the facial expression such as parted lips, dimples, and eye cuts. The quality of the bisque should be smooth, free from a lot of peppering (tiny black specks) or conspicuous firing lines. However, remember that factories sold many heads with small manufacturing defects because they were in the business of producing playthings, not works of art. These small defects, if they do not detract from the beauty of the doll, do not devalue it. It is perfectly acceptable to have light speckling, light surface lines, firing lines in inconspicuous places, darkened mold lines, slightly uneven eyecuts, or a very light cheek or nose rub. The complexion should be subdued and evenly tinted, not harsh and splotchy. The painting of the lips, eyebrows and eyelashes should show artistic skill. When the eyes are painted, look for shading and white dot highlights. On a doll with molded hair, individual brush strokes, especially around the face, give a more realistic look and would be a desirable detail.

If an antique doll has a wig, the hair, if not vintage, should be appropriate to the age of the doll. An antique doll should not have a synthetic wig; it should have a good quality mohair or human hair wig. If an antique doll has glass eyes, they should be antique eyes, not new replacements. New eyes change the whole look of an antique doll and should never be used. The eyes should have a natural eye color and contain some threading in the irises to give them a lifelike appearance.

Condition

Condition is the all-important factor in doll pricing. Examine the head carefully. If it is bisque with an open dome, shining a light inside the head can reveal hairlines and repairs. It is easy to carry a small light in your handbag, but if you are buying from a dealer, always ask if you can light the head or if he would

prefer to do it for you. If a bisque or china head has damages, then of course, it will devalue the doll. Whether or not to buy a damaged head with price adjustment is a very personal decision. Some collectors will not buy anything with damage. Some will buy if they love the face and the doll is priced according to the damage. You have to decide what is right or wrong for you. On the introductory page to the Antique & Vintage Dolls section, I have given a list of how much a specific damage could affect a doll's "book price."

Since antique dolls have been around for quite a while and have probably been played with, you have to assume that there will be some wear and aging. A bisque doll head may have a light nose or cheek rub, small "wig pull," tiny flake on the earring hole, some normal wear and soil on the body, dust in the wig, or light wear and aging on the clothing and shoes. These are expected and would not detract from the value. A china head may have wear on the

16in (41cm) Alexander cloth *David Copperfield*, all original. For additional information, see page 196. *Howard & Jan Foulke.*

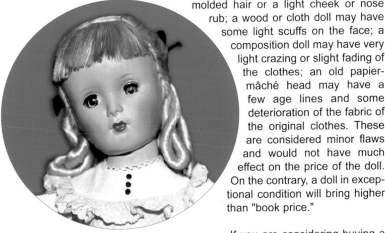

molded hair or a light cheek or nose rub; a wood or cloth doll may have some light scuffs on the face; a composition doll may have very light crazing or slight fading of the clothes; an old papier-mâché head may have a few age lines and some deterioration of the fabric of the original clothes. These are considered minor flaws and would not have much effect on the price of the doll. On the contrary, a doll in exceptional condition will bring higher than "book price."

4in (36cm) Alexander hard plastic *Amy* with loop curls, all original. For additional information, see page 203.
Howard & Jan Foulke.

If you are considering buying a doll that needs a lot of repair, such as restringing or body repair like rebuilding fingers, resetting eyes, reworking joints, take the cost of the repairs into account when deciding on a price. These repairs can add up at the doll hospital, and even if you do your own repairs, you should count your time and materials for them. If a doll needs to have an appropriate wig and clothing, that is an additional expense to consider.

Because their material is so susceptible to the atmosphere, American composition dolls in perfect condition are very seldom found. Even those that weren't played with often might not have been stored properly, which could cause crazing and soiling of clothes. The "book price" for a composition doll is based upon a minimum of crazing, very good complexion color, original uncombed hair in factory set, and original clothes in very good condition (slight fading is acceptable). An unplayed-with doll, all original and boxed, with minimal crazing will bring a premium of at least 50 percent over "book price."

The newer a doll is, the more nearly perfect it must be to bring "book price." So, hard plastic and vinyl dolls must have perfect hair in the original factory set and clothes completely original, fresh and unfaded. Skin tones should be natural with good cheek color. Mildew or a musty odor really devalues the doll. Mildew often makes the complexion color splotchy and is very difficult to get rid of, so avoid it unless you like challenges. Mint collectible dolls never removed from their original boxes will bring a premium of 25 to 50 percent over "book price" unless they are specifically priced as mint-in-box or mint-on-card (MIB or MOC).

Body

Whether the doll is antique or modern, check to make sure that the head and body go together and are correct for each other. As for antique dolls, some companies, such as Kestner, Jumeau, Steiner, and Handwerck, stamped their bodies, so you should always check to be sure those brands have marked bodies. Many dolls are now entering the market from old collections assembled years ago. Some of these contain dolls that were "put together" before there was much information available about correct heads and bodies. If you get a mismatch head and body, you really don't have a complete doll as far as value is concerned, so this is a very important fact to check. You also need to look at all of the body parts to be sure they go with each other. You do not want a body with mixed parts from several makers or periods. Minor damage or repair to an original old body does not affect the value of an antique doll. An original carefully

12in (31cm) cloth Georgene Novelties *Miss America*, all original. For additional information, see page 39.
Howard & Jan Foulke.

repaired or even recovered body is preferable to a new body. Do not pay "book price" for a doll with a new body, because the only value the doll has as an antique is in its head and clothes if they are vintage. A rule of thumb is that an antique head is worth about 40 to 50 percent of the complete doll "book price." A rare head could be worth up to 80 percent. Collectors do not like completely repaired old bodies because it is difficult to tell if the parts are original to each other. A little soil and aging is preferable to a repaint.

As for composition and plastic dolls, they too should be checked to make sure the body and all parts are original to the head. Some of these dolls are now fifty to seventy years old and have been passed around and owned by quite a few different people, so anything could have happened to them along the way. Never assume that everything is ok. Check it out before you buy it.

Clothing and Originality

Since antique fabrics are so fragile and continue to deteriorate as the years go by, it is really difficult to find antique dolls in original clothes. And, if you do find one, you can expect to pay fifty to a hundred percent or more over "book price" for an antique doll with original clothing, shoes and hair. Even faded, somewhat worn or carefully mended original or appropriate old clothes, are preferable to new ones. Some dealers specialize in selling vintage doll clothing and accessories. Good old leather doll shoes can bring $65-85 per pair; a lovely Victorian white-work dress can cost $95. Good old mohair doll wigs can bring from $25 to $250. If you have to replace clothing and cannot find appropriate vintage clothes or if you just like to dress your dolls, you should look for or make clothes that are of the proper style for the age of the doll and are made of fabrics that would have been available when the doll was produced. There are many reference books and catalog reprints that you can consult showing dolls in original clothing. Several commercial companies and many individual entrepreneurs sell appropriate clothes for old dolls. Doll shows and the internet are excellent sources for vintage clothing.

It is often very difficult to determine whether or not an antique doll is totally original — whether the head and body and all other parts of the doll, including wig, eyes and clothes, have always been together. Any part of the doll or its costume could have been changed over the years. Many dolls labeled as "all original" are simply dolls wearing vintage and appropriate clothing, wigs, shoes and stockings. Some dealers and collectors are "embellishing" more expensive dolls by taking original clothing and wigs from cheaper dolls to further enhance the value of the most costly ones. If you are paying for an all-original doll, be sure that it really is as stated.

Group of 5½-9in (14-23cm) German china frozen charlottes. For additional information, see page 84.
Kay Jensen Antique Dolls.

Dolls with trunks of clothing should be inspected carefully to determine whether or not the clothes actually go with the doll, or whether they are simply an assembled wardrobe for the doll. A little common sense goes a long way in deciding whether the clothes are of the proper fit, fabric, style and age for the doll. The same is true for accessories. Pricing is vastly higher for a doll with an original trousseau, easily two to three times "book price." An assembled wardrobe is nice, but it's only worth the value of the clothes individually.

Boxed sets of dolls and accessories need to be examined very closely, as some charming sets of newly assembled old items are being offered as totally original for very, very high prices. Collectors who buy these as genuine are very disappointed when they discover that these are fake sets, even though all of the parts may be vintage. If you buy them, knowing what they are, because you enjoy and love them, that's fine.

Of course, very occasionally, when you can find these ensembles which are genuine, they are the ultimate in doll collecting.

Reproductions

Unfortunately, reproductions are becoming an increasing problem, especially to those who collect all-bisque dolls. Lots of reproductions and fakes are coming to the United States, many of them via the internet, from Germany. They are usually represented as vintage stock coming from the old Hertwig factory, but they are not. They are presented on a card, usually dressed as pairs in sailor outfits, as bunnies, as cook and maid, etc. I have seen several boxed sets of twelve in quite

14in (36cm) Kathe Kruse *Ingebord*, Doll IX with synthetic head, U.S. Zone Germany, all original. For additional information, see page 130.
Howard & Jan Foulke.

13in (33cm) 1850s china with glass eyes and waves framing face. For additional information, see page 71.
Kay Jensen Antique Dolls.

attractive clothes, which, at first look, appear to be vintage clothes, but close examination reveals them simply to have been made by some clever seamstress. Some tiny dolls are presented six on an old cardboard card. These sets are very appealing and cleverly put together, so it's not surprising that collectors are mistaking them for antiques. Another often-seen reproduction is an all-bisque googly, mold number 217. This is the same mold number as a genuine antique Kestner googly, but it has a different face and footwear from the original. I have also seen lots of glass-eyed all-bisque children about 4 inches, as well as all-bisque Heubach children, a Kewpie girl with molded hat, military nodders, a jester, Max & Moritz, snow babies, and a darling wooden cart with a papier-mâché goat and all-bisque children in a box. These items are now turning up at shows and in auctions in the United States as they get disseminated into the general doll market. Unfortunately, we will be haunted with them for a long time to come. So if you do buy small dolls, be wary about them. Once you recognize them, you will have no trouble realizing that they are fakes, so do not let them deter you from collecting the genuine articles. Collectors of Gebruder Heubach character dolls need to be especially careful of reproductions. Even as late as a few years ago, some employees of the old Heubach porcelain factory were still making a few dolls from the old molds. Usually the face color is a little harsher on the newer dolls. It's hard to pinpoint exactly, but you just get a feeling that it is not quite right.

Visual Appeal

Sometimes, particularly at auction, you see a doll bring well over its "book price" simply because of the way it looks. It may not even be in original clothes. Usually, it is because someone had the ability to choose just the right wig, clothes and accessories to enhance the doll's visual appeal. They made it look so good you could describe it only in absolutes -- "sooo cute," or "absolutely adorable," "drop-dead gorgeous," "unbelievably real," or "beyond stunning." But sometimes, though, the visual appeal comes from the face of the doll itself. It may be the way the teeth are put in, the placement of the eyes, the tinting on the face, or the sharpness of the molding. Or it may not be any of those specific things; it may just be what some collectors refer to as the "presence" of the doll — that indefinable quality that makes it the best for you. You can't put a price tag on that. To you, it's worth whatever you want to pay for it.

And finally, my last tip: do your homework. This guide has a lot of information about dolls in addition to prices, but if you are interested in a certain type of doll or manufacturer, you should do additional research on that type of doll. There are many specialized books on the doll market that give information about specific manufacturers or doll periods or types of dolls. I have listed many of the ones that I use most often in the Bibliography at the end of this book. You should also read several doll magazines because often they can often give you the latest and most specific information on your particular interests. And, of course, last but not least important — you should look at as many dolls as possible "in person." Visit museum collections, spend lots of time "just looking" at doll shows, and go to the United Federation of Doll Clubs annual convention, if possible, where you will see rare and wonderful dolls. With all of this help, you will have the knowledge and ability to assemble an outstanding doll collection. Have fun doing it!

24in (61cm) Kammer & Reinhardt child doll.
For additional information, see page 109.
Howard & Jan Foulke.

17in (43cm) Arranbee composition *Nancy Lee*, all original.
For additional information, see page 214.
Howard & Jan Foulke.

Selling Dolls

You may have found a few dolls in your mother's attic and want to sell them because no family members are interested in keeping them, or you may be a collector with a few dolls to sell because your tastes have changed, or you may be the executor of an estate that contains a large doll collection. No matter the situation, you need to know how to go about selling the dolls, so here are a few guidelines to help you out.

Before you can actually offer them for sale, you need to identify your dolls and get an idea of their value. Of course, if you have a whole collection to sell, you might not want to go this individual route, but then again, you might enjoy it. If not, skip right down to the section about dealers and auctions. Each provides a simple way for disposing of a whole collection at once.

Now back to inspecting your dolls. Examine them one by one for any identifying marks, stamps or labels. Look on the back of the head, on the front or back shoulder plate along the bottom edge, on the front and back of the body, even on the bottom of the foot or sole of the shoe. If you are lucky, you will find a name that you can look up in this book. If not, page through the book with your doll in front of you, looking for a similar doll. After you have identified it, check out the prices listed and decide what you might ask for your doll. Keep in mind that as a private person you are probably not going to be able to get the retail or "book price," but it is important to know what the potential value of the doll is.

Next you have to consider the condition, which is vitally important in evaluating a doll, and be very realistic about any flaws. If you have a 1930s composition 18in (46cm) Shirley Temple with combed hair, no clothing, faded face with crazing and a piece off of her nose, do not expect to get the "book price" of $750-800 for her because that price is for an excellent doll, with original clothes, in unplayed-with condition, if purchased from a dealer. Your very used doll is probably worth only $50 because it will have to be purchased by someone who wants to restore it.

21in (53cm) Effanbee composition *Historical Doll*, all original. For additional information, see page 253.
Rosemary Kanizer.

If you have an antique doll with a perfect bisque head, but no wig, no clothes, and the body in pieces (but all there), you can probably expect to get about half of its "book price." If it is a very desirable doll, you might get 75 percent, if you find the right buyer. If your antique doll has a perfect bisque head with original wig, clothing and shoes, you can probably get up to 75 percent of its "book price."

If you are selling a hard plastic 1950s Toni doll, she will have to be in excellent condition with original unfaded clothes, good facial color, and hair in original factory set to bring "book price." If your doll has been played with, has her hair combed, still has her original dress (but it's faded and soiled), and has lost her shoes, you can expect to get 25 to 35 percent of her "book price." As to actually selling the dolls, the easiest place to start is your local newspaper. Check to see if anyone is advertising to purchase dolls; many collectors and dealers do so. If that doesn't work, you can place an ad for your doll. You might also look in the paper for any antique shows in your area. If a dealer has dolls, ask if he might be interested in buying your dolls. Also, you could inquire at antique shops in your area about dealers who specialize in dolls. You will probably get a higher price from a doll specialist than a general antiques dealer because the specialist will be more familiar with the market for a specific doll. You can also check the website of the National Antique Doll Dealers Association at www.nadda.org for someone near you.

Consigning your dolls to an auction is another possibility. If it is a common doll, it will probably do quite well at a local sale. If it is a more rare doll, consider sending it to one of the auction houses that specialize in selling dolls; most of them will accept even one doll if it is a valuable one, and they will probably get the best price for you. Since auctions have really become an important part of doll buying and selling, we have given some more specific tips for auction dealing in the next chapter. You can find an auctioneer specializing in dolls by searching online, reading their ads in the doll magazines that are sold in bookstores or on newsstands, or networking with doll dealers and collectors.

If you are online, you might try selling your dolls on one of the auction services, such as eBay. You will need to have a digital camera or scanner or provide photographs, which are very important to online selling. You should decide on a reserve, a minimum price you will accept, just in case it is a slow auction week. If you decide on this route, it's a good idea to do a search of completed auctions to see what prices dolls like yours are bringing. You can then get an idea of just how to present your doll to its best advantage. If it sells, you will have to pack it carefully for shipping. Wrap it in tissue paper, then bubble wrap and surround it with peanuts in a sturdy cardboard box. If it has a bisque head with glass or sleep eyes, you should stuff the head with tissue paper to protect the eyes from falling out during shipping. Improper packing of the head is the most common cause of shipping damage to antique bisque head dolls.

If you cannot find your doll in this guide, you should consider having it professionally appraised. This will involve your paying a fee to have the doll evaluated. I provide this service, and you can contact me through my web site www.janfoulke.com. For more detailed information about buying and selling dolls, check out my book *Doll Buying and Selling* also available on my web site.

21½in (54cm) Simon & Halbig 749 child on French body.
For additional information, see page 172.
Kay Jensen Antique Dolls.

Selling Dolls at Auction

If you're thinking of selling a valuable doll or an entire collection, auctions can be a very attractive means of marketing, provided that your dolls are offered through a reputable professional auction firm, one experienced in selling dolls. Since auctions are becoming such an important way for collectors to buy and sell dolls, I asked the international auction company of James D. Julia, Inc., of Fairfield, Maine, to provide some guidelines to collectors looking to sell their dolls at auction. James D. Julia has a doll division with knowledgeable doll experts and usually conducts two specialized doll sales each year.

Advantages of Selling at Auction

A professional doll auction company has the same interest you have in selling the dolls, which is to get the greatest price for each item since the company's commission is based on the total amount of the sale. If you have a large collection, an auction allows for the marketing of the entire collection at one time, essentially turning it into cash in a relatively short period of time. A professional doll auction company would have an extensive marketing program, exposing your dolls to a large number of the right clients. Not only would a professional auction company utilize print advertising and produce a quality catalog, they would also maintain a website and offer the dolls on the internet for both left bids and live internet bidding. This will give your dolls maximum worldwide exposure. Auctions can be a professional, convenient, and highly lucrative means of turning your doll or dolls into cash.

Reputation

It's important for a doll auction company to be professional, but it also must have a good reputation. Ask the company for references. Also talk to doll dealers and other doll collectors, and check with the attorney general's office or auction licensing division within the state where the auction house exists. Learn as much as you can about the auction company. The more information you have, the better your experience will likely be.

Expertise

If you're selling valuable dolls, you want to be sure to use a doll auction company that has experts on staff or uses knowledgeable consultants. Some auction houses offer a conservation service. If valuable dolls need restoration before an auction, some houses will make arrangements to have the work done for the consigner.

Marketing

In order for you to get the biggest return from your collection, it's imperative that the auction house have an aggressive marketing program. Ask about where they advertise, how large their ads are, and do they have a mailing list and send out a brochure.

Catalog

Today, more than ever, people buy from their armchair rather than from the auction room. Consequently, a good doll auction catalog is imperative. Be sure the auction house prepares a quality catalog that will take the product to the potential buyer wherever they are in the world. Review several of the auctioneer's catalogs.

Good quality photos will obviously make an impression on the buyer and potentially make you more money. Well-written, informative and detailed descriptions will generate more excitement, greater participation, and more money for you. A guarantee of the description can influence a bidder into spending more money.

Website

The internet has become one of the most significant marketing tools in recent history. A professional auction house will have a well-established site to promote itself and your dolls.

Results

One of the best ways of measuring an auction company is to look at their catalogs and the types of items they've sold. If they frequently sell the types of things you have, and have done reasonably well with them, it's a good indication that they may do well for you.

Auction Contracts

If you enter into an agreement with an auction company, you must be positive you have a well-documented contract. This should cover all of the details you and the auctioneer have agreed upon including the commission structure, and any special terms or marketing agreements. It should have a concise inventory with an estimated value on each of the lots. Make sure the auctioneer is bonded and insured, and ask how you would be compensated in the event of damage or loss of your items.

Commission Rates

Nearly all large auction houses in North America today charge two fees: a seller's commission and a buyer's premium. The auctioneer retains both of these fees. For the seller's commission, some auctioneers have a set firm rate, but others will negotiate the rate, depending upon the quality and value of the doll or collection.

Competitive Quotes

If your doll or collection is a relatively valuable one, you should speak with at least two well-known auction firms to get quotes and insight into how they will market your dolls.

Terms & Conditions

Ask about the auction house's terms for the buyer. Although most auction houses sell lots "as is, where is," a select few give a specific guarantee as to description and condition as given in the catalog. Obviously with such a guarantee, you will probably get more absentee and internet bidding, possibly giving you a greater return.

Participation

Ask how buyers can participate. A professional auction house will offer many ways — phone bidding, absentee bidding, left bids through their web site, live participation via the internet, and inclusion of their catalog on eBay, all in addition to live bidding in the auction room. Obviously, the more ways buyers can bid, the greater will be your return.

Buying Dolls at Auction

Going to a doll auction is a fun and entertaining way to add dolls to your collection. If you haven't gone to one, you really should try it. Auctions are a great meeting place for collectors and dealers to interact with each other, a wonderful place for studying dolls, and a possible opportunity to acquire a bargain. Most collectors and dealers really enjoy the thrill of the auction, but there are some who prefer to buy in a less pressured atmosphere, such as a show or shop. For those collectors who have never attended an auction, I asked the auction firm of James D. Julia to provide some tips especially for first-time auction goers. Even if you are a seasoned auction buyer, you will find these suggestions very helpful.

Before You Go

Find out what the auctioneer has by sending for the catalog or viewing the items on his website. If there are only one or two items in which you are interested, you may wish to call in advance to get some further details about the condition of those items to be sure that they meet your standards. You don't want to travel a great distance for nothing. Look through the catalog and mark the items you are interested in. Read the conditions of the auction, which the auctioneer prints in the catalog. You will want to know what the buyer's premium (the auctioneer's percentage added onto your bid) is so you can take that into account when you bid. Find out how you can pay, whether by cash, check or credit card. Don't forget to pack your flashlight and magnifying glass if you are buying antique dolls.

Conditions of Sale

Read the auctioneer's conditions of sale that he prints in the catalog. This is extremely important. Some auctioneers sell "as-is, where-is" and they seriously mean it. If you buy the lot, pay for it, and then find a crack or discover that it is not as advertised, you still own it. Some auctioneers will offer a guarantee or some kind of limited warranty, or will allow returns under certain circumstances: these could be damage to a bisque head or a repair to a papier-mâché head that wasn't mentioned in the catalog and you didn't notice during the preview, or an item was damaged after you looked at it. Determine these conditions before you bid. This is even more important if you are an absentee buyer, are bidding via telephone or internet, or have left a bid and don't have an opportunity to examine the item in person.

Preview

The dolls will be on display prior to the auction so that you can look at them. Arrive in time to allow yourself plenty of time to examine the items that you have selected from the catalog and would like to purchase. Look at them very critically and carefully, using your flashlight to check the bisque heads and your magnifying glass as well. Check the bodies, too. Make notes in your catalog about the negatives and positives of each item. Allow time to look at any items that are your second choices as consolation prizes if you don't get your original picks. It's easy to focus your attention on only three or four items, and when the price soars far beyond what you're willing to pay, go home empty-handed. You really shouldn't buy apparent bargains that you haven't examined beforehand to determine the condition. It's very tempting to bid on something that seems like it's going cheaply, but there is always the possibility that you won't be happy with it if you haven't looked it over in advance. So do your homework and be prepared!

Determine your Bid Price in Advance

Auctions can be a very impulse-oriented forum. To best ensure that you won't get carried away and pay far more than you wish to, after you finish your previewing, go somewhere quiet to review your notes and the catalog and decide the maximum you will pay for each doll you have marked. Many people write in code so someone can't look over their shoulder and see what they intend to bid. Regardless, make notes for yourself as to what your maximum price will be. Auctions are very fast-paced; most auctioneers sell 65-90 items an hour. Consequently, when your lot comes under the hammer, you may have only 30 or 50 seconds in which to participate, so it's better to be prepared.

During the Sale

Sit as close to the front as possible and pay attention to what is being said. Sometimes an auctioneer will announce a last-minute change in condition from the podium, which can have a major impact on value.

After the Sale

Pay for and pick up your purchase. Examine it one last time to be sure no damage occurred to it after you previewed it. Make sure you have any accessories that go with it, including hat, shoes and socks, etc., that can easily fall off during handling. Leave with a smile on your face!

Antique & Vintage Dolls

Dolls in this section are listed alphabetically by maker, by material, or sometimes by trade name. Dolls are arranged in chronological order by date within a main entry, earliest dolls coming first.

Values given in this section are retail prices for clean dolls of good quality in very good overall condition: no cracks, chips, or repairs to porcelain heads, and with proper antique bodies and appropriate wigs and clothes. Papier-mâché, wood and cloth dolls may have light wear, fading and soil, but must have original paint and proper vintage bodies.

You can use this chart as a guide for assessing how condition can affect the price of an antique doll with a bisque or china head:

Eye flake or neck flakes	less 10-15%
Cheek rubs	less 10-15%
Hairline in back or under wig	less 30-35%
Head broken and glued	less 65-75%
Repair not involving facial features	less 50-60%
Repair involving facial features	less 75%
Repair on shoulder plate	less 35-40%
Body in poor condition	less 35%
Naked, wigless, dirty, unstrung	
Common doll	less 50-65%
Rare doll	less 25-35%
All original body, clothes, shoes, and wig	
in excellent condition	add 50-150%
Especially nice vintage clothes, wig, and shoes	add 25-50%

22in (56cm) Kammer & Reinhardt 115a toddler.
Mary Barnes Kelley Collection.

Alabama

History Ella Smith Doll Co., Roanoke, AL, 1889-1925.

Trademark Alabama Indestructible Doll

Description All cloth, molded face with oil-painted complexion, hair and features, applied ears, tab-jointed shoulders and hips, flat derrière, painted shoes and stockings, appropriate clothes.

Comment Very desirable American dolls, may have some wear and crazing, but must have original paint. A few may be found with bare feet or with wigs. Dolls with molded ears and bobbed hairdo are later examples.

Mark Various stamps on body including	Pat. Nov. 9, 1912 No. 2 ELLA SMITH DOLL CO.

18½in (47cm) *Alabama Indestructible Doll.*
Gloria & Mike Duddlesten.

Early doll, applied ears
12-15in (31-38cm) $1,400-1,600
21-24in (53-61cm) $2,500-3,000
Black, 14-19in (36-48cm) ....$6,600°
Wigged, 24in (61cm) ....$3,000-3,500°

Later doll, molded ears
14-15in (36-38cm) $900-1,000
21-24in (53-61cm) $1,500-1,800
Black, 14-19in (36-48cm) ....$3,000°

°Few price samples available.

Alexandre

History Henri Alexandre, Paris, France, 1888-1892; Tourrel, 1892-1895; Jules Steiner and successors, 1895-1901.
Trademark Bébé Phénix
Description Bébé with perfect bisque socket head, French jointed composition and wood body may show wear, closed mouth, paperweight eyes, appropriate clothes and wig.
Comment H.A. marked dolls are seldom found. Bébé Phénix marked dolls are more readily available; some may have one-piece arms and legs; the face is popular.

H.A. Bébé. 1889-1891.
    17-19in (43-48cm) ....$5,000-5,500°

Mark
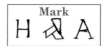

Bébé Phenix. 1889-1900.
    12-14in (31-36cm) $2,800-3,200
    17-18in (43-46cm) $3,400-3,600
    22-23in (56-58cm) $4,000-4,500
    Open mouth, 17-19in (43-48cm) $1,800-2,200

Mark

Bébé Phenix.
James J. Julia, Inc.

All-Bisque Dolls
French and French-type

History Various French and German porcelain factories, Ca. 1880-on.
Description Perfect all-bisque doll with joints at shoulders and hips, slender limbs, swivel neck, glass eyes, mohair wig, closed mouth, molded footwear, original parts, appropriate clothes.
Comment The French name for these small dolls is *Mignonnette*. Those with smiling faces were made by Simon & Halbig for the French trade. Dolls are usually not marked, but may have size numbers. Dolls with bare feet or joints at elbows and knees are rare and very desirable. Dolls with original clothes will be higher. 8-inch and above sizes are very rare with few prices available.
Mark Usually none, sometimes numbers or **BTE**.

Early *Mignonnettes*
Ca. 1880-1900.

5-5½in (13-14cm)	$2,000-2,500
6-6½in (15-16cm)	$2,650-3,250
7½in (19cm)	$4,300
8in (20cm)	$5,000-6,000
9¼in (24cm)	$9,000

Bare feet

5-5½in (13-14cm)	$2,500-2,800
7in (18cm)	$5,000-5,500

Jointed elbows, 5-5½in $5,500-6,000
Molded blue bonnet,
    5in (13cm) at auction $7,700
F.G. face, bare feet
    7in (18cm) $5,000-6,000
    8in (20cm) damage,
       at auction $4,620
Oriental, 5-5½in (13-14cm) $2,000-2,500
Black, 5-5½in (13-14cm) $2,000-2,500
Painted eyes, all original clothes
    4-4½in (10-12cm) $1,000-1,100
    2½in (6cm) blue boots $225-275
Round face, German made for French
trade, original French style clothes,
    4½-5½in (11-14cm) $850-950

5½in (14cm) *Mignonnette*,
all original.
Howard & Jan Foulke.

Later Models
1910-1930.

S.F.B.J., long tan stockings
    6in (15cm) $575-675
J.V., high black boots
    6in (15cm) $450-500
    8½in (22cm) $650-750

8¼in (21cm) *Mignonnette*.
Howard & Jan Foulke.

6½in (17cm) Hetwig & Co. all-bisque boy with molded clothes. *Howard & Jan Foulke.*

7in (18cm) early all-bisque girl with painted eyes, stiff hips and bootines. *Howard & Jan Foulke.*

German

> **History** Various porcelain factories, including Hertwig & Co; Alt, Beck & Gottschalck; J.D. Kestner; Kling; Simon & Halbig; Hertel, Schwab & Co.; Bähr & Proschild; Limbach. Consult the company names for additional all-bisque listings. 1880-on.
>
> **Comment** All-bisque dolls are very hot on the current market. The early models by Kestner and S & H are extremely desirable. See those entries for additional listings. Prices are for perfect dolls with proper matching parts. Always check to be sure the parts are correct. Size numbers, if any, should match. Watch out for reproductions, as they are rampant on the internet.
>
> **Mark** May be incised with Germany, mold and size numbers, or perhaps a paper label stomach.

All-Bisque with molded clothes
1890-1910. Good quality.

3½-4in (9-10cm)	$85-100
5-6in (13-15cm)	$150-175
7in (18cm)	$210-235

All-Bisque Slender Dolls
Ca. 1900-on. Stationary neck, slender arms and legs; glass eyes; molded shoes or boots and stockings; many in regional costumes.

3¾-4in (9-10cm)

Folk costumes	$150-165
School clothes	$200-225
5-6in (13-15cm)	$250-275

5¼in (13cm) 149 all-bisque with
pink stockings.
Howard & Jan Foulke

4½in (11cm) all-bisque with
blue boots.
Howard & Jan Foulke

Swivel neck, 4in (10cm)
 10a or 39/11 ....$225-250
 5½in (14cm) 13a $350-400
Black or Mulatto
 4-4½in (10-12cm) $300-350
 with swivel neck, 5in (13cm) $550
**Round face, swivel neck, two-strap heeled shoes, pegged shoulders
and hips, 4½-5½in (11-14cm)**
 Re-dressed $375-425
 Original clothes $750-850

All-Bisque with painted eyes

1880-1910. Stationary neck, molded and painted shoes and stockings; fine
quality work.
 1¼-1½in (3-4cm) original crocheted clothes $75-95
 1½-2in (4-5cm) $65-75
 4in (10cm) $175-200
 5in (13cm) $200-225
 6-7in (15-18cm) $275-300
 Swivel neck, 4-5in (10-13cm) $250-300
Early style bootines, yellow or blue boots or shirred hose
 4-5in (10-13cm) $225-275
 6-6½in (15-16cm) $375-425
 8in (20cm) $750-850
Long black or brown stockings, tan slippers
 4¼in (11cm) $375
 5in (13cm) $425-450
 6in (15cm) $500-550

All-Bisque with glass eyes

Ca. 1890-1910. Stationary neck, molded and painted shoes and stockings;
fine quality work.
 3in (8cm) $275-325*
 4½-5in (11-13cm) $275-325*

*Allow $50-$150 extra for yellow boots or unusual footwear and/or especially fine quality.

```
6in (15cm) .........................................$325-375*
7in (18cm) .........................................$425-475*
8in (20cm) .........................................$550-600*
9in (23cm) .........................................$750-800*
10in (25cm).........................................$900-1,000*
12in (31cm) ........................................$1200*
```
Early style model, stiff hips, shirred hose or bootines
```
    3in (8cm) .......................................$325-350
    4½in (11cm) ....................................$350-400
    6in (15cm) .....................................$550-575
    7in (18cm) .....................................$750-850
    8-8½in (20-21cm)  ...........................$1,200-1,300
```
Long black or white shoes, tan shoes
```
    5in (13cm) .....................................$575-675
    7½in (19cm) ...................................$900-950
```

All-Bisque with with swivel neck and glass eyes
Ca. 1880-1910. Molded and painted shoes or boots and stockings; fine quality.
```
    3¼in (8cm) .............$350-375**
    4-5in (10-13cm) ........$400-500**
    6in (15cm) ............$600-650**
    7in (18cm) ............$700-750**
    8in (20cm) ...........$950-1,150**
    9in (23cm) .........$1,400-1,500**
    10in (25cm) ..........$1,800-2,000
```
Early Kestner or Simon & Halbig-type
```
    4½-5in (12-13cm) ..$1,900-2,200
    6in (15cm) ............$2,250
    7in (18cm) .......$2,350-2,500
    8in (20cm) .......$2,750-3,000
    9in (23cm) .......$3,250-3,500
    10in (25cm) ......$3,600-3,800
```
With swivel waist, 8in (20cm)
```
at auction ...............$20,000
```
With jointed knees
```
    6in (15cm) at auction ...$4,400
    8½in (22cm) at auction ..$8,225
```
#102 (so-called Wrestler)
```
    5½in (14cm) .....$2,000-2,200
    8½-9in (22-23cm) ..$3,500-4,000
```
#120 (Bru-type face),
```
    8½in (22cm) .....$4,500-5,000°
```
Bare feet
```
    5½-6in (14-15cm) ..$2,400-2,600
    8in (20cm) .......$4,700-5,200
    11in (28cm) ...........$9,000
```
Round face, bootines
```
    6in (15cm) .......$1,500-1,650
    8in (20cm) .......$2,400-2,500
```
Long black stockings, tan slippers, 7½in (19cm) $1,250-1,400
Simon & Halbig 886 and 890 ....See page 172.

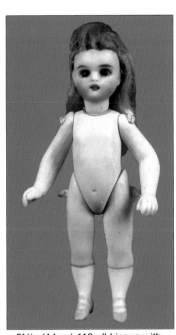

5½in (14cm) 118 all-bisque with glass eyes and swivel neck.
Howard & Jan Foulke

---

*Allow $50-$150 extra for yellow boots or unusual footwear and/or especially fine quality.
**Allow $100-$150 extra for yellow boots or unusual footwear.
°Few price samples available.

25

All-Bisque Baby
Ca. 1900-on. Jointed at shoulders and hips, curved arms and legs; molded hair, painted features.
- 2½-3½in (6-9cm) $75-95
- 4-5in (10-13cm) $125-175
- **Fine early quality, blonde molded hair**
  - 3½-4½in (9-11cm) $160-185
  - 6-7in (15-18cm) $250-300
  - 13in (33cm) $900-1,000
- Immobile, 5-6in (13-15cm) $160-195

All-Bisque Character Baby
Ca. 1910. Jointed at shoulders and hips, curved arms and legs; molded hair, painted eyes; very good quality.
- 3½in (9cm) $85-95
- 4½-5½in (11-14cm) $150-175
- 7in (18cm) $275-300
- 8in (20cm) $350-400
- Molded white shift, 6in (15cm) $300
- Swivel waist, molded suit, 7in (18cm) at auction $2,640
- **#830, #391, and others with glass eyes**
  - 4-5in (10-13cm) $275-325
  - 6in (15cm) $400-450
  - 8in (20cm) $600-650
  - 11in (28cm) $850-950
- **Swivel neck, glass eyes**
  - 6in (15cm) $625-675
  - 8in (20cm) $800-1,000
  - 10in (25cm) $1,000-1,100
- **Swivel neck, painted eyes**
  - 5-6in (13-15cm) $325-375
  - 8in (20cm) $575-625
  - 11in (28cm) $800-900
- Mildred, the Prize Baby, 5in (13cm) $5,000
- Baby Darling #497, 6in (15cm) $850
- **Limbach (clover mark)**
  - 4-5in (10-13cm) $55-85
  - 7in (18cm) $110-135
  - 11-12in (28-31cm) fine quality $550-650

All-Bisque Character Dolls with Glass Eyes
Ca. 1910. Excellent quality with proper parts.
- **#150, 155**
  - 5-6in (13-15cm) $400-500
  - 7in (18cm) $650
  - 8in (20cm) at auction $1,100
- **#156**
  - 5-6in (13-15cm) $400-500
  - 7in (18cm) $750
- #602, swivel neck, 5½-6in (14-15cm) $550-650
- #79, pierced nose, 4½in (12cm) $500-550
- #609, 22, 4½in (12cm) $425-450
- **Orsini girls**
  - Glass eyes, 5in (13cm) $2,800-3,100
  - Glass eyes, 7in (18cm) ....$4,500-5,500°
  - Painted eyes, 5in (13cm) $1,200-1,300

°Few price samples available.

5in (13cm) Limbach all-bisque baby.
Howard & Jan Foulke.

8in (20cm) 156 all-bisque character girl, probably by Kestner.
Howard & Jan Foulke.

2⁷/₈ (7cm) pink bisque character
girl, probably by Hertwig.
Howard & Jan Foulke.

5in (13cm) immobile all-bisque
baby, probably by Kestner.
Howard & Jan Foulke.

#222 Our Fairy, glass eyes,
    5in (13cm) $500-600
    8½in (22cm) $875-900
    11in (28cm) $1,800
  Baby Bud, glass eyes, wig, 7in (18cm) $900-1,000

All-Bisque Character Dolls
1913-on. Painted eyes; all in good condition with proper parts.
  Pink bisque
    2-3in (5-8cm) $45-55
    5in (13cm) $100-110
    Glass eyes, wig, 2¾in (7cm) $85-95
    Girl with molded hair bow loop, 2½in (6cm) $75

Thumbsucker, 3in (8cm) $225-250
Chubby
   4½in (11cm) $210-240
   6in (15cm) $325-375
HEbee, SHEbee
   5in (13cm) $650
   7in (18cm) $850
     Boxed $950
Bunny Tot, Horsman, 6in (15cm)
   at auction $1,650
Peterkin, 5-6in (13-15cm) $275-375
Little Imp, 5in (13cm) $150
Happifats, 4in (10cm) boy
   and girl pair $450-500
Happifats Baby, 3¾in (10cm) .$250-275
Elfie, 4½in (12cm) at auction $825
Wide Awake
   5in (13cm) $200
   11in (28cm) $800-900
Little Annie Rooney, 4in (10cm) . .$300
September Morn, Grace Drayton,
   4in (10cm) $2,500
   7in (18cm) at auction $4,000
Max & Moritz,
   3¾in (9cm) pair $2,000
   4½in (11cm) molded clothes pair $2,500
Cupid or Sister, 5½in (14cm) $80-90
Snowflake (Oscar Hitt), 2½in (6cm) $250
#790, 791, 792, 5½-6in (14-15cm) $450-500
#150, 160, 165,
   3¾in (10cm) $200-225
   5½-6in (14-15cm) $275-300
#168, 4¼in (11cm) $350

4in (10cm) all-bisque SHEbee
with pink shoes and HEbee
with blue shoes.
Howard & Jan Foulke.

Later All-Bisque with painted eyes

Ca. 1920. Many by Limbach (clover mark) and Hertwig & Co.; some of
pretinted bisque; mohair wig or molded hair; molded and painted one-strap
shoes and white stockings; all in good condition, with proper parts.
   3½in (9cm) $55-65
   4½-5in (12-13cm) $95-110
   6in (15cm) $150-160
   7-8in (18-20cm) $200-225

All-Bisque "Flapper" (tinted bisque)

Ca. 1920. Molded bobbed hair with loop for bow, painted features; long yellow
or lavendar stockings, one-strap shoes with heels; all in good condition, with
proper parts, very good quality.
   5in (13cm) $325-350
   6-7in (15-18cm) $450-500
     Glass eyes $600-650
   Standard quality, 4-5in (10-13cm) $135-165

All-Bisque Baby

Ca. 1920. Pink bisque, curved arms and legs; all in good condition, with proper parts.

"Candy Baby" 2½-3in (6-8cm)
Original factory clothes $95-110
Naked $45-50
Two-face, swivel neck, 4in (10cm) $150-175

All-Bisque "Flapper"

Ca. 1920. Pink bisque with molded bobbed hair; original factory clothes; all in good condition, with proper parts.

3in (8cm) $90-100
Molded hat $250
Molded bunny ears cap $350
Aviatrix, flight suit $250-300
Swivel Waist, 3½in (9cm) $350
Wigged, 3½in (9cm) $95-125
Adult, 5¾in (14cm) $250-275

All-Bisque Nodder Characters

1920-on. Many made by Hertwig & Co. Nodding heads, elastic strung, molded clothes; all in good condition.

3-4in (8-10cm) $25-40
Comic characters ....$45 up*
Dressed Animals $150-175
Dressed Teddy Bears $200-225
Santa $200-225
Dutch Girl, 6in (15cm) $150-165

3¼in (8cm) all-bisque flapper girl with molded hat, all original. *Howard & Jan Foulke.*

3½in (9cm) all-bisque *Orphan Annie* nodder with her dog *Sandy*. *Howard & Jan Foulke.*

*Depending on character and rarity.

All-Bisque Immobiles

Ca. 1920. Molded clothes; in good condition.

Adults and children, 1½-2¼in (4-6cm) $25-35
Children, 3¼in (8cm) $55-65
Santa, 3in (8cm) $125-135
Children with animals on string, 3in (8cm) $165-185

Jointed Animals

Ca. 1910-on. All-bisque animals, wire-jointed shoulders and hips; original crocheted clothes; in good condition.

Rabbit, 2-2¾in (5-7cm) $475-525
Bear, 2-2½in (5-6cm) $450-500
Cat, 2in (5cm) $450-500
Frog, Monkey, Pig $600-700
Bear on all fours, 3¼in (8cm) $225-275

5in (13cm) all-bisque Occupied Japan children, all original.
Howard & Jan Foulke.

Made in Japan

History Various Japanese porcelain factories. Ca. 1915-on.
Comment Quality varies widely, so look for the best example. Paint is not usually fired in, so features and color may disappear if washed.
Mark Incised Made in Japan or NIPPON, perhaps a paper label on stomach.

Baby, white, 4in (10cm) $30-33
All-original elaborate outfit $50-65
Two-face, crying and sleeping $150-175
Black, 4-5in (10-13cm) $45-50
Bye-Lo Baby, 6in (15cm) $100-125
Betty Boop-type
4-5in (10-13cm) $15-20
6-7in (15-18cm) $25-30

Black Character Girl, molded hairbow loop, 4½in (12cm) $30
Bride & Groom, boxed set, 4in (10cm) $50
Buster Brown, 2¾in (7cm) $40
Child
    4-5in (10-13cm) $25
    6-7in (15-18cm) $30-35
    5½in (14cm) wigged "Nippon," excellent quality $65-75
    5½in (13cm) Occupied Japan pair, all original $75-95
    With animal on string, 4½in (12cm) $30
    Stiff with molded clothes, 3-4in (8-10cm) $8-12
        Boxed set of five $60
    6-7in (15-18cm) $25
Cho-Cho San, 4½in (12cm) $60
Circus Set, boxed, 11 pieces $150-175
Comic Characters, 3-4in (8-10cm) .... $20 up*
Mickey Mouse $175-225
"Nippon" Characters, 4-5in (10-13cm) $85-95
    JolliKids, 3½in (9cm), pair $175
    Happifats, 3½in (9cm), pair $275
    Girl with molded hat and shoes, 5¼in (13cm) $95
    Kewpie, Rose O'Neill, 3½in (9cm) $45-55
    Soldier, Molded clothes, 4½in (12cm) $195
    Baby in Bath Tub, 2½in (6cm) $55
Nodders, 4in (10cm) $20-25
Old Woman in Shoe, Boxed set $225-250
Orientals, 3-4in (8-10cm) $15-20
Queue San, 4in (10cm) $70-80
Shirley Temple, 5in (13cm) $100-125
Skippy, 5½in (14cm) $95-110
Snow White, boxed set $400-600
Teddy Bear, 3in (8cm) $40-50
Three Bears, boxed set $250-300
Three Little Kittens, Boxed set $350
Three Little Pigs, each $35-40
Wedding Set, Boxed, three pieces, 4½in (13cm) $75-85

Alt, Beck & Gottschalk

History Alt, Beck & Gottschalck porcelain factory, Nauendorf, near Ohrdruf, Thuringia, Germany, 1854-on.

Comment ABG is one of the oldest makers of doll heads, producing them over a long period of time, ranging from china heads of the 1880s to characters of the 1920s. Quality is usually excellent, with some slippage in the later dolls. All prices are for perfect china or bisque heads on appropriate vintage bodies with vintage clothing and wigs.

China Shoulder Heads

Ca. 1880. Black or blonde-haired china head; old cloth body with china limbs. Mold numbers such as 784, 1000, 1008, 1028, 1046, 1142, 1210 and others.

Mark

784 X 6

    16-18in (41-46cm) $250-300
    22-24in (56-61cm) $350-400
    28in (71cm) $500-600

*Depending on rarity.

Bisque Shoulder Heads

Ca. 1880. Molded hair, closed mouth; cloth body with bisque lower limbs. Mold numbers such as 890, 990, 1000, 1008, 1028, 1064, 1142, 1254, 1288, 1304.

Painted eyes

10in (25cm) all original	$250
15-17in (38-43cm)	$300-350*
22-23in (56-58cm)	$425-475*

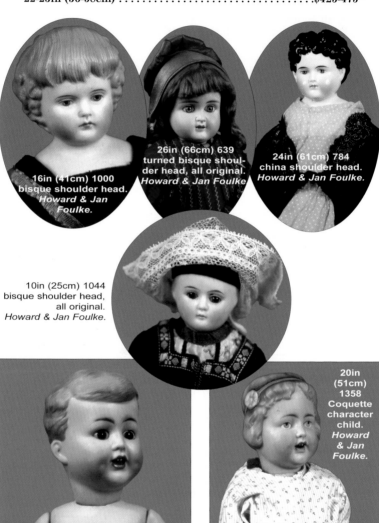

16in (41cm) 1000 bisque shoulder head. *Howard & Jan Foulke.*

26in (66cm) 639 turned bisque shoulder head, all original. *Howard & Jan Foulke*

24in (61cm) 784 china shoulder head. *Howard & Jan Foulke.*

10in (25cm) 1044 bisque shoulder head, all original. *Howard & Jan Foulke.*

12in (30cm) 1357 character child. *Howard & Jan Foulke.*

20in (51cm) 1358 Coquette character child. *Howard & Jan Foulke.*

*Allow extra for unusual or elaborate hairdo or molded hat.

Glass eyes
  9-11in (23-28cm) $275-300*
  14-16in (36-41cm) $375-475*
  22in (56cm) $650-750*
  #990, pink mob cap and #998, white mob cap, 20in (51cm) ...$1,000
  #894, blue scarf, glass eyes, 21in (52cm) $1,500
  #1024, molded orange bonnet, 17½in (44cm) ....$2,100°
  #1022, short blonde curly hair, molded blue hair band,
  molded necklace with orange pendant,
  glass eyes, 22in (56cm) $1,650
  #974, long wavy hair, exposed ears, glass eyes,
  23in (58cm) $1,250
  #996, lavendar and white head scarf, 6in (15cm) head only ..$1,200
  #1288, molded hair, glass eyes, 7½in (19cm) head only $600
  Blue cap, pierced ears, necklace, 17in (43cm) $1,200

Bisque Shoulder Heads

Ca. 1885-on. Turned shoulder head, wig, glass eyes, closed mouth; kid or cloth body. Mold numbers, such as **639, 698, 870, 1032, 1123, 1235.**

Mark

6 9 8 ✖ 9

with "DEP" after 1888.

  17-19in (43-48cm) $350-450
  23-25in (58-64cm) $500-600
  With open mouth
    16-18in (41-46cm) $225-275
    21-23in (53-58cm) $325-375
  #911, 916, swivel neck, closed mouth,
    20-23in (51-58cm) $1,100-1,200
  #912, 21-23in (53-58cm) $1,000-1,100

Child Doll

Perfect bisque head, open mouth; ball-jointed body.
#1362 Sweet Nell

Mark

ABG
1362
Made in Germany
2

  14-16in (36-41cm) $300-350
  19-21in (43-53cm) $375-425
  23-25in (58-64cm) $450-500
  29-30in (74-76cm) $600-700
  36in (91cm) $1,200
  #630, closed mouth, 23in (58cm) $1,900-2,200
  #911, closed mouth, 16in (41cm) $1,500-1,600
  #938, closed mouth, 22in (56cm) ....$3,500-4,000°
  #989, closed mouth, 23in (58cm) ....$4,500°
  #989, open mouth, 15in (38cm) ....$1,850°

All-Bisque Girl

1911. Chubby body, molded white stockings, blue garters, black Mary Janes.
Mold #83 over #100, 125, 150 or 225 Our Darling
  5-6in (13-15cm) $175-225
  7in (18cm) $250-300
  8in (20cm) $425-475

All-Bisque Baby

  8½in (21cm) swivel neck, closed mouth ....$900-1,000°
  #29-14 character baby, glass eyes, swivel neck,
    6in (15cm) ....$650-700°

°Few price samples available.
*Allow extra for unusual or elaborate hairdo or molded hat.

Character

Ca. 1910-on. Some with open nostrils; composition body.

#1322, 1352, 1361

10-12in (25-31cm)	$225-250
16-18in (41-46cm)	$325-375
22-23in (56-58cm)	$500-550

Toddler

8-10in (20-25cm) five-piece body	$750-800
14-16in (36-41cm)	$550-650

#1329, 1321, 17-18in (43-46cm) $1,200-1,500
#1357, 16-18in (41-46cm) $1,000-1,100
#1358, coquette, 20in (51cm) ....$2,200°
#1407 Baby Bo Kaye, 8in (20cm) $1,350
#1431 Orsini, earthenware baby, 24in (61cm) $800-900
#1450, smiling child, 14in (36cm) ....$16,000-$17,000°

Mark

AB
1322
Made in Germany

Louis Amberg & Son

History Louis Amberg & Son, New York, NY, 1907-1929.
Comment Amberg imported German bisque heads and manufactured composition dolls. Prices are for dolls in excellent condition with perfect bisque and appropriate vintage bodies and clothes. Composition dolls should have original clothes, but may have light crazing and wear.

15in (38cm) *Newborn Babe*, marked head and body.
Howard & Jan Foulke.

Newborn Babe, Bottle Babe, My Playmate

Ca. 1914-on. Painted hair, sleep eyes; soft cloth body.
Mold **886** by Recknagel. Mold **371** with open mouth by Marseille.

Length

9-10in (23-25cm)	$200-225
13-14in (33-36cm)	$350
17in (43cm)	$450

Mark

L·A·B·S·
371·3/0 D·R·G·M·
Germany

THE ORIGINAL
NEWBORN BABE
(C) Jan 4th 1914 - No. G 45020
AMBERG DOLLS
The World Standard

°Few price samples available.

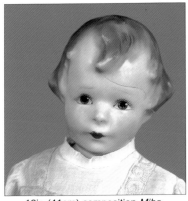

16in (41cm) composition *Mibs*.
Howard & Jan Foulke.

Bisque head *Baby Peggy*.
James D. Julia, Inc.

Charlie Chaplin

1915. Composition portrait head, molded mustache; straw-filled cloth body with composition hands; original clothes; all in good condition with wear. Mark Cloth label on sleeve.

    22in (56cm) $600-650

AmKid

1918. Composition shoulder head, sleep eyes, wig; kidolene body, composition arms.

    22in (56cm) $100-125

Mibs

1921. Composition shoulder head designed by Hazel Drucker with wistful expression, molded blonde or reddish hair; cloth body with composition arms and legs with painted shoes and socks; appropriate old clothes; all in good condition.

> Mark None on doll; paper label only:
> **"Amberg Dolls Please Love Me I'm Mibs"**

    16in (41cm) $850-950

Mibs 1921.

    Bisque shoulder head only, at auction $650

All-Bisque Mibs

    3in (8cm) $225-250
    4¾in (12cm) $250-300
    6in (15cm) $400-450

Baby Peggy

1923. Composition head, molded brown bobbed hair or brown mohair wig, smiling closed mouth; appropriately dressed; all in good condition.

> Mark
> "19 © 24
> LA & S NY
> Germany
> —50—
> 982/2"

    20in (51cm) $750-850

Baby Peggy

1924. Perfect bisque head by Armand Marseille with character face, brown bobbed mohair wig, brown sleep eyes, closed mouth; composition or kid body, fully-jointed.

#982 or 983, shoulder head, 20in (51cm) $1,200-1,400
#972 or 973 socket head, 18-22in (46-56cm) $2,000-2,200

All-Bisque Baby Peggy

3in (8cm) $325-350
5½in (14cm) $500-550
4½in (12cm) wigged $475-525

Vanta Baby

1927. A tie-in with Vanta baby garments. Composition or bisque head with molded and painted hair, sleep eyes, open mouth with two teeth..

Bisque head

    10in (25cm) $400-450
    20-22in (51-56cm) $750-800
Composition head, excellent condition,
    18-20in (46-51cm) $275-325
All original in tagged clothes $450

> **Mark** Bisque Head
>
> Vanta Baby
> L ABS · ¾ D.R.G.M.
> Germany.

It (Edwina or Sue)

1928. All-composition with round ball joint at waist. Inspired by the "It" girl, Clara Bow.

14in (36cm) $275-325

Tiny Tots Body Twists

1928. All-composition with large round ball joint at the waist.

8in (20cm) $100-125
Little Amby, all original with paper label, at auction $300

Sunny Orange Maid

1924. Composition/cloth; molded "orange" hat; orange dress.

14in (36cm) all original $500-600

Peter Pan

1928. All-composition with round ball joint at waist. 14in (36cm).

Original Peter Pan outfit $375
Re-dressed $200-225

Georgene Averill (Madame Hendren & Georgene Novelties, Inc.)

> **History** Averill Manufacturing Co. and Georgene Novelties, Inc., New York, NY 1915-on.
>
> **Comment** Georgene Averill imported German bisque heads and manufactured composition and cloth dolls. She used the trademark *Madame Hendren* for her composition dolls. Prices are for dolls in excellent condition with perfect bisque and appropriate vintage bodies and clothes. Composition dolls should have original clothes, but may have light crazing and wear.

Bonnie Babe

1926. Bisque heads by Alt, Beck & Gottschalck; cloth bodies by K & K Toy Co.; distributed by George Borgfeldt & Co., New York. Perfect bisque head with smiling face, open mouth with two lower teeth; cloth body with composition arms (sometimes celluloid) and legs often of poor quality; all in good condition. Mold #1386 or 1402.

Mark
Copr. by
Georgene Averill
1005/3652
Germany
1386

Length:

12-13in (31-33cm)	.........................$500-600
16-18in (41-46cm)	.........................$600-700
22-23in (56-58cm)	......................$1,000-1,200
Composition body, 8in (20cm) tall	...............$1,250°
Celluloid head, 16in (41cm) tall	...............$400-450°

All-Bisque Bonnie Babe

1926.

5in (13cm)	...............................$1,000-1,100
7in (18cm)	...............................$1,500-1,600

Rag or Tag

All-bisque dog or cat with swivel neck, glass eyes; molded booties, crocheted yarn tail. Tag is mold 891.

Mark Incised
"RAG TRADE MARK Copr.
By Georgene Averill
890 Germany."

5in (13cm)	...............$3,500°
Boxed, at auction	...........$4,725

Allie Dog

Bisque dog head by Alt, Beck & Gottschalck, glass eyes, smiling open mouth with teeth and tongue; cloth or fur body.

Mark
"ALLIE DOG Copr.
By Georgene Averill
Germany 1405."

12-15in (31-38cm)	............$7,000-7,500

22in (56cm) *Bonnie Babe*.
Howard & Jan Foulke.

15in (38cm) *Allie Dog*.
Connie & Jay Lowe.

°Few price samples available.

Sunny Boy and Girl

Ca. 1927. Celluloid "turtle" mark head; stuffed body with composition arms and legs; appropriate or original clothes; all in good condition.

15in (38cm) $275-325

Composition Dolls

All appropriately dressed in good condition.

Mme. Hendren Character, Ca. 1915- on. Original tagged felt costume, including Dutch children, Indians, cowboys, sailors,

10-14in (25-36cm) $100-150

Mama and Baby Dolls, Ca. 1918-on. Composition with cloth bodies; names such as *Baby Hendren* and *Baby Georgene*

15-18in (38-46cm) $200-225

22-24in (56-61cm) $275-325

Dolly Reckord, 1922. Record-playing mechanism in torso, with records, 26in (66cm) ....$600-$700

14½in (37cm) body twist *Dimmie.* Howard & Jan Foulke.

14in (36cm) *Nurse Jane*, all original. Howard & Jan Foulke.

Grace G. Drayton, 1920s,

Chocolate Drop with yarn pigtails, 14in (36cm) $575

Bobby, 14in (36cm) $250-300

Whistling Doll, 1925-1929. Doll whistles when feet are pushed up or head is pushed down, 14-15in (36-38cm)

Dan, sailor or cowboy $200-250

Black Rufus or **Dolly Dingle** ....$450-$475

Snookums, 1927, 14in (36cm) ....$350-$375

Body Twists, 1927, Dimmie and Jimmie with a large round ball joint at waist, 14½in (37cm) $275-325

Dimmie, all original with tag $450

Patsy-type Girl, Peaches, 1928

14in (36cm) $225-250

17-18in (43-46cm) $300-350

Lenci-type Girl, Ca. 1930. Lenci-style, composition face (some flocked); original felt and organdy clothes, may have Val-Encia tag,

19in (48cm) ....$400-$500°

Little Cherub, 1937. Designed by Harriet Flanders; original clothes.

16in (41cm) $250-300

12in (31cm) painted eys $175-200

°Few price samples available.

Cloth Dolls

Original clothes; all in excellent condition, clean with bright color.

Children or Babies
- 12in (31cm) $100-115
- 24-26in (61-66cm) $175-225

International and Costume Dolls
- 12in (31cm) $75-85
- Mint-in-box with wrist tag $110-135

Wedding Party, 5 dolls $600

Girl Scout or Brownie, 13in (33cm)
- with complete outfit ....$225-$250

Becassine
- 8in (20cm) $300-350
- 13-15in (33-38cm) $600-700

Uncle Wiggily or Nurse Jane, 18-20in (46-51cm) $550-650

Comic Characters
- Little Lulu $400-500
- Nancy, Sluggo, Tubby Tom, 14in (36cm) $500-600

Topsy Turvy, Topsy & Eva, 10in (25cm) $150-175

Kris Kringle, Vinyl face, 10in (25cm) boxed with tag $145

Maud Tousey Fangel, 1938.
- Snooks, Sweets, Peggy-Ann, Marked "M.T.F." Bright color, all original
  - 12-14in (31-36cm) $550-600
  - 17in (43cm) $750-800
  - 22in (56cm) $1,000-1,100

Grace G. Drayton, good clean condition, some wear acceptable.
- Chocolate Drop, 1923. Brown cloth with three yarn pigatils.
  - 11in (28cm) $400-450
  - 16in (41cm) $450-500
- Dolly Dingle, 1923, 11in (28cm) $300-350
  - 16in (41cm) $450-500
  - 10in (25cm) double-faced $750

Vinyl Dolls

Baby Dawn, Ca. 1950. Vinyl and cloth, all original and
- excellent, 19in (48cm) $200-250

14in (36cm) *Nancy* and *Sluggo*, all original. *Gidget Donnelly.*   14in (36cm) *Little Lulu*, all original. *Howard & Jan Foulke.*

Baby Bo Kaye

History Bisque heads by Alt, Beck & Gottschalck; bodies by K & K Toy Co., distributed by George Borgfeldt & Co. 1925.

Comment A very desirable character designed by J.K. Kallus. See the Cameo section for other delightful Kallus designs.

Description Perfect bisque head with flange neck on original cloth body, molded hair, glass eyes, open mouth with two lower teeth, composition limbs. Appropriate clothes.

> **Mark** Incised on bisque head
> **Copr. By J.L. Kallus Germany 1394/30**

#1394, 1457, bisque head, 16-19in (41-48cm) $2,400-2,800
Celluloid Head, 16in (41cm) $650-750
#1407 bisque head, composition body, 7½in (19cm) $1,350
All-Bisque, swivel neck, molded pink or blue shoes and white socks, may have paper sticker on torso
    5in (13cm) $1,500-1,650
    6in (15cm) $2,000

Babyland Rag

History E.I. Horsman, New York, NY, some dolls made by Albert Brückner, 1893-on.

Comment All prices are for dolls in very good condition with good color, original clothes and very light soil and aging.

Description All cloth with hand-painted or printed features, mohair wig, original cotton clothes, leather shoes and socks.

Marks None

Early face, hand-painted features
    13-15in (33-38cm) $550-650
        Fair condition $300-350
    22in (56cm) $1,000
        Fair condition $450-500
    30in (76cm) $2,000-2,200
    Black, 15in (38cm) $750-850
        22in (56cm) $1,500-1,600
    Topsy Turvy,
        13-15in (33-38cm) $700-800
    Buster Brown,
        30in (76cm) $2,200
Life-like face, printed features,
    13-15in (33-38cm) $500-600
        Fair condition $300-325
    Topsy Turvy,
        14in (36cm) $500-600
Babyland Rag-type, lesser quality
    14in (36cm)
        black or white $250-350
Brückner Rag Doll, stiffened mask face
    12-14in (31-36cm)
        White $210-235
        Black $350-400

18in (46cm) *Baby Bo Kaye.*
Gloria & Mike Duddlesten.

15in (38cm) Babyland Rag with
life-like face.
Howard & Jan Foulke.

14in (36cm) black Brückner doll,
all original.
Yvonne Baird.

Topsy Turvy $450-500

| Mark PAT'D JULY 8ᵀᴴ 1901 |

Dollypop, and others with flat printed face,
12in (31cm) $225-250

Bähr & Pröschild

History Bähr & Pröschild, porcelain factory, Ohrdruf, Thuringia, Germany, made heads for Bruno Schmidt, Heinrich Stier, Kley & Hahn and others. 1871-on.

Comment This early maker produced very fine quality bisque heads. The closed-mouth child dolls are very desirable. Dolls before 1910 are marked only with a series 200 or 300 mold number, sometimes with dep. Open-mouth dolls often have 6 teeth.

Description Perfect bisque socket head with flattened crown having two or three small holes and closed mouth, paperweight glass eyes, pierced ears, vintage mohair wig. Jointed composition and wood body with straight wrists. Appropriate vintage clothes. Later open-mouth dolls have sleeping eyes and a jointed composition or baby body.

14in (36cm) 224 child.
Howard & Jan Foulke.

17in (43cm) 340 child.
Howard & Jan Foulke.

Belton-type Child Doll

Ca.1880. Solid dome head with flat top having two or three small holes, paperweight eyes, closed mouth, pierced ears; wood and composition jointed body with straight wrists. Mold numbers in 200 series.

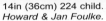

| Mark Mold number with dep. |

12-14in (30-36cm) $1,750-2,000
18-20in (46-51cm) $2,300-2,600
24in (61cm) $3,00-3,200

Child Doll

Ca. 1888-on. Open mouth with four or six upper teeth: jointed composition body (many of French-type). Mold numbers in 200 and 300 series.

Mark Mold number with dep. OR

$$B_8 P$$
$$340\text{-}4$$

#204, 239, 273, 275, 277, 289, 297, 300, 325, 340, 379, 394
and other socket heads
    12-13in (30-33cm) $400-450
    16-18in (41-46cm) $500-550
    22-24in (56-61cm) $650-750
#208, 209, 8-8½in (20-21cm) **jointed body with**
    molded shoes $900-1,000
#224 **(dimples)**
    14-16in (36-41cm) $550-600
    22-24in (56-61cm) $900-1,000
#246, 309 **and other shoulder heads on kid bodies**
    16-18in (41-46cm) $350-400
    22-24in (56-61cm) $450-500
#302, 325, **swivel neck, kid body**
    17in (43cm) $525-550
    20in (51cm) $600-650
#320, **swivel waist body, 17in (43cm)** $1,000

All-Bisque Girl

Yellow stockings (heart mark)
    5in (13cm) $375-425
    7in (18cm) $550-600

8½in (21cm) 585 toddler. *Howard & Jan Foulke.*

18in (46cm) 137 Belton-type child. *Howard & Jan Foulke.*

Character Baby

1910-on. Smiling baby face, open mouth; composition bent-limb baby body. Mold #585, 604, 624, 678, 619, 620 and 587.

12-14in (31-36cm)	$300-350
17-19in (43-48cm)	$450
23-25in (58-64cm)	$600-650

Toddler, fully-jointed body

12-13in (31-33cm)	$650-700
22in (56cm)	$1,000

Toddler, five-piece body

10-12in (25-31cm)	$550-600
14in (36cm)	$550
#425 All-bisque baby, 5½-6in (13-15cm)	$300-350

Mark

Belton-type (So-called)

History Various unidentified German porcelain factories, such as Bähr & Pröschild. 1875-on.

Comment Dolls with the French-style faces are particularly desirable.

Description Perfect bisque socket head with solid flattened crown having one, two or three small holes for stringing or attaching wig, glass paperweight eyes, closed mouth, pierced ears, mohair wig. Wood and composition jointed body with straight wrists. Appropriate vintage clothes.

Mark Mold or size numbers only.

Belton-type Child Doll

Bru-type face, 12-14in (30-35cm)	$3,000-3,500

French-type face, fine early quality (some mold #137 or #183)

13-15in (33-38cm)	$1,900-2,200
18-20in (46-51cm)	$2,300-2,600
22-24in (56-61cm)	$3,000-3,200

German-type face, good quality
8-9in (20-23cm) five-piece body $850-950
12in (31cm) $1,200-1,300
15-17in (38-43cm) $1,400-1,600
20in (51cm) $2,000-2,200
#200 Series, Bähr & Pröschild .... See page 42.
TR 809, 17in (43cm) $1,400-1,600

C.M. Bergmann

History C.M. Bergmann doll factory, Waltershausen, Thuringia, Germany. Heads manufactured by Armand Marseille; Simon & Halbig; Alt, Beck & Gottschalck and perhaps others. Distributed in the U.S. by Louis Wolf & Co., NY. 1888-on.

Comment This factory produced mainly child dolls. The most desirable are those with heads made by Simon & Halbig and the rare #612 charcter baby.

Description Perfect bisque head, glass sleeping eyes, open mouth, vintage wig. Composition ball-jointed body. Appropriate clothing.

Trademarks Cinderella Baby (1897), Columbia (1914), My Gold Star (1926).

12½in (32cm) Incised CMB child with head made by Simon & Halbig. *Howard & Jan Foulke.*

Child Doll
Ca. 1889-on.
#1916, heads by A.M. and unknown makers
10in (25cm) $400
14-16in (36-41cm) $250-275
20-22in (51-56cm) $350-375
25in (64cm) $400
28-29in (71-74cm) $500
32-33in (81-84cm) $550-650
35-36in (89-91cm) $800-900
39-42in (99-111cm) $1,700-2,000
Heads marked "Simon & Halbig"
10in (25cm) $500-600
13-15in (33-38cm) $400-450
18-20in (46-51cm) $375-400
23-24in (58-61cm) $450-500
29-30in (81-91cm) $550-650
35-36in (81-91cm) $1,200-1,400
39in (99cm) $2,300-2,500
Eleonore, 25in (64cm) $550-650
#612 Character Baby, open-closed mouth or
open mouth with tongue, 14-16in (36-41cm) $3,000
#134 Character Toddler, 12in (31cm) $950

Mark

C.M.BERGMANN
Made in Germany

C.M.BERGMANN
SIMON&HALBIG
10

Bisque

French
(Makers Not Listed Separately)

Marked B.M. Bébé
1880-1895. Alexandre Mothereau. Perfect pressed bisque socket head, closed mouth, paperweight eyes; French wood and composition jointed body; appropriate clothing; all in good condition.

    12-15in (31-38cm) $11,000-12,500
    28-29in (71-74cm) $22,500
    33in (84cm) $28,000

20in (51cm) H Bébé.
Kay Jensen Collection.

Marked F.R. Bébé
Ca. 1880s. Falck & Roussel. Perfect bisque socket head, closed mouth, paperweight eyes; French wood and composition body; appropriate clothing; all in good condition.

    10in (25cm) $9,000
    16-18in (41-46cm) $14,000-17,000

Marked H. Bébé
Ca. late 1870s. Possibly by A. Halopeau. Perfect pressed bisque socket head of fine quality, cork pate, good wig, paperweight eyes, pierced ears, closed mouth; French wood and composition jointed body with straight wrists; appropriate clothing; all in excellent condition.

Mark
2 • H

SIZE	0 = 16½in (42cm)	2 = 19in (48cm)	3 = 21in (56cm)	4 = 24in (6lcm)

    21-24in (53-61cm) $65,000-75,000

18in (46cm) Huret child, wood body.
James D. Julia, Inc.

Huret Child
Ca. 1878. Maison Huret. Perfect bisque head; appropriate clothing; all in excellent condition.
Gutta-percha body,
    18in (46cm) $70,000-80,000
Wood body, 19in (48cm)
    at auction $48,875

Marked J. Bébé
Ca. 1880s. Joseph Louis Joanny. Perfect pressed bisque socket head, paperweight eyes, closed mouth; French wood and composition body; appropriate clothing; all in good condition.

22in (56cm) J Bébé.
Kay Jensen Collection.

    12in (31cm) $3,500
    17-18in (43-46cm) $5,000-5,500
    22in (56cm) $6,500-7,500

45

Marked J.M. Bébé

Ca. 1880s. Perfect pressed bisque socket head, good wig, paperweight eyes, closed mouth, pierced ears; French composition and wood body; appropriate clothing; all in good condition.

Mark
5

23in (58cm) $15,000-18,500

Marked M. Bébé

Mark
M
4

Mid 1890s. Perfect bisque socket head, good wig, closed mouth, paperweight eyes, pierced ears; French jointed composition and wood body; appropriate clothing; all in good condition. Some dolls with this mark may be **Bébé Mascottes**.

19-23in (48-58cm) $3,100-3,500

Marked Bébé Mascotte

1890-1897, May Freres Cie; 1898-on, Jules Nicholas Steiner. Perfect bisque socket head, closed mouth, paperweight eyes; pierced ears; jointed composition and wood body; appropriate clothing; all in good condition.

10-12in (25-31cm) $2,250-2,500
19-20in (48-51cm) $3,600-3,700
24in (61cm) all original, at auction $4,500

Pintel & Godchaux Bébé.
James D. Julia, Inc.

11in (28cm) Pan-type Bébé.
Kay Jensen Collection.

Marked A. Marque Character Doll

1916. Perfect bisque head with wistful character face (one face only) sculpted by Albert Marque, appropriate wig, paperweight eyes, closed mouth; jointed composition body of special design with bisque lower arms and hands, straight wrists; appropriate clothes. Original clothes were made by Paris designer Margaines-Lacroix. All in excellent condition.

22in (56cm) one size only $192,500

Marked P.D. Bébé

1878-1890. Petit & Dumoutier, Paris. Perfect bisque head with good wig, paperweight eyes, closed mouth, pierced ears; jointed composition body (some with metal hands); appropriate clothes; all in good condition.

Mark
P.2.D.

16in (41cm).....................................$11,000-13,000
19-23in (48-58cm) $18,500

Marked P.G. Bébé

Ca. 1880-1899. Pintel & Godchaux, Montreuil, France.
Perfect bisque socket head, good wig. paperweight eyes,
closed mouth: jointed French composition and wood body;
appropriate clothing: all in good condition.

Marks	
B	**A**
P9G	**P7G**

Trademark: *Bébé Charmant*
20-22in (51-56cm) $2,500-2,800
Open mouth, 18-20in (46-51cm) $1,400-1,600

Marked PAN Bébé

Ca. 1887. Henri Delcroix, Paris and Montreuil-sous-Bois (porcelain factory). Perfect bisque socket head, good wig. paperweight eyes, closed mouth, pierced ears; French composition and wood body; appropriate clothes; all in good condition.

Mark
PAN
2

SIZE   2 = 12in (31cm)   10 = 27in (68cm)   11 = 28½in (72cm)

12in (31cm) $6,000-7,000

Marked Van Rosen

Ca. 1912. Character dolls made from a bisque-like material; glass eyes, wig.
17-19in (43-48cm) $9,000-10,000
Black $18,000

Marked J. Verlingue Bébé

Ca. 1915-1921. Montreuil. *Petite Française Liane.* Perfect bisque head, sleeping eyes, good wig, open mouth; jointed composition body.
16in (41cm) $350-400
26in (66cm) $600-650

For lady and fashion dolls *(poupées)* see pages 82-84.

German
(Unmarked or Makers Not Listed Separately)

History Various German porcelain and doll factories. 1860s-on.
Mark Some numbered, some "Germany," some both.

Shoulder head with molded hair

Ca. 1880. Tinted bisque shoulder head with beautifully molded hair (usually blonde), closed mouth: original kid or cloth body. bisque lower arms; appropriate clothes; all in good condition.

American Schoolboy
   12-14in (31-36cm) $400-450
   17-20in (43-51cm) $600-650
Composition body, socket head, 11-12in (28-31cm) $550-650
Boy or girl. painted eyes, 14-16in (36-41cm) $300-400
Boy or girl, glass eyes, 16in (41cm) $600-650
Lady, painted eyes, 12-14in (31-36cm) $300-350
Lady, glass eyes, fancy blonde hairdo,
   20in (51cm) at auction $1,320

16in (41cm) bisque bonnet
or hatted doll.
Howard & Jan Foulke.

20in (51cm) shoulder head child
with molded hair.
Private Collection.

5in (13cm) 1880s doll
house doll with
molded bangs.
Howard & Jan Foulke.

19in (48cm) unmarked shoulder
head child with closed mouth.
Howard & Jan Foulke.

18in (46cm) child incised R & B
made by Rempel & Breitung.
Howard & Jan Foulke.

Hatted or Bonnet Doll

Ca. 1880-1920. Bisque shoulder head, molded bonnet; original cloth body with bisque arms and legs: good old clothes or nicely dressed; all in good condition.

Standard quality, 8-9in (20-23cm)	$130-165
11-13in (28 33cm)	$225-250
15in (38cm)	$300-350
18in (46cm)	$450-500
Fine quality, 18-22in (46-56cm)	$1,000 up*
All-bisque, 4½in (12cm)	$150-175
7in (18cm)	$225-250

Dolls' House Doll

Ca. 1890-1920. Man or lady bisque shoulder head: cloth body, bisque lower limbs: original clothes or suitably dressed; all in nice condition.

4½-7in (12-18cm)

Molded hair, glass eyes, ca. 1870	$450-500
Girl with bangs, ca. 1880, all original	$210
Victorian man with mustache	$200-225
Victorian lady, all original	$200
Lady with glass eyes and wig	$350-400
Man with mustache, original military uniform	$1,600
Chauffeur with molded cap	$350-400
Black man	$650-700
Maid, all original	$110-135
1920s man or lady	$100-125
1920s man with molded hat, all original	$225

Child Doll with closed mouth

Ca. 1880-1890. Perfect bisque head, good wig, glass eyes; nicely dressed; all in good condition, excellent quality.

Kid or cloth body

17-19in (43-48cm)	$300-400**
23-25 in (58-64cm)	$550-650**

#50, shoulder head

14-16in (35-41cm)	$500-600
22in (56cm)	$1,250-1,300

#132, 120, 126, Bru-type face

13-14in (33-36cm)	$2,500-2,800
19-21 in (48-53cm)	$3,800-4,000

#51, swivel neck shoulder head, 17-19in (43-48cm) $900-1,100
#86, Bru-type nurser, 13in (33cm) at auction $1,000

Lady doll, swivel neck, original fashion clothes,

19-20in (48-51cm)	$2,000-2,500

Composition body (German look)

11-13in (28-33cm)	$1,250-1,350
16-19in (41-48cm)	$1,650-1,850

#136 (French look)

12-15in (31-38cm)	$1,900-2,100
19-21in (48-53cm)	$2,500-2,800

E.G. (Ernst Grossman)

16in (41cm)	$2,600
21in (53cm)	$4,000

*Allow extra for unusual style.   **Allow 30 percent extra for swivel neck fashion-type model.

5in (13cm) unmarked Simon &
Halbig-type child, all original
crepe paper outfit.
Howard & Jan Foulke.

9½in (24cm) unmarked
character baby.
Howard & Jan Foulke.

Child Doll with open mouth "Dolly Face"

1888-on. Perfect bisque head, good wig, glass eyes, open mouth; ball-jointed composition body or kid body with bisque lower arms; dressed; all in good condition. Very good quality; including dolls marked "G.B." and "K" inside "H," "L.H.K.," "P.Sch.," "D&K."

12-14in (31-35cm)	$300-350
18-20in (46-51cm)	$375-400
23-25in (58-64cm)	$450-500
30-32in (76-81cm)	$700-800
#50, 51, square teeth, 14-16in (36-41cm)	$750-850

#444, 478, 422, 457

17in (43cm)	$400-450
23-25in (58-64cm)	$500-600
35in (81cm)	$1,200

Standard quality; including My Sweetheart, Princess, My Girlie, My Dearie, Pansy, Viola, G & S, MOA and A.W.

18-20in (46-51cm)	$225-250
24-26in (61-66cm)	$350-375
32-33in (81-84cm)	$450-500

Small Child Doll

1890 to World War I. Perfect bisque socket head, set or sleep eyes; five-piece composition body; cute clothes; all in good condition.

Very good quality (Simon & Halbig-type)

5-6in (13-15cm)	$275-300
8-10in (20-25cm)	$350-400

Fully-jointed body,

7-8in (18-20cm)	$600-650

Closed mouth, 4½-5½in (12-14cm)

all original	$400-450
8in (20cm)	$700-750

Standard quality

5-6in (13-15cm)	$100-125

8-10in $175-200
#39-13, five-piece mediocre body, original clothes
  5in (13cm) glass eyes $175-200
  Painted eyes $90-100
#12a, #13a Georg Bruchlos, glass eyes, mediocre body,
  original clothes, 5in (13cm) $175-200

Globe Baby
1898. Carl Hartmann.
  8in (20cm) $325
  8in (20cm) all-original clothes and wig $400-450
  12in (31cm) $450-550

Character Baby
Ca. 1910-on. Perfect bisque head, good wig or solid dome with painted hair, sleep eyes. open mouth; composition bent-limb baby body; suitably dressed; all in good condition. Including dolls marked "G.B.," "S&Q," "P.M." and "F.B."
  9-10in (23-25cm) $150-200
  14-16in (35-41cm) $225-250
  19-21in (48-53cm) $300-350
  23-24in (58-61cm) $400-450
  My Sweet Baby, 23in (58cm) toddler . . . . $1,000-$1,200°

6½in (16cm) *Phyllis*
711/5 character
shoulder head.
Howard & Jan Foulke.

Character Doll
Ca. 1910-on. Perfect bisque head, jointed composition body; dressed; all in good condition.
#111, 18-20in (46-51cm) . . . . $20,000°
#120, painted eyes, open/closed mouth,
  16in (41cm) at auction $5,720
#125, smiling, 13in (33cm)
  at auction . . . . $6,000-7,000°
#128, 18-20in (46-51cm) . . . . $25,000°
#159, 23in (58cm) $1,150
#163, 14in (36cm) $450-500
#213, Bawo & Dotter, 12in (31cm)
  at auction $7,250
#214, Bawo & Dotter, 17in (43cm) . . $11,500
#221, toddler, 16in (41cm) . . . . $2,500°
#411, lady shoulder head,
  14in (36cm) . . . . $3,500°
#616, F.B. lady, 18in (46cm) Nurse . . $7,750°
#711, Phyllis, 6½in (16cm) head only . $650°
#838, P.M. "Coquette,"
  11-12in (28-31cm) $550-600

Infant, unmarked or unidentified maker
Ca. 1924-on. Perfect bisque head; cloth body; dressed; all in good condition. Baby Weygh, IV and others.
  10-12in (25-31cm) long $185-210
  15-18in (38-46cm) long $300-350
  #1924, composition body, 9in (23cm) $185-210
  HvB, 15in (38cm) long $350-400
  Gerling Baby, 17in (43cm) long $450
  K & K Mama Doll, 23in (58cm) $300-400

°Few price samples available.

Japanese (Caucasian Dolls)

History Various Japanese porcelain factories, imported through New York distributors, such as Morimura Brothers, Yamato Importing Co. and others. 1915-on.

Comment Japanese factories stepped in to fill the void created during World War I when imports from Germany were cut off. Quality is spotty so choose carefully.

Description Perfect bisque socket head, glass sleeping eyes, open mouth, wig or solid dome head with painted hair. Jointed composition or kid body for child; bent-limb composition body for character baby. Appropriate clothing.

Mark

Character Baby
    9-10in (23-25cm) $110-125*
    13-15in (33-38cm) $150-200*
    19-21in (48-53cm) $275*
    24in (61cm) $400*
    Hilda **look-alike, RE Nippon, 19in (48cm)** $500-600*
    Heubach Pouty look-alike, F.Y Nippon 300 Series,
        17-18in (43-46cm) $500-600*

Child Doll
    14-16in (36-41cm) $200-250
    20-22in (51-56cm) $275-325
    26-28 in (66-71cm) $400-450

22in (56cm) Morimura Brothers child.
Kay Jensen Antique Dolls.

13in (33cm) circle dot Bru *Bébé.*
Private Collection.

Black Dolls**

History Black bisque dolls were made by both French and German porcelain factories from their regular molds or specially designed ones with Negroid features. Complexions range from light brown to very dark. Most of the black cloth dolls are American made, except for the popular English Golliwogs. Ca. 1880-on.

Comment Black dolls are very popular with collectors. The best examples of the bisque dolls are those with specially designed faces, rather than simply black-tinted versions of white dolls.

*Do not pay as much for doll with inferior bisque head.
**Also see entry for specific maker or for material of doll.

10½in (27cm) A-3 Steiner *Bébé*.
Private Collection.

19in (48cm) and 6½in (16cm)
Gebruder Kuhnlenz 34 dolls.
Howard & Jan Foulke.

Black Bisque Doll

Ca. 1880-on. Perfect bisque socket head; composition or sometimes kid body in a matching color; cloth bodies on some baby dolls; appropriate clothing.

French Makers:
B.M., closed mouth, 15in (38cm) Portrait doll,
  all original, at auction $17,600
Bru: Circle Dot, 17in (43cm) $50,000
Poupée Peau, 17in (43cm) original Eastern
  or African costume $8,000-9,000
Danel, Paris Bébé, closed mouth 19in (48cm) at auction $6,875
E.D., closed mouth, 20in (51cm) $5,200
Eden Bébé, open mouth, 15in (38cm) $2,000
Jumeau
  Bébé, open mouth
    10in (25cm) $1,650
    13in (33cm) $2,200-2,300
    20in (51cm) $3,100-3,300
  DEP, open mouth, 16in (41cm) $2,000
Poupée Peau, 15in (38cm) original Eastern costume $9,000
Lanternier, 18-20in (46-51cm) $950-1,250
S.F.B.J. #301, fully-jointed body
    10in (25cm) $1,100-1,200
    16in (41cm) original Eastern costume $1,500-1,600
Steiner, Figure A, 15-16in (38-41cm) open mouth $3,000-3,500
Van Rosen character, 15in (38cm) ....$18,000°

German Makers:
#120, Bru-type mulatto, closed mouth,
    10-12in (25-31cm) ....$3,200-3,800°
Bähr & Pröschild #277, 12in (30cm) $1,000
Belton-type 179, 14in (36cm) $3,000-4,000
Gebrüder Heubach #7657, Shoulder head only $625
H. Handwerck, 18-21in (46-53cm) $1,200-1,400
E. Heubach
  #399, 414, 452
    7½in (19cm) toddler $400-425
    10-12in (25-30cm) $500-550
  #444, 13in (33cm) $650
  #463, 10-12in (25-30cm) $750
  #300, 6in (15cm) $450-500

°Few price samples available.

11in (28cm) knitted wool doll. *Howard & Jan Foulke.*

13in (33cm) Arts & Crafts Studio, all cloth with mask face, all original. *Connie Blain.*

9in (23cm) Loveleigh Novelty walnut head doll, all original. *Howard & Jan Foulke.*

Kämmer & Reinhardt, Child, 16in (41cm) $1,500-1,700
  #100 Baby, 11in (28cm) $700-800
    19in (48cm) $1,500-1,800
  #101, 13-14in (33-36cm) ....$4,000-4,500°
  #126, toddler, 8-9in (20-23cm) $1,250
  #192, 21in (53cm) ....$2,500-2,650°
J.D. Kestner, Child, 16in (41cm) closed mouth pouty $7,000
  Hilda, 18in (46cm) ....$4,000-4,500°
Kuhnlenz #34, 7-9in (18-23cm) fully-jointed $750-850
  8½in (21cm) five-piece body, all-original
    Mammy with baby $650-700
    19-20in (48-53cm) $6,500
K & W 134 character toddler, 15-17in (38-43cm) $500-550
Armand Marseille, #341, cloth body, 10-12in (25-31cm) $300
  #351, composition body
    8-12in (20-31cm) $350-400
    14-16in (38-41cm) $500
    21in (53cm) $650-700
  #362, composition body, 15in (38cm) $700-800
  #1894, 10in (25cm) fully-jointed $500-600
Recknagel, #126 infant, 10½in (26cm) $300
  #188 character baby, 11in (28cm) $350
S PB H, Hanna, 7-8in (18-20cm) $275-325
  #1923 child, 19-20in (48-51cm) $900-1,000
Simon & Halbig
  #739, 20in (51cm) $1,500-1,800
  #949, open mouth, 19in (48cm) at auction $3,520
  #969, 16in (41cm) at auction $3,850
  #1009, 19-21in (48-53cm) $2,000-2,200
  #1069, 15in (38cm) $2,700
  #1078, 1079, 15in (38cm) $1,100-1,200
  #1301, character, 20in (51cm) ....$33,000°
  #1358, 22in (56cm) $10,000
  #1368, 14in (36cm) $4,000
Unmarked Child
  Simon & Halbig quality, five-piece body
    3in (8cm) $350

°Few price samples available.

```
4-5in (10-14cm) ...........................$450-$500
Ordinary quality
   8-9in (20-23cm) five-piece body ...............$300-$350
   10-13in (25-33cm) jointed body ...............$400-$500
```

All-Bisque
Glass eyes, wig
```
3¾in (9cm) ..........................................$425
5in (14cm) .......................................$550-575
Kestner, swivel neck, bare feet, 6in (15cm) ...............$1,850
Simon & Halbig 886
4½in (11cm) .....................................$600-700
7in (18cm) ....................................$1,450-1,650
G.K. 61, swivel neck, 3½in (9cm) ..........................$575
5in (13cm) ..........................................$900
5½in (13cm) mulatto .............................$1,300
7in (18cm) mulatto ...............................$2,200
#31, closed mouth, 9½in (24cm) .....................$3,500°
Molded shorts, 5-6in (13-15cm) ........................$500-600
Hertwig character, 2¾in (6cm) .............................$95
```

Cloth Black Doll*
Ca. 1880-on. American-made cloth doll with black face, painted, printed or embroidered features; jointed arms and legs; original clothes; all in good condition.
```
Primitive, Painted or embroidered face ...........$1,000-2,000**
Stockinette (so-called Beecher-type), 20in (51cm) ..........$3,200
1930s Mammy, 18-20in (46-51cm) .....................$500-600**
WPA, Molded cloth face, 22in (56cm) .................$1,200-1,500
Alabama-type, 24in (61cm) .........................$2,500-3,500
Chase Mammy, 26in (66cm) ...........................$10,000°
Chase Child, 13in (33cm) at auction .....................$16,450
Knitted wool, 11-12in (28-31cm) .......................$150-200
Mask Face, 1940s, 13in (33cm) .........................$150-175
```

Golliwogg
Ca. 1925-1930.English cloth character; all original: very good condition.
```
18in (46cm) ..........................................$425-525
16-18in (41-46cm), ca. 1950 ...........................$225-325
```

Black Papier-mâché Doll
Ca. 1890. By various German manufacturers. Papier-mâché character face, arms and legs, cloth body; glass eyes; original or appropriate clothes; all in good condition.
```
12-14in (31-36cm) ....................................$350-450
18-20in (46-51cm) character with broad smile .........$1,200-1,500
```

Black Low-Fired Pottery
Ca. 1930. English and German. Molded curly hair.
```
16in (41cm) ..........................................$500-600
```

Walnut Head Folk Doll
Ca. 1940s. Loveleigh Novelty Doll, Grantville, GA.
```
8-11in (20-28cm) caricature faces ......................$175-275
```

°Few price samples available.
*Also check under manufacturer, if known.
**Greatly depending on appeal.

Bleuette

History Mascotte of the French girl's magazine *La Semaine de Suzette*. 1905 - 1906. Extensive wardrobe could be purchased, or made from patterns printed in the magazine. All dolls produced for Gautier-Languereau by S.F.B.J. doll factory. If a doll is any size other than those indicated, she is not a *Bleuette*.
Comment *Bleuette* is extremely popular expecially with collectors who love to sew clothing for her. *Bleuette* enthusiasts have their own newsletters, web sites, chat rooms and special gatherings during other doll events. An original Gautier-Languereau dress will bring $200-300, and up to $450 for an unusual outfit.

Premiere Bleuette
Ca. 1905. Bisque head with Jumeau Face, open mouth, stationary blue eyes; jointed composition and wood body; appropriate clothing.

> **Head Mark 2 or 1 or both.**
> **Body Mark 2 on back, 1 on feet.**

$10^{5/8}$in (27cm) only $4,000-5,000

2nd Series Bleuette
Ca. 1905-1915. Bisque head from Fleischmann mold, open mouth, stationary blue or very dark eyes; jointed compostion and wood body; appropriate clothing.

> **Head Mark 6/0**
> **Body Mark 2 on back, 1 on feet.**

$10^{5/8}$in (27cm) only $1,500-1,800

S.F.B.J. Bleuette
Ca. 1915-1928. Bisque head, blue or very dark stationary or sleeping eyes, open mouth; jointed composition and wood body; appropriate clothing.

> **Head Mark SFBJ 60 Paris 8/0 or SFBJ 301 Paris 1**
> **Body Mark 2 on back, 1 on feet.**

$10^{5/8}$in (27cm) only $2,300-2,800

Unis Bleuette
Ca. 1920's. Bisque head, blue or very dark stationary or sleeping eyes, open mouth; jointed composition and wood body; appropriate clothing.

> **Head Mark 71 Unis France 149 60 8/0 or Unis France 301 1**
> **Body Mark 2 on back, 1 on feet.**

$10^{5/8}$in (27cm) only $2,100-2,600
Not as nice quality bisque $1,200-1,600

1933-on.

> **Head Mark 71 Unis France 149 301 1 ¼**

$11^{3/8}$in (29cm) only $1,200-1,600

Premiere *Bleuette.*
Kay Jensen Antique Dolls.

Unis Bleuette

Ca. 1928-1933. Composition head, blue or very dark sleeping eyes, jointed composition and wood body; appropriate clothing.

> **Head Mark** **71 Unis France 149 301 1 ¼**
> **Body Mark** **2** on back, **1** on feet.

10⁵/₈in (27cm) only $400-600

1933-on.

> **Head Mark** **71 Unis France 149 301 1 ½ or 1 ¼**

11³/₈in (29cm) only $400-600

SFBJ 60 8/0 *Bleuette.*
Howard & Jan Foulke.

Fleishman 6/0 *Bleuette.*
Howard & Jan Foulke.

Bru

History Bru Jne & Cie., Paris and Montreuil-sous-Bois, France. 1866-1899.

Comment For most antique doll collectors owning a Bru doll would be the ultimate possible thrill, as it is considered a very top-of-the-line doll and quite prestigious. The most desirable Bru Jne models have a molded tongue and the Chevrot hinged legs.

Description Perfect bisque socket head on shoulder plate with paperweight eyes, closed mouth, pierced ears, mohair wig, cork pate. Original leather bodies except as noted and appropriate vintage clothes.

Poupée (Fashion Lady)

Ca. 1866-on. Gusseted kid lady body.

Smiling face, sizes A (11in [28cm]) to O (36in [91cm])

14-16in (35-41cm)	.$3,500-4,000*
20-21 in (51-53cm)	.$5,500-6,000*
28in (71cm)	.$8,000-9,000
Wood arms, 16in (41cm)	.$4,900-5,100*

Wood body, naked

15-17in (38-43cm)	.$6,000-6,800*
21in (53cm)	.$9,000

Oval face, incised with numbers only; shoulder plate sometimes marked "B. Jne & Cie."

12-13in (31-33cm)	.$2,800-3,000*
15-17in (38-43cm)	.$3,500-3,800*
20-21in (51-53cm)	.$4,400-4,900*
Wood body, naked, 16in (41cm)	.$5,500

Surprise Doll, Two faces, 17in (43cm) at auction $15,000

Fashion Boots $450

Marked Breveté Bébé

Ca. 1879-1880. Skin wig, paperweight eyes with shading on upper lid, closed mouth with while space between lips, full cheeks, pierced ears; gusseted kid body pulled high on shoulder plate and straight cut with bisque lower arms (no rivet joints).

Mark Size number only on head. Oval sticker on body:

or rectangular sticker like Bébé Bru one, but with words Bébé Breveté.

SIZE:	5/0 = 10½in (27cm)	0 = 15in (38cm)	2 = 18in (46cm)
	2/0 = 14in (36cm)	1 = 16in (41cm)	3 = 19in (48cm)

11in (28cm)	.$13,000-15,000
14-16in (35-41cm)	.$16,000-18,000
19-22in (48-56cm)	.$22,000-23,000

Bébé Modèle

Ca. 1879.

Breveté face, wood body, 18in (46cm) $35,000

*Allow extra for original clothes.

17in (43cm) Bru *poupée.*
Private Collection.

13½in (34cm) *Bébé Bru Breveté.*
Kay Jensen Antique Dolls.

Marked Crescent or Circle Dot Bébé

1879-1884. Deep shoulder plate with molded breasts, cork pate, attractive wig, paperweight eyes with eye shadow, closed mouth with slightly parted lips, molded and painted teeth, plump cheeks, pierced ears; gusseted kid body with bisque lower arms (no rivet joints).

Mark

sometimes
with "BRU Jne."

APPROXIMATE SIZE CHART FOR CIRCLE DOT AND BRU JNE BÉBÉS:

0 = 11in (28cm)	5 = 17in (43cm)	12 = 30in (76cm)
1 = 12in (31cm)	8 = 22in (56cm)	14 = 35in (89cm)
2 = 13m (33cm)	10 = 26in (66cm	

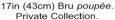

10½in (26cm)	$13,000-14,000
13-14in (33-35cm)	$15,000-17,000
18-19in (46-48cm)	$20,000-22,500
24in (61cm)	$26,500-28,500
31in (79cm)	$32,000-35,000

Marked Nursing Bru (Bébé Têteur)

Ca. 1878-1898. Perfect bisque head, shoulder plate, open mouth with hole for nipple, mechanism in head sucks up liquid, operates by turning key; nicely clothed; all in good condition.

Early model, 1879 Breveté face, 13-15in (33-38cm) $18,000
Other early models, 13-15in (33-38cm) $12,000-14,000
Later model, 13-15in (33-38cm) $8,000-9,000

Bébé Gourmand

Ca. 1880.
18in (46cm) ....$26,500°

Bébé Musique

17in (43cm) with trunk and trousseau, at auction $56,000

°Few price samples available.

Marked Bru Jne Bébé

Ca. 1884-1889. Deep shoulder plate with molded breasts, cork pate, attractive wig, paperweight eyes, closed mouth, molded tongue, pierced ears; gusseted kid body with scalloped edge at shoulder plate, bisque lower arms with lovely hands, kid over wood upper arms, hinged elbow, all kid or wood lower legs.

Mark "BRU Jne"
Body Label:

> BÉBÉ BRU BTE   S.G.D.G.
> Tout Contrefacteur Sera Saisiet Poursuivi
> conformement a la Loi

10in (25cm)	**$25,000**
12-13in (31-33cm)	**$21,000-22,000**
15-17in (38-43cm)	**$25,000-28,000**
23-24in (58-61cm)	**$30,000-32,000**
27in (69cm)	**$37,000**

Late model, no molded tongue
14in (36cm)	**$10,000-12,000**
18-20in (46-51cm)	**$13,500-15,000**
Marked Bru Shoes	$800-900
Bru factory dress and hat	$1,700-2,000

Marked Bru Jne R Bébé

Ca. 1889-1899. Perfect bisque head on a jointed composition body.

Mark BRU JNE R 9

Body Stamp: "Bebe Bru" with size number.

Closed mouth
11-13in (28-33cm)	**$2,200-2,600**
19-21in (48-53cm)	**$6,000-7,000**
27in (69cm)	**$9,000**

Bébé Respirant (breather), 1892, 19in (48cm) $10,000

Open mouth
12in (31cm)	**$1,500-1,800**
20-21in (51-53cm)	**$3,000-4,000**

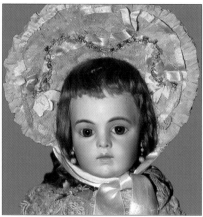

25in (63cm) *Bébé Bru* Jne 9.
Kay Jensen Antique Dolls.

27in (69cm) *Bébé Bru* Jne 11.
Connie & Jay Lowe.

Bucherer

History A. Bucherer, Amriswil, Switzerland, 1921.
Trademark Saba Figures
Comment Bucherer characters are sought-after by a devoted group of collectors in the United States and Europe. Internet sales are very brisk.
Description Composition character head, metal ball-jointed body with large composition molded shoes. All prices are for a doll in excellent condition in original clothing. 8in (20cm) average size.

> **Mark on Torso**
> MADE IN SWITZERLAND
> PATENTS APPLIED FOR

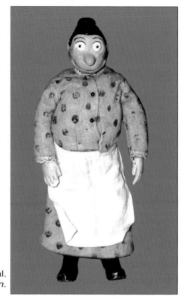

Bucherer *Mama Katzenjammer*, all original.
Wayne Jensen Collection.

Bescassine $300
Mutt & Jeff, **each** $250-300
Maggie & Jiggs, **each** $700-800
Man or lady in provincial costume $450-500
Occupational characters: fireman, clown, black butler,
    aviator, baseball player, policeman, sailor, soldier
    and others. $400-650
Comic characters: *Katzenjammers, Happy Hooligan,*
    Charlie Chaplin, Aggie, Jimmy Dugan, Puddin' Head
    and others $400-650

Bye-Lo Baby

History Bisque heads by J. D. Kestner, ABG, Kling & Co. and Hertel, Schwab & Co. Composition heads by Cameo Doll Co. All-bisque dolls by J. D. Kestner. Celluloid heads and dolls by Karl Standfuss. Unauthorized wooden heads by Schoenhut. Cloth bodies and assembly by K & K Toy Co. Composition bodies by Konig & Wernicke. Designed by Grace Storey Putnam. Distributed by George Borgfeldt. 1922-on.
Comment These babies though not rare are very popular with collectors today. They were the first realistic infant doll, and became an instant best seller. Models with bisque heads were made in seven sizes from 9 to 20 inches. Original white lawn baby gowns have a Bye-Lo tag.
Description Perfect bisque head with sleeping eyes. Original stamped Bye-lo cloth body with curved legs (a very few with "swing" legs) and celluloid hands. Vintage baby clothes.

17in (43cm) head circumference *Bye-lo Baby.*
Howard & Jan Foulke.

Bisque Head Bye-Lo Baby
Ca. 1923. Mold #1373 (ABG).
Head circumference,
   7½in-8in (19-20cm) $300-350
   9-10in (23-25cm) $250-275
   12-13in (31-33cm) $300-350
   15in (38cm) $450-550
   17in (43cm) $650-700
   18in (46cm) $750-800
   Tagged Bye-Lo gown $50
   Bye-Lo pin $65-75
   Bye-Lo blanket $40-50
#1369 (ABG) socket head on composition body, some
   marked "K&W", 12-13in (30-33cm) long $600-700
   Painted eyes, 12-13in (30-33cm) long $600
#1415, smiling with painted eyes, 13½in (34cm)
   head circumference ....$4,000°

Composition Head
Ca. 1924.
   12-13in (31-33cm) head circumference
      All original with tag $250-300
      Re-dressed $150

Celluloid Head
   10in (25cm) head circumference $200-250

Painted Bisque Head
Late 1920s.
   12-13in (31-33cm) head circumference $200-250

Wooden Head
   (Schoenhut) 1925 ....$1,700-2,000°

Vinyl Head
   1948, 16in (41cm) $90-100

Wax Head
   1922, 16in (41cm) $700-900

Baby Aero or Fly-Lo Baby
#1418, bisque head, 11in (28cm) ....$2,800-3,200°
Composition head, original costume, 12in (31cm) $800-900

All-Bisque Bye-Lo Baby
Ca. 1925-on. Solid head with molded hair and painted eyes; jointed shoulders and hips, some with pink or blue shoes.

    4-5in (10-13cm) $250-300
    6in (15cm) $350-400
    8in (20cm) $550-650
Solid head with swivel neck, glass eyes, jointed shoulders and hips
    4-5in (10-13cm) $525-575
    6in (15cm) $675-725
    8in (20cm) $950-1,000
Head with wig, glass eyes; jointed shoulders and hips
    4-5in (10-13cm) $600-650
    6in (15cm) $750--850
    8in (20cm) $1,250

Mark
6 - 13 ½
Copr. by
Grace S. Putnam
Germany

Action Bye-Lo Baby, immobile, in various positions, painted features,
3in (8cm) $250-300

All-Celluloid
4in (10cm) $275-325

8in (20cm) all-bisque *Bye-lo Baby* with wig and glass eyes. *Howard & Jan Foulke.*

Catterfelder Puppenfabrik

History Catterfelder Puppenfabrik, doll factory, Catterfeld, Thuringia, Germany. Founder Carl Troutman. Bisque heads made by J. D. Kestner and others. 1894-on.

Comment The C.P. character children are very rarely found and are eagerly sought-after by collectors of rare characters.

Description Perfect bisque socket head, sleeping or glass eyes, mohair wig or molded hair. Jointed composition body or bent-limb baby body. Appropriate vintage clothes.

Child Doll, #264 (Kestner)
Ca. 1902-on.
    14-17in (36-43cm) $350-400
    25in (64cm) $600

Mark
C P
208 / 45
Deponiert

°Few price samples available.

Character Child
Ca. 1910-on.
#207, 210, 215, 217, 219, 220
14-18in (36-46cm) $4000-5000up

Character Baby
Ca. 1910-on.
#200, 201, 208
    14-16in (36-41cm) $275-325
    19-21in (48-53cm) $400-500
#201 toddler 5-piece body
    8-10in (20-25cm) $650-750
#262, 263 (Kestner)
    15-17in (38-43cm) $325-375
    20-22in (51-56cm) $450-550
#262 toddler 5-piece body
    18in (46cm) $500-600

17in (43cm) 207
character, all original.
Richard Saxman Antiques

Celluloid Dolls

History Rheinische Gummi und Celluloid Fabrik Co. (turtle symbol); Buschow & Beck, (Minerva trademark, helmet symbol); E. Maar & Sohn, (Emasco trademark, 3M symbol); Cellba (mermaid symbol), all in Germany; P.R. Zask (ASK in triangle) in Poland; Petitcolin (eagle symbol), Société Nobel Française (SNF in diamond), Neuman & Mars (dragon symbol), Société Industrielle de Celluloid (Sicoine), all in France. Parsons-Jackson Co. in the United States; Cascelloid Ltd. (Palitoy) in England; Moto & Tomokichi Sekiguchi (3 lobed flower), Royal Co. Ltd (fleur-de-lis), Sato Sankichi (SS inside a Rhombus), all in Japan. 1900-on.
Comment Celluloids are in a slow mode in the United States, but are still very popular in Australia and Europe.
Mark As indicated above, also with the marks of J.D. Kestner, K & R, Bruno Schmidt, Käthe Kruse and König & Wernicke.

Celluloid Shoulder Head Child Doll
Ca. 1900-on. Cloth or kid body, celluloid or composition arms; dressed; all in good condition.
    Painted eyes, 16-18in (41-46cm) $85-110
    Glass eyes, 19-22in (48-56cm) $150-175
    Original provincial costume, 12-14in (30-36cm) $150-160
        Boy/girl pair $350-400

All-Celluloid Child Doll, Painted Eyes
Ca. 1900-on. Jointed at neck, shoulders and hips; all in good condition.
    4in (10cm) $25-35
    7-8in (18-20cm) $40-50
    10-12in (25-31cm) $65-85
    14-15in (36-38cm) $100-125
    Googly, 5in (12cm) $175-200
    Billy & Betty walkers, pair $150
    Tommy Tucker-type character, 12-14in (31-36cm) $125-135

Billy & Betty celluloid "walking" dolls with "finger" legs, all original. *Howard & Jan Foulke.*

French with original provincial costume by LeMinor, Poupées Magali and others

8in (20cm) $50-55
12-14in (31-36cm) $100-135
19in (48cm) $175-225
SNF pair with molded provincial costumes, 9in (23cm) $250

12in (30cm) celluloid shoulder head on cloth body, all original. *Howard & Jan Foulke.*

13½in (34cm) all-celluloid *Poupée Bretonne*, all original. *Howard & Jan Foulke.*

All-Celluloid Child, Glass Eyes
12-13in (31-33cm) $110-125
15-16in (38-41cm) $165
18in (46cm) $195
21in (53cm) $225
Turtle Mark Black Toddler, 16in (41cm) $250-350
Marie-France, by Petitcolin, smiling character, all original
    18in (46cm) $350-400
    Boxed, in child's dress $565
K★R 717 or 728, 14-16in (36-41cm) $350-450

All-Celluloid Baby
Ca. 1910-on. All in good condition.
6-8in (15-20cm) $40-45
10-12in (25-31cm) $85-95
15in (38cm) $125-135
21in (53cm) $165-195
SNF black baby, 16-18in (41-46cm) $300-350
Asian baby, 10in (25cm) $250-300

All-Celluloid, Made in Japan
Ca. 1920s.
Molded clothes
    4-5in (10-12cm) $40-50
    8-9in (20-23cm) $100-125
Child with pedestal legs, jointed arms, 6-7in (15-18cm) $15-20
Baby
    8-10in (20-25cm) $30-40
    24in (61cm) $150-165
Occupied Japan
    Chubby toddler character, 6½in (17cm) $85-95
    Baby, 24in (61cm) $100
    Bride & Groom, 3in (8cm) molded clothes $35-40

Parsons-Jackson, Stork Mark
11½in (29cm) baby $125-150
14in (36cm) toddler $250
With molded shoes and socks $300-325

Celluloid Head Infant
Ca. 1920s-on.Baby head with glass eyes; cloth body, appropriate clothes; all in good condition.
12-15in (31-38cm) $100-125

Celluloid Socket Head Doll
Ca. 1910-on. Wig, glass eyes, sometimes flirty, open mouth with teeth; ball-jointed or bent-limb composition body; dressed; all in good condition.
K★R 701, child, 12-13in (31-33cm) ....$900-1,100°
K★R 717, child, flapper body, 16-18in (41-46cm) $500-550
K★R 700, baby, 14-15in (36-38cm) $250-275
K★R 728
    12-13in (31-33cm) baby $200-250
    23in (38cm) baby $400-450
    14-15in (36-38cm) toddler $300-350
    18in (46cm) flapper $500-550
F.S. & Co. 1276, 17in (43cm) baby $200-250

°Few price samples available.

Chad Valley

History Chad Valley Co. (formerly Johnson Bros., Ltd.), Birmingham, England. 1917-on.

Comment The most popular models of this firm are the British Royal Children, Princesses Margaret and Elizabeth and Prince Edward, and the Mabel Lucie Attwell *Bambinos*. Dolls must be clean with good color and original clothes.

Description All cloth, usually felt face and velvet body; jointed neck, shoulders and hips, mohair wig, glass or painted eyes.

Mark Cloth label usually on foot: "HYGIENIC TOYS Made in England by CHAD VALLEY CO. LTD."

Chad Valley Doll

Characters, painted eyes, 10-12in (25-31cm) $75-95
Characters, glass eyes, 10-12in (25-31cm) $150-175
   17-20in (43-51cm) $500-1,500*
Children, painted eyes, 9in (23cm) $110-135
   13-14in (33-36cm) $300-325
   16-18in (41-46cm) $450-500
   Smiling face, 14-15in (36-38cm) $300-350
Children, glass eyes, 16-18in (41-46cm) $500-600
Royal Children, glass eyes, 16-18in (41-46cm) $1,000
Mabel Lucie Attwell, glass inset side-glancing eyes,
   smiling watermelon mouth, 15-17in (38-43cm) $650-750
Snow White Set, Dwarfs, 10in (25cm) each $200-225
   Snow White, 16in (41cm) $500-600
   Complete Set $2,500-3,000

16in (41cm) Palace Guard.
Diane Costa

Martha Chase

History Martha Jenks Chase, designer and manufacturer, Pawtucket, RI. 1889-on.

Comment Dolls should be clean and may have some minor wear and scuffs, but must have original paint. Chase made special hospital babies and adults for use in nurses' training.

Description Stockinet head and limbs painted with oils, large painted eyes and thick upper eyelashes, rough-stroked hair to provide texture. Sateen slip-covered cloth body jointed at shoulders, hips, elbows and knees; later dolls at hips and shoulders only; some bodies completely painted. Appropriate vintage clothing.

Mark Stamped on left leg or under left arm
Chase Stockinet Doll
or
Chase Hospital Doll
PAWTUCKET, R.I.
MADE IN U.S.A.

Chase Doll

Baby, 13-15in (33-38cm) $350-400*
17-20in (43-51cm) $450-500*
24-26in (61-66cm) $550*
Hospital Baby, 19-20in (49-51cm) $450-500
Child, molded bobbed hair
12-15in (31-38cm) $1,000-1,200
20in (51cm) $1,500-1,600
Boy with side part and side curl, 15-16in (38-41cm) . . . .$3,000°
Lady, 13-15in (33-38cm) $1,300-1,500
Man, 15-16in (38-41cm) . . . .$3,000°
Black Mammy. $10,000
Black child, at auction $16,450
Hospital Lady, 64in (163cm) $700-800
Alice in Wonderland character set, six dolls $67,000
George Washington, 24in (61cm) all original $5,500-6,500

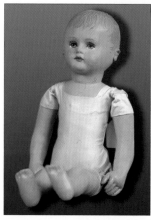

Label from original Chase box.
Howard & Jan Foulke.

24in (61cm) child.
Howard & Jan Foulke.

*Allow extra for a doll in excellent condition or with original clothes.
°Few price samples available.

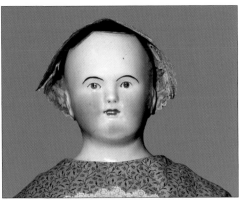

23in (58cm) Jacob Petit china head,
marked J.P. Par Brevet.
Kay Jensen Antique Dolls.

China Heads
French

History Various French doll firms, some heads may have been made in Germany. 1850s-on.

Comment The early heads by Jacob Petit are very rare and desirable. They are marked Par Brevet or JP on the front edge or inside. For Rohmer and Huret *poupées* see the French Fashion-type section.

Description Perfect china shoulder head with open crown, cork pate, and mohair wig or solid dome with painted hair, glass or painted eyes and eyelashes, feathered eyebrows, closed mouth. Shapely kid fashion body, may have china arms curved to above elbow. Appropriate vintage clothes.

Poupée with wig,
    12-13in (31-33cm) $2,800-3,200
    16-17in(41-43cm) $3,600-4,000
Painted black hair,
    6-7in (15-18cm) $450-500
    12in (31cm) $1,100
    16in (41cm) $2,500-2,800
    Jacob Petit, black painted pate, 22in (56cm) ....$,5000
Sèvres *Marquisette*, 1917-1918, 20in (51cm) at auction $4,620

English

History Possibly made in Rockingham area, Ca. 1840-1860.

Comment Although many collectors attribute these dolls as English, the origin is really unknown, and they may very well have been made elsewhere. The most desirable models have their original china limbs. Value goes down considerably if the limbs have been lost.

Description Perfect china shoulder head with flesh tint, bald head may have a molded slit for inserting wig, human hair wig, painted features, closed mouth. Cloth body with china lower limbs with holes to attach them to the cloth, bare feet. Appropriate vintage clothes.

19-22in (48-56cm) $3,000-4,000
Without china limbs $1,200-1,500

German

> **History** Made by various porcelain factories, such as Alt, Beck & Gottschalck; Kling & Co.; Hertel, Schwab & Co.; K.P.M.; Dressel & Kister; Dornheim, Koch & Fischer; Hertwig & Co., and others. 1840s-on.
> **Comment** The heads with unusual and fancy hairstyles are the best, and usually the earliest models. Glass eyes are unusual and desirable. Most china heads are ladies, but during the 1880s, child heads were designed. Blonde hair is more unusual than black.
> **Description** Perfect china shoulder with molded hair, may have pink tinted complexion. Vintage cloth body may have china arms and legs. Appropriate vintage clothing.
> **Mark** Usually none, but perhaps incised with mold or size numbers or Germany.

1840s Hairstyles

China shoulder head with black molded hair; may have pink tint complexion.

20in (51cm) kinderkopf.
Howard & Jan Foulke.

Hair swept back into bun
    5in (13cm) $600
    13-15in (33-38cm) $2,000-2,600
    18-21in (46-53cm) $3,200-4,200
Fancy braided bun,
    22-24in (51-61cm) $5,000-6,000
Long curls, early face,
    21in (53cm) $3,400
Kinderkopf (child head)
    10½in (27cm) $800-900
    18-22in (46-56cm) $2,500-2,800
Wood jointed body, china lower limbs
    5-6in (13-15cm) $1,800-2,200
    11in (28cm) $4,000-5,000
Molded Hat, Damen head,
    16in (41cm) at auction $10,575
K.P.M.
    Brown hair with bun, 16-18in (41-46cm) $6,500-7,000
    Brown hair with side curls, 14in (36cm) $5,000-5,500
    Young man, brown hair
        16-18in (41-46cm) $4,500
        22-23in (56-58cm) $7,000-8,000
    Boy, cafe-au-lait hair, head only
        4½in (11cm) $3,300

1850s Hairstyles

China shoulder head (some with pink tint), molded black hair (except bald).

16in (41cm)
1850s china with
Greiner-style hairdo
and brown eyes.
*Howard & Jan
Foulke.*

    Morning Glory, brown hair with molded flowers
        21in (53cm) $6,500-7,500
        27in (69cm) $10,000-11,000
    Bald Head, some with black areas on top, proper wig. Allow extra for original human hair wig in fancy style.
        Fine quality
            12in (31cm) $700-750
            15-17in (38-43cm) ...$1,000-1,200
            22-24in (56-61cm) $1,700-1,900
            19in (48cm) glass eyes $2,100

20in (51cm) china head with coiled bun.
Howard & Jan Foulke.

Standard quality
    13in (33cm) $500-550
    16-17in (41-43cm) $750-800
    20-22in (5 1-56cm) $900-1,000
Covered wagon with blue eyes
    5-7in (13-18cm) $275-300
    17-20in (43-51cm) $700-800
    24-26in (61-66cm) $1,000-1,100
    19in (48cm) wood body $3,000
Covered wagon with brown eyes, 20-22in (51-56cm) ...$1,100-1,300
Greiner-style with brown eyes
    14-15in (36-38cm) $1,300-1,500
    19-22in (48-56cm) $2,000-2,200
Greiner-style with glass eyes
    15-16in (38-41cm) ....$3,850°
    22in (56cm) ....$4,800°
Waves, framing face, brown eyes
    20-21in (51-53cm) $2,000-2,200
    With glass eyes, 18-21in (46-53cm) $3,000-3,500
Alice Hairdo, with molded headband,
    22-24in (56-61cm) $900-1,000
Sophia Smith, long curls, brown eyes,
    18-22in (46-56cm) $2,100-2,500
Lydia, 28in (71cm) $7,500
Molded Hat, 20in (51cm), long blond curls $4,500
Young Victoria, 18in (46cm) $2,500
Child or Baby, flange swivel neck; taüfling body with china
or papier-mâché shoulder plate and hips, china lower limbs; cloth
midsection (may have voice box) and upper limbs,
    10in (25cm) $3,000-4,000
Child with Alice Hairstyle, 12in (31cm) $4,000-5,000

°Few price samples available.

1860s and 1870s Hairstyles

China shoulder head with black molded hair (a few blondes); old cloth body may have leather arms or china lower arms and legs.

Plain style with center part (so-called flat top and high brow)
4½in (11cm) $150-175*
6-7in (15-18cm) $165-185*
14-16in (36-41cm) $250-300*
19-22in (48-56cm) $350-400*
24-26 in (61-66cm) $450-500*
28in (71cm) $600-700*
34-35in (86-89cm) $800-900
Molded necklace, 22-24in (56-61cm) $600-700
Molded blouse, 17in (43cm) $950
Blonde hair, 18in (46cm) $425-475
Brown eyes, 20-22in (51-56cm) $600-700
Swivel neck, 15½in (40cm) $1,500
Youthful face, 20-23 in (51-58cm) $550-600
All-china Child, jointed shoulders and hips
3½in (9cm) $900
9in (23cm) $3,800-4,000
Mary Todd Lincoln with snood
14-15in (36-38cm) $850
18-21in (46-53cm) $1,000-1,100
Blonde hair, fancy snood, 20-21in (51-53cm) $1,500
Conta and Boehme
19in (48cm) $700-800
Molded bonnet, applied flowers, poor quality,
20in (51cm) $500
Young Man, 21in (53cm) $1,300-1,500
Dolley Madison, with molded bow
21-24in (53-61cm) $450-550
Blonde hair, pierced ears, 22in (56cm) $750-800
Adelina Patti
13-15in (33-38cm) $425-475
19-22in (48-56cm) $650-725
14in (36cm) original body and limbs $600
Dagmar-type, 18in (46cm) $800
Jenny Lind
12in (31cm) $850
21-24in (53-61cm) $1,600-1,800
Currier & Ives, long hair on shoulders, 15in (38cm) $600
Curly Top
14in (36cm) black hair $600
19in (48cm) tan hair $900
Grape Lady, 18in (46cm) $2,200-2,500
Spill Curl
19-22in (48-56cm) $900-1,100
Café-au-lait color with black hair band, 24in (61cm) $1,430
Fancy Hair Styles
Light brown hair, fancy green and white snood,
20in (51cm) $2,400
Curls on forehead, high curls in back,
18½in (47cm) $2,500
High loose bun, brushmarks, pierced ears,
14in (36cm) $3,300

*Allow 50% more for all-original body and clothes.

24in (61cm) china head with so-called
Alice hair style with molded head band.
Howard & Jan Foulke.

12in (30cm) china head with molded bun, so-called Jenny Lind.
Howard & Jan Foulke.

1880s Hairstyles

China shoulder head with black or blonde molded hair. Many made by Alt,
Beck & Gottschalck or Kling & Co.

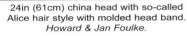

14-16in (36-41cm)	$225-275
21-23in (53-58cm)	$350-400
28in (71cm)	$500-550
Head only, 5in (13cm)	$125-150
Bawo and Dotter, "Pat. Dec. 7/80," 18-20in (46-51cm)	$350-400

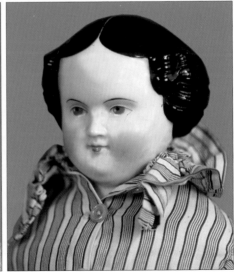

11½in (29cm) china head with
blonde hair and molded snood.
Private Collection.

24in (61cm) 1860s china head with brown eyes.
Howard & Jan Foulke.

1890s Hairstyles

China shoulder head with black or blonde molded wavy hair; allow extra for a lithographed body.

4½in (11cm) $55-60
8-10in (20-25cm) $75-85
13-15in (33-38cm) $100-125
19-21in (48-53cm) $150-200
24in (61cm) $250
Open mouth, 10in (25cm) $175-200
Molded bonnet,
    8-10in (20-25cm) $125-150
Molded "Jewel" necklace
    22in (56cm) $400-425
    8½in (21cm) $150-165
Black Man, 12in (31cm)
    at auction $1,050
Jester, molded hat,
    14-17in (36-43cm) $650-750

Dressel & Kister

Ca. 1890-1920. China shoulder head with varying hairdos and brush-stroked hair; delicately painted features; cloth body with china arms having beautifully molded fingers. Often used as ornamental dolls in only half form as for a boudoir lamp or candy box.

13in (33cm) ....$1,500 up
Heads only $675-750

Dressel & Kister china head.
Private Collection.

Pet Name

Ca. 1905. Made by Hertwig & Co. for Butler Bros., New York. China shoulder head, molded yoke with name in gold; black or blonde painted hair (one-third were blonde). Used names such as **Agnes, Bertha, Ruth, Dorothy, Edith, Esther, Ethel, Florence, Helen, Mabel, Marion** and **Pauline**.

12-14in (30-36cm) $50-175
18-21in (46-53cm) $250-300
24in (61cm) $350

Cloth, Printed

History American companies, such as Cocheco Mfg Co., Lawrence & Co., Arnold Print Works, Art Fabric Mills and Selchow & Righter. English companies, such as Dean's Rag Book Co. 1896-on.

Comment These dolls were printed on fabric to be cut out and sewn at home. The child dolls in printed underwear were dressed. All prices are for dolls in very good condition with bright color and vintage clothing if appropriate.

Mark Foot may be stamped with a patent date, but the mark was usually on the fabric part which was discarded after cutting.

Dolly Dear, Merry Marie, Improved Foot Doll, Standish No Break Doll and others with printed underwear

7-9in (18-23cm) $50-65
16-18in (41-46cm) $90-100
22-24in (56-61cm) $125-135

Uncut sheet
   13in (33cm) doll $90-100
   20in (51cm) doll $125-135
Black Child, Art Fabric, 18in (46cm) $150-175
Children with Printed Outer clothes, Ca. 1903.
   12-13in (31-33cm) $90-110
   17in (43cm) $125-150
Aunt Jemima Family, 1924, four doll set $220
Baby's Ball, 1910 Art Fabric $300
Brownies, 1892, Palmer Cox, marked on foot,
   8in (20cm) $65-75
   Uncut sheet of 6 .... $225
Buster Brown & Tige $275
Christmas Stocking, 1907, Saalfield $715
Cream of Wheat Rastus, 1922. .... $90
Cresota Flour Boy $275
Duck & Ducklings, 1910, Elms & Sellon $200
Foxy Grandpa, 1903, Wheaton $125
E.T. Gibson, 1912, red bathing costume $200
Ida Gutsell, 1893, Cocheco $225-250
Kelloggs
   4 Fairyland Dolls, 1928 .... $220
   Snap, Crackle & Pop, uncut set $125
   Dandy the Duck, 1935, uncut $85
   Freckles the Frog, 1935, uncut $100
   Goldilocks & Bears, 1935, uncut $150
Red Riding Hood, 1892, Arnold, uncut $225
Rooster, 1892, Arnold, uncut $525
Tom Thumb, 1907, Selchow & Righter $65
Topsy, 1892, Arnold Print Works $135
Mothers' Congress, 1900. 17in (43cm) faded $650
Pillow Dolls, 1920s-1930s, printed and hand-embroidered,
   16in (41cm) $40-50
Gerber Baby, 1940s, 8in (20cm) pair $220

8in (20cm) printed cloth girl.
Howard & Jan Foulke.

Columbian Doll

History Emma and Marietta Adams, Oswego, NY, 1891-1910 or later.

Comment Columbian dolls are prized for their primitive look and beautiful painting. Especially desirable are dolls painted by Emma before her death in 1900. Dolls may have some wear and fading, but no repaint or touch-up.

Description All-cloth with hand-painted hair and features on a flat face, painted limbs. Appropriate vintage clothes.

Mark Stamp on back of body

Before 1900   **COLUMBIAN DOLL**
     EMMA E. ADAMS
     OSWEGO CENTRE, N.Y.
After 1906   **COLUMBIAN DOLL**
     MANUFACTURED BY
     MARIETTA ADAMS RUTTAN
     OSWEGO, N.Y.

15in (38cm) **$6,000-7,000**	
19-23in (48-58cm) **$8,000-10,000**	
23in (58cm), some wear .**$4,000-4,200**	
20in (51cm), quite worn **$2,200**	

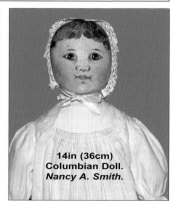

**14in (36cm)
Columbian Doll.
Nancy A. Smith.**

Danel, Later Jumeau

History Danel & Cie, Paris and Montreuil-sous-Bois, France, 1889-1892. Jumeau 1892-1895.

Comment Jumeau won a lawsuit in 1892 against Danel and took over his trademarks *Paris Bébé* and *Bébé Française*.

Description Perfect bisque socket head, glass paperweight eyes, closed mouth, pierced ears. French composition and wood jointed body. Appropriate vintage clothes.

Paris Bébé

Ca. 1889-1892. A copy of a Jumeau doll.
    11in (28cm) **$2,500**
    18-20in (46-51cm) ..**$3,500-3,800**
    24-26in (61-66cm) ..**$4,200-4,500**

Mark	
Incised on head	**Tête Déposé** **Paris Bébé**
Stamp on body	[Eiffle Tower symbol] PARIS BÉBÉ **Brévete**

Paris Bébé

Character face developed by Jumeau for use with this trademark after 1892.
    18-19in (46-48cm) **$4,500-5,500**
    26-28in (66-71cm) **$7,000-8,000**

Bébé Française

1891.

Mark Incised on head: **B 9 F**

    14-16in (36-41cm) **$3,700-4,000**
    23-25in (58-64cm) **$5,200-5,700**

26in (66cm) DEP with
closed mouth.
Kay Jensen Antique Dolls.

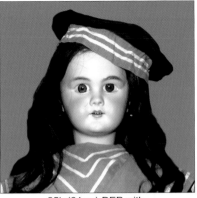

25in(64cm) DEP with
open mouth.
Gloria & Mike Duddlesten.

DEP

History Closed-mouth DEP is often found on a marked Jumeau body, but the origins are unclear. Open-mouth DEP head sometimes found with a Tête Jumeau red stamp was made by Simon & Halbig German porcelain factory for SFBJ's Jumeau line.

Comment These models are very popular with collectors. Allow at least $200 extra for a Jumeau flowered shift.

Description Perfect bisque socket head, glass eyes, pierced ears, vintage mohair wig. French jointed composition and wood body, sometimes with Jumeau label or stamp. Appropriate vintage clothes.

| Mark DEP |
| 8 |

DEP Closed-Mouth Bébé

Ca. 1890. Closed mouth, paperweight eyes, upper and lower painted eyelashes.

12in (31cm) $1,500-1,600
15in (38cm) $2,000-2,100
18-20in (46-51cm) $2,500-3,200
25-27in (63-68cm) ....$,3800-4,200

DEP Open-Mouth Bébé

Ca. 1900-on. Deeply molded eye socket, sleep eyes, painted lower eyelashes, upper hair eyelashes.

9½-10in (24-25cm) $1,000
13-15in (33-38cm) $900-950
18-20in (46-51cm) $1,050-1,200
23-25in (58-64cm) $1,300-1,500
29-30in (74-76cm) $1,800-2,000
35in (89cm) $2,500-2,600
10in (25cm) trousseau
        boxed set $2,500

31in (79cm) *Paris Bébé.*
Linda Kellerman.

Door of Hope

History Handmade by girls at the Door of Hope Mission, Shanghai, China. Heads made by carvers from Ning-Po. 1901-on.
Comment These high-quality dolls are extremely popular with collectors. There are 25 dolls in the series with authentic costuming for different classes of Chinese people.
Description Carved wood head with painted and/or carved hair. Cloth body, some with stubby cloth arms, some with carved hands. Original handmade clothes. Dolls in excellent colorful condition.
Mark May have **Made in China** label.

11-13in (28-33cm)

Adult	$900-1,500
Amah	$700-800
Amah with Baby	$1,700-2,000
Bride, old style with face veil	$1,500
Bride, new style	$2,000
Manchu Lady, carved headdress	$5,000-7,000
Policeman	$2,000-3,000
Priest	$,2000-3,000
Young lady, side part	$2,300

6½in (16cm) Door of Hope Child, all original.
Connie & Jay Lowe.

Dressel

History Cuno & Otto Dressel, doll factory and verlager (distributed items made by other doll factories), Sonneberg, Thuringia, Germany. Bisque heads made by Armand Marseille, Simon & Halbig, Ernst Heubach, and Gebrüder Heubach. 1700-on.
Comment The Dressel factory had a long production history. Collectors favor the Jutta dolls and the #1469 flapper lady. Quality varies, so be sure to look for the best example you can find.
Description Perfect bisque socket head on composition body or shoulder head on kid body. Appropriate clothing.

Marked Holz-Masse
Ca. 1875-on. Papier-mâché or composition shoulder head; cloth/composition body. See page 153.

Child Doll
Ca. 1893-on. Perfect bisque head, good wig, glass eyes, open mouth.

Composition body

16-18in (41-46cm)	$225-250
22-24in (56-61cm)	$275-325
32in (81cm)	$500-550
38in (96cm)	$1,200-1,500

Marks

1896
C.O.D. 9 DEP

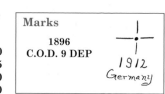

1912
Germany

#93, 1896, kid body

    15-16in (38-41cm) $165-200
    19-22in (48-56cm) $225-250
Character-type face, similar to
K★R 117n
    16in (41cm) $650-750
    20-22in (51-56cm) $900-1,100
    34in (86cm) $1,800-2,000

Label on box of Dressel child.

12in (31cm) Dressel child,
all-original and boxed.
Howard & Jan Foulke.

19in (48cm) Dressel character
boy with composition head.
Howard & Jan Foulke.

Portrait Series

1896. Perfect bisque heads with portrait faces, glass eyes, some with molded mustaches and goatees; composition body; original clothes; all in good condition. Some marked "S" or "D" with a number.
Uncle Sam,
    13in (33cm) $1,500
    17in (43cm) $2,800
Admiral Dewey and Officers
    8in (20cm) $750-850
    15in (38cm) $1,800-2,200
Teddy Roosevelt,
    13iin (33cm) $6,500
Buffalo Bill, Hexe, Farmer, Old Rip,
    8-10in (20-25cm) $500-650

Marked Jutta Child

Ca. 1906-1921. Perfect bisque socket head, good wig, sleep eyes, open mouth, pierced ears; ball-jointed composition body. Head made by Simon & Halbig. Mold 1348 or 1349.
    14-16in (36-41cm) $450-475
    19-21in (43-53cm) $500-550
    24-26in (61-66cm) $600-650
    30-32in (76-81cm) $800-900
    38-39in (96-99cm) $2,500-2,800

20in (51cm) *Jutta* 1349 child.
Howard & Jan Foulke.

Mark
1349
Jutta
S & H
6

Character Child
Ca. 1909-on. Perfect bisque socket head (glazed inside), mohair wig, painted eyes, closed mouth; ball-jointed composition body.

Mark

COD
$\text{A}/2$

 10-12in (25-31 cm) ....$1,500-1,800°
 16-18in (41-46cm) $3,000
 Limbach 8679 pouty, glass eyes,
  14in (36cm) ....$1,800-$2,000°
 Composition head
  19in (48cm) ....$2,600-$3,000°
  13in (33cm) wear on nose and lips $1,300

Marked C.O.D. Character Baby
Ca. 1910-on. Perfect bisque character face with wig or molded hair, painted or glass eyes; jointed baby body.
 12-14in (31-36cm) $200-225
 17-19in (43-48cm) $300-325
 23-24in (58-61cm) $400-450

Marked Jutta Character Baby
Ca. 1910-1922. Perfect bisque socket head, good wig, sleep eyes, open mouth: bent-limb composition baby body; dressed; all in good condition.

Mark

Jutta
1914.

5½

 Simon & Halbig
  16-18in (41-46cm) $400-450
  23-24in (58-61cm) $600-700
  Toddler, fully-jointed body, 18-20in (46-51cm) $800-900
 Other Makers (Armand Marseille, E. Heubach)
  16-18in (41-46cm) $300-350
  23-24in (58-61cm) $400-450

Lady Doll
Ca. 1920s. Bisque socket head with young lady face, good wig, sleep eyes, closed mouth; jointed composition body in adult form with molded bust, slim waist and long arms and legs, feet modeled to wear high-heeled shoes.
 #1469, 14in (36cm)
  Naked $2,000-2,500
  Original clothes $3,000-3,500

E.D. Bébé

History Etienne Denamur, Paris, France. 1889-on. **Comment** Dolls with the Jumeau look and signed "E.D." are Jumeau factory dolls produced when

Mark E 10 D
DÉPOSÉ

Emile Douillet was director of the Jumeau firm, 1892-1899. They do not have the word "Déposé" under the "E.D." They are priced in the Jumeau section. E.D. quality varies, so choose carefully.

Description Perfect bisque head, mohair wig, blown glass eyes, pierced ears. Wood and composition jointed body. Appropriate clothes.

 Closed mouth
  15-17in (38-48cm) $2,400-2,500
  22-24in (56-61cm) $3,200-3,500
  28in (71cm) $3,800
 Open mouth
  18-20in (35-51cm) $1,500-1,600
  25-27in (64-69cm) $1,900-2,100

°Few price samples available.

E.D. Bébé.
James D. Julia, Inc.

Eden Bébé

History Fleischmann & Blodel doll factory, Paris, France. 1890-1899. SFBJ 1899-on.
Comment Quality varies, so choose carefully. Pay 35% less for heads on 5-piece composition bodies.
Description Perfect bisque head, mohair wig, blown glass eyes, pierced ears. Wood and composition jointed body. Appropriate clothes.

Marked Eden Bébé

Ca. 1890.
Closed mouth
14-16in (36-41cm) $1,500-1,700
21-23in (53-58cm) $2,000-2,200
Open mouth, 19-20in (48-51cm) $1,200-1,300

Mark
EdenBebe
PARIS
9
DE POSE

26in (66cm) Eden Bébé.
Private Collection.

French Fashion-Type (Poupée)

History Various French firms, most in or near Paris. Ca. 1850-1930. See also Bru, Jumeau, Gaultier, Gesland and China Heads, French. **Comment** Poupées are beautiful lady dolls in elegant fashionable clothes. Only a few porcelain factories, such as Gaultier and Blampoix, produced the bisque heads and parts used for them. The numerous doll shops and small factories made their own bodies, wigs and clothes, but bought the porcelain parts from the large suppliers. **Description** Perfect head of fine quality bisque, swivel or stationary neck, blown glass eyes, closed mouth, pierced ears, mohair wig. French kid leather body, sometimes with bisque arms or jointed wood body. All prices are for a doll in very good condition in appropriate clothing. Allow extra for bisque lower arms.

Kid body (*poupée peau*)
    12-13in (31-33cm) $1,900-2,200*
    15-16in (38-41cm) $2,650-3,000*
    18-19in (46-48cm) $3,350-3,650*
    21in (53cm) $4,200-4,500*
    33in (84cm) $6,000-6,750*
Bisque arms and lower legs,
    16in (41cm) $6,500*
Painted eyes, stiff neck,
    16-17in (41-43cm) $1,800-2,200*
Wood body (*poupée bois*),
    16-18in (41-46cm) $6,200-6,800*

12½in (32cm) *poupée peau*, all original.
Kay Jensen Antique Dolls.

E.B. Poupée
E. Barrois, 1862-1877. | Mark E 1 DÉPOSÉ B |
    Kid body
        14-16in (36-41cm) $2,800-3,200*
        19-20in (48-51cm) $3,600-3,900*
        23in (58cm) $4,500-4,750*
    Open mouth, 18in (46cm) $6,000-7,000
    Wood body, 18in (46cm) $6,500

B.S. Poupée.
Ainé Blampoix (Senior). 1855-1870.
    Kid body, 16in (41cm) $3,000-3,500

Clément, Pierre Victor
1866-1875.
    Hollow leather body, 17in (43cm) $8,000-9,000

A. Dehors
1866. Portrait face, swivel neck, bisque lower arms.
    17in (43cm) $18,000-19,000

*Allow up to 50% extra for fancy original clothes.

Duval-Denis
Early 1860s. Early white bisque shoulder head, kid body.

18in (46cm) $5,500

Huret Poupée
Maison Huret. 1850-1920.

China or bisque shoulder head, 16-17in (42-43cm)

    Kid body $15,000-20,000

    Wood body $20,000-25,000

    Gutta-percha body $20,000-25,000

      Rare face with painted teeth $93,500

      Original fashion dress $1,500-2,500

Signed chair, 12in (31cm) $1,500

Signed table, 8in (20cm) $1,500

17in (43cm) Huret *poupée peau*, with painted eyes.
Nancy A. Smith.

L.D. Poupée
Louis Doléac & Cie. 1881-1908.

16-17in (42-43cm), Kid body $4,000-5,000

Wood body, distinctive face $10,000

Lavallée-Peronne, Mme.
A La Poupée de Nuremberg.

Wood body, 17in (43cm) $6,500

    Lily (La Poupée Modele), at auction $14,300

Martin, Benoit
1863. Wood, metal and gutta-percha body.

    La Poupée Phenix, 17in (43cm) at auction $8,800

Radiquet and Cordonnier
1880. *Poupée-statuette.* Molded breasts, bisque arms, one bent at elbow, bisque lower legs, original signed stand.

17in (43cm) $12,500-13,500

Rohmer Poupée
1857-1880. China or bisque swivel or shoulder head.

16-18in (41-46cm) $4,000-4,500

Simonne Poupée
1863-1878.
Kid body, 16-17in (41-43cm) $3,300-3,800
Wood body, 18in (46cm) $6,500-7,500

Terrene Poupée
1863-1890.
Kid over metal body, 17in (43cm) $6,000-6,500

Period Clothes for a Poupée
Dress $500-1,000
Boots $300-350
Elaborate mohair wig $350-400
Plain mohair wig $150-250

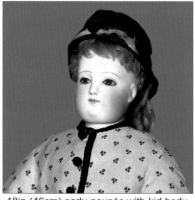

18in (46cm) early *poupée* with kid body
and bisque arms and legs.
Kay Jensen Antique Dolls.

5½-9in (13-23cm) Frozen Charlottes.
Kay Jensen Antique Dolls.

Frozen Charlotte (Bathing Doll)

History Various German porcelain factories. Ca. 1850s to early 1900s.
Comment These early dolls were called "bathing dolls" because
children played with them in water and at the beach. Many of the
smaller ones were light and could float.
Description All china doll, black or blonde molded hair, painted features; arms extended, legs separated but not jointed; perfect condition,
good quality.
Mark Usually none.

Frozen Charlotte
2-3in (5-8cm) $50-65*
4-5in (10-13cm) $140-165*
6-7in (15-18cm) $200-225*
9-10in (23-25cm) $275-325*
14-15in (36-38cm) $550-600
17in (43cm) $700-750
Pink tint, early hairdo
    2½-3½in (6-9cm) $300-325
    3½in (9cm) *café-au-lait* hair $425
    5in (13cm) $425-450
    8-10in (20-25cm) $800-1,000

*Allow extra for pink tint, fine decoration and modeling, unusual hairdo.

Pink tint with bonnet
   3½in (9cm) $400-450
   5in (13cm) $525-575
Black china, 5in (13cm $165-195
Black boy, molded turban and pants, 3in (8cm) $275-300
Black boy, molded shift, 5in (13cm) $300-350
Blonde hair, molded bow, 5½in (14cm) $200-225
Wig, lovely painted boots, 5in (13cm) $200-225
All-Bisque
   Child, 5in (13cm) $150-175
   Parian-type (1860s style), 5in (13cm) $225-250
   Alice style with pink boots, 5in (13cm) $325-375
   Fancy hairdo and boots, 4½in (11cm) $275-300
   Molded clothes, 3¼in (9cm) $225
   Early boy, blonde hair, 9in (23cm) $450-500

Fulper

History Fulper Pottery Co., Flemington, NJ, porcelain factory, for doll factories, such as Amberg or Horsman. 1918-1921.

Comment Collectors of American dolls are particularly interested in examples from this company, one of the few American porcelain factories to produce bisque doll heads. A particularly pretty example will be higher. Quality varies, so choose carefully.

Description Perfect bisque head, wig, set or sleep eyes, open mouth; kid or composition body. Appropriate clothes.

Mark

AMBERG
DOLLS
THE WORLD
STANDARD

MADE IN
U.S.A.

16in (41cm) Fulper character baby.
Howard & Jan Foulke.

Fulper Child Doll
Kid body, 18-21in (46-53cm $225-250
Composition body
   16-18in (41-46cm) $250-300
   22-24in (56-61cm) $325-375
Character Baby
   16-18in (41-46cm) $275-300
   22-24in (56-61cm) $375-400
Toddler, 22in (56cm) $550-650
Molded hair, 16in (41cm) ....$3,500-4,000°

°Few price samples available.

Gaultier

History François Gauthier (name changed to Gaultier in 1875). St. Maurice, Charenton, Seine, Paris, France. 1860-1899. SFBJ 1899-on. **Comment** Gaultier made heads and porcelain parts only, not bodies. Quality of F.G. heads varies with early models being finer and more desirable. Of all of the French *poupées*, those by F.G. are the most easily found. The "block letter" *bébés* are very popular with collectors.

F.G. Fashion Lady (Poupée Peau)

Ca. 1860-1930. Perfect bisque swivel head on bisque shoulder plate, original or good French wig, lovely glass stationary eyes, closed mouth, ears pierced; original kid body, kid arms with wired fingers or bisque lower arms and hands.

Mark "F.G." on side of shoulder.

```
10-11 in (26-28cm) ....$1,500-1,650*
12-13in (30-33cm) ......$1,600-1,800
16-17in (41-43cm) .....$1,900-2,200*
20in (51cm) .........$2,500-2,700*
23-24in (58-61cm) .....$3,000-3,200*
29-30in (71-76cm) ......$4,500-5,000
35in (89cm) ...............$6,500
37in (94cm) ................$7,200
```

Wood body, (*Poupée Bois*),
   16-18in (41-46cm) . .$4,800-$5,200
Late doll in ethnic costume,
   8-9in (20-23cm) $750-850
Painted eyes,
   16-17in (41-43cm) ...$1,800-2,000
Painted eyes, molded hair,
   13in (33cm) $2,600-2,800
Man with molded mustache,
   13in (33cm) $3,000

18in (46cm) Gaultier *poupée peau.*
Howard & Jan Foulke.

APPROXIMATE SIZE CHART	
3/0 = 10½in (27cm)	3 = 17in (43cm)
2/0 = 11½in (29cm)	5 = 20in (51cm)
1 = 13½in (34cm)	6 = 22in (56cm)
2 = 15in (38cm)	

F.G. Bébé, "Block Letter" Mark

Ca. 1879-1887. Perfect bisque swivel head, large bulgy paperweight eyes, closed mouth, pierced ears.

Mark F.7.G.

Composition body
```
10in (25cm) .........$4,600-4,900
13-15in (33-38cm) ....$4,500-4,800
18-20in (46-51cm) ....$5,500-6,000
22-23in (56-58cm) ....$6,100-6,200
27-28in (69-71cm) ....$6,800-7,200
33-35in (84-89cm) .....$7,500-8,000
```
Kid body
```
10in (25cm) .........$5,000-5,200
13-14in (33-36cm) ....$5,000-5,500
17-19in (43-48cm) ..........$6,250
22in (56cm) .........$7,000-7,500
```

21in (53cm) Gaultier *bébé*, block letter mark on kid body. *Kay Jensen Antique Dolls.*

*Allow up to 50% extra for original clothes.

F.G. Bébé, "Scroll" Mark

Ca. 1887-1900. Bisque head, beautiful large set eyes; composition body.

Closed mouth, very good quality bisque

5-6in (13-15cm) $750-800
15-17in (38-43cm) $3,000-3,300
22-24in (56-61cm) $3,800-4,100
27-28in (69-71cm) $4,500-5,000
32in (81cm) $5,500

Open mouth

14-17in (38-43cm) $1,750-1,950
20-22in (51-56cm) $2,100-2,400
31in (79cm) $3,300-3,600

Mark

Gesland

History E. Gesland, Paris, France. 1860-1928. Heads by François Gaultier.

Comment The early faces are the most desirable. All Gesland dolls are fairly difficult to find. Choose "scroll" mark faces carefully as the quality varies.

Description Perfect bisque swivel head, mohair wig, paperweight eyes, closed mouth, pierced ears. Stockinet body on metal frame with bisque hands and legs for the poupées and composition for the *bébés*.

Mark Head: **F.G.**
Body Sometimes stamped "E. Gesland."

Fashion Lady (Poupée)

Early face, 16-20in (41-51cm) $5,500-6,200*
F.G. face
14in (36cm) $3,600-3,800*
16-20in (41-51cm) $4,000-4,500*
24in (61cm) $5,500-5,700*
28in (71cm) $6,000-6,500
Body only, for 14in (36cm) $1,100

Bébé

Beautiful early face
14-16in (36-41cm) $5,200-5,500
22-24in (56-61cm) $6,200-6,500
29-30in (71-76cm) $7,300-7,500
"Scroll" mark face
14-16in (36-41cm) $3,000-3,300
22-24in (56-61cm) $4,000-4,500
31in (79cm) $4,800-5,200

17½in (45cm) Gesland *poupée*, all original.
Private Collection.

*Allow up to 50% extra for original clothes.

7in (18cm) Goebel character girl.
Howard & Jan Foulke.

Goebel

History F & W Goebel porcelain factory, Coburg, Thuringia, Germany. 1879-on.
Comment This factory produced mostly porcelain novelties and small dolls. Still in business today, it is famous for the Hummel figurines.
Description Perfect bisque socket head, composition body.

Marks

"B" plus number
"Germany"
sometimes A, C, G, H, K, S, SA & T

Goebel Child Doll
1895 on.
    #120 or B
        16-18in (41-46cm) $275-300
        23-25in (58-64cm) $325-350

Goebel Character Baby
Ca. 1910.
        13-15in (33-38cm) $200-225
        19-21in (48-53cm) $325-350

Goebel Character Doll
Ca. 1910. Molded hair in various styles, some with ornamentation, some with hats; character face with painted features; papier-mâché five-piece body.
        6½in (7cm) $200-250

9½in (24cm) Goebel B5 character baby.
Howard & Jan Foulke.

Googly-Eyed Dolls

History J.D. Kestner; Armand Marseille; Hertel, Schwab & Co.; Heubach; H. Steiner; Goebel and other German and French firms. Ca. 1911-on.
Comment Googlies are probably the most popular doll type. Nearly all collectors have at least one googly. Prices are for dolls with vintage wigs and clothes.

All-Bisque Googly

Jointed at shoulders and hips, molded shoes and socks; mohair wig, glass eyes, impish mouth; undressed.

Glass Eyes
    #217, 501, 330 and others
        4½-5in (11-13cm) $700-750
        5½-6in (14-15cm) $850-950
    #189, 192 swivel necks
        4½-5in (11-13cm) $850-975
        5½-6in (14-15cm) $1,050-1,150
        7in (18cm) $1,350-1,450
Baby, 4½in (12cm) $550-600
    #112 Kestner, jointed elbows and knees, swivel neck
        5in (13cm) $3,250
        7in (18cm) . . . .$4,500°
    #111 Kestner, jointed elbows and knees, stiff neck,
        5½in (13cm $2,850-3,250
    S.W.C. #405, 6½in (17cm) . . . .$1,350°
    K★R 131, 7in (18cm) . . . .$3,500-3,800°
Painted eyes, molded hair or wigged
    #217, 179 and others
        4½in (12cm) $400
        6in (15cm) $550-600
        7in (18cm) $650-700
    S.W.C. #408, 5in (13cm) $350-450
    #218, baby with wig, 6in (15cm) $525

4½in (11cm) S.W.C. all-bisque googly with glass eyes.
Howard & Jan Foulke.

9in (23cm) A.M. 252 googly with top knot.
Howard & Jan Foulke.

Painted Eyes, Composition Body

Perfect bisque swivel head; five-piece composition toddler or baby body; cute clothes.
A.M., E. Heubach, Goebel, R.A.
      6½-7½in (16-19cm) $400-450*
      9-10in (23-25cm) $750*
      12in (31cm) $1,000*
#252 A.M., Kewpie-type baby
      9in (23cm) . . . .$1,200-1,400°
Gebrüder Heubach
      6-7in (15-18cm) $575-625*
      7in (18cm) Winker $850-900
      9in (23cm)
        top knot $1,700-1,900
#262 E.H., 7in (18cm) $900

°Few price samples available.   *Allow extra for unusual models.

13in (33cm) A.M. 323 googly.
Howard & Jan Foulke.

9in (23cm) A.M. 200 googly.
Private Collection.

Glass Eyes, Composition Body

Perfect bisque head; original composition body; cute clothes; all in nice condition.

A.M. #323 and other similar models by H. Steiner, E. Heubach, Goebel and Recknagel

> 7-8in (18-20cm) $850-900
> 10in (25cm) $1,200-1,400
> 13in (33cm) $2,000-2,250
> Baby body, 10-11 in (25-28cm) $1,000-1,200

Armand Marseille

> **#253 (watermelon mouth)**
> > 7-8in (18-20cm) $1,100-1,300
> > 11in (28cm) $2,000-2,300
> > 13½in (34cm) $3,500
> **#200, 9-11in (23-28cm)** $1,600-1,800
> **#240, 10in (25cm)**
> > toddler $3,000-3,200
> **#241, 10in (25cm)** ....$3,500°

Bähr & Pröschild 686,
> 7in (18cm) ....$2,500°

Demalcol (Dennis, Malley & Co., London, England),
> 9-10in (23-25cm) $750-850

Max Handwerck (Elite)
> Molded hat,
> > 10-13in (25-33cm) ... $1,700-1,800
> Uncle Sam $2,500
> Double-faced $2,200

Hertel, Schwab & Co.
> **#163, red molded hair**
> > 15in (38cm) baby ...$6,000-6,500
> > Toddler
> > > 12in (31cm) $5,000
> > > 16in (41cm) $7,000-7,500
> **#165, Baby**
> > 11-12in (28-31cm) ..$3,200-3,500
> > 16in (41cm) $5,500

**Kammer & Reinhardt
131 googly.**
*Courtesy of John
Clendenien.*

Toddler
 11-12in (28-31cm) $4,500
 16in (41cm) $6,500
 26in (66cm) at auction $23,000
#172
 Baby, 15in (38cm) ....$7,500°
 Toddler, 18in (46cm) ....$12,000°
#173
 Baby
  10-11 in (26-28cm) ....$3,500-3,800°
  16in (41cm) ....$6,000-6,500°
 Toddler
  10-12in (26-31cm) ....$4,000-5,000°
  16in (41cm) .... $7,000-7,500°
Ernst Heubach
 #291, 7in (18cm) matching pair with
  dimples, at auction $2,800
 #310, 13-14in (33-36cm) at auction $4,000-4,500
 #322, 8½-9in (21-23cm) $2,100-2,400
Gebrüder Heubach
 Einco
  11in (28cm) five-piece body $3,500-3,800
  18in (46cm) at auction $13,500
 Elizabeth, 7-9in (18-23cm) $1,850
 #8678, 9573
  6-7in (15-18cm) $900-1,000
  9in (23cm) $1,500
 #10542, 8in (20cm) $900-1,000
Oscar Hitt, 13in (33cm) at auction $26,000
K★R 131, 15-16in (38-41cm) $10,000-11,000
J.D.K. 221
 12-13in (31-33cm) $5,800-6,800
 16½in (43cm) largest size $13,000-14,500
Kley & Hahn 180, 16½in (43cm) ....$3,500°
Limbach SK, 8in (20cm) ....$2,800°
P.M. 950, 11in (28cm) ....$3,100-$,300°
S.F.B.J. #245
 8in (20cm), five-piece body $2,200-2,500
 15in (38cm) ....$4,500-4,600°
Schieler, 15in (38cm) ....$3,200°

Disc Eyes
DRGM 954642 black or white.
 11-12in (28-31cm) .... $900-1,200°

Composition Face
1911-1914. Hug Me Kids, Little Bright Eyes and other trade names. Round all-composition or composition mask face, wig, round glass eyes looking to the side, watermelon mouth; felt body; original clothes; all in very good condition.
 10in (25cm) $650-700
 12in (31cm) $850-950
 16in (41cm) $1,000-1,250

Greiner

History Ludwig Greiner of Philadelphia, PA, U.S.A. 1858-1883, but probably as early as 1840s.
Comment Greiner obtained the earliest known U.S. Patent for a doll head. His dolls are well-respected by collectors of papier-mâché dolls. The '58 label dolls are most desirable. Look for dolls with old bodies. Some wear on the head is expected, but no repaint. Some patches on the body are acceptable.
Description Papier-mâché shoulder head with black or blonde molded hair, painted features; vintage cloth body with leather arms. Appropriate vintage clothing.

Mark Paper label on back shoulder:
GREINER'S
IMPROVED
PATENT HEADS
Pat. March 30th '58
Or
GREINER'S
PATENT DOLL HEADS
No 5
Pat. Mar. 30 '58. Ext. '72

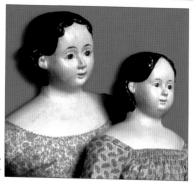

Two large Greiner dolls with '58 labels.
Private Collection.

Marked Greiner
'58 Label
- 15-17in (38-43cm) $900-1,000
- 20-23in (51-58cm) $1,250-1,500
- 28-30in (71-76cm) $1,750-2,000
- 38in (97cm) $2,800

Much worn
- 20-23in (51-58cm) $650-750
- 28-30in (7 1-76cm) $850-950

Glass eyes: 20-23in (51-58cm) $2,200-2,500

'72 Label
- 19-22in (48-56cm) $600-650
- 29-31 in (71-79cm) $900-1,000
- 35in (89cm) $1,100-1,200

Heinrich Handwerck

History Heinrich Handwerck, doll factory, Waltershausen, Thuringia, Germany. Heads by Simon & Halbig. 1855-on.
Trademarks Bébé Cosmopolite, Bébé de Réclame, Bébé Superior.
Comment Handwerck dolls are easy to find, but all-original examples are very desirable and will bring 50% or more over listed prices. Bodies should be stamped in red on lower back side or side torso.
Description Perfect bisque socket head, mohair wig, sleep eyes, open mouth, pierced ears. Composition ball-jointed body with Handwerck stamp. Appropriate vintage clothing.

Handwerck Child Doll

Ca. 1885-on.

#69, 79, 89, 99, 109, 119 or no mold #:

10-12in (25-31cm), all original	$600-700
14-16in (36-41cm)	$450-500
19-21in (43-53cm)	$450-500
23-25in (58-64cm)	$500-550
28-30in (71-76cm)	$600-700
32in (79cm)	$750-850
36-38in (91-101cm)	$1,800-2,300
42in (107cm)	$3,500

Bébé Cosmopolite, 19in (48cm) all original,
boxed $800-1,000

Ladies' Home Journal "Daisy," blonde mohair wig,
blue eyes, 18in (46cm) only $1,500

#139 and other shoulder heads, kid body

16-18in (41-46cm)	$250-275
22-24in (56-61cm)	$300-350

#79, 89, closed mouth

18-20in (46-51cm)	$2,300-2,500°
24in (61cm)	$2,800-3,200°

#189, open mouth

6½in (16cm), fully-jointed body	$700-800
18-20in (46-51cm)	$900-950

Marks

HANDWERCK
HALBIG
Germany

139.29
0
)H(

22in (56cm) H. Handwerck 99 child,
all-original.
Howard & Jan Foulke.

22in (56cm) Max Handwerck child.
Private Collection.

Max Handwerck

History Max Handwerck, doll factory, Waltershausen, Thuringia, Germany. Some heads by Goebel. 1900-on.

Trademarks Bébé Elite, Triumph-Bébé.

Comment Some of the Max Handwerck girls have almost a character look to their faces. Some heads were made by the Goebel porcelain factory. Quality varies, so choose carefully.

Description Perfect bisque socket head, good wig, sleeping eyes, pierced ears. Original composition ball-jointed body or baby body. Appropriate clothes.

°Few price samples available.

Max Handwerck Child Doll
#283, 287, 297

16-18in (41-46cm)	$200-250
22-24in (56-61cm)	$300-350
31-32in (79-81cm)	$600-700
#421, 21in (53cm)	$500-550

Bébé Elite Character Baby
19-21in (48-53cm)	$325-350

Mark

Max Handwerk
Bebe Elite
B 90/ 185
b
germany

Hertel, Schwab & Co.

History Hertel, Schwab & Co., porcelain factory, Stutzhaus, near Ohrdruf, Thuringia, Germany. 1910-on.

Comment This porcelain factory, though a latecomer to the industry, made excellent quality heads for doll factories, including Kley & Hahn and König & Wernicke.

Description Perfect bisque shoulder head, painted or sleeping glass eye, mohair wig or molded hair. Jointed composition or bent-limb baby body.

21in (53cm) H.S.&Co. 136 child.
Howard & Jan Foulke.

Character child 141 with unusual open mouth.
James D. Julia, Inc.

Marks   Made
in
Germany
136/10

152

3

Marked Character Baby
Ca. 1910.

#130, 142, 150, 151, 152

10-12in (25-31cm)	$200-225*
15-17in (38-43cm)	$250-350*
19-21in (48-53cm)	$375-400*
24-25in (61-64cm)	$500-550*
#150, all-bisque, 6in (15cm)	$400-450
#142, all-bisque, painted eyes, 11in (28cm)	$850-900

*Allow 25 percent extra for a jointed toddler body.

#159, two faces, 10in (25cm) at auction $750-850
#125 (so-called Patsy Baby), 12-13in (30-33cm) $950-1,000
#126 (so-called Skippy)
    9in (23cm) baby $850
    16in (41cm) toddler $1,500

Child Doll
Ca. 1910. Good quality jointed composition body (some marked "K & W").
  Mold #136
      7in (18cm) five-piece body $250-275
      18-20in (46-51cm) $300-350
      24-25in (61-64cm) $400-450

All-Bisque #208 Prize Baby
Glass eyes, wig.
    4in (10cm) $200-225
    7in (18cm) $350-400
    8½in (21cm) $625-650

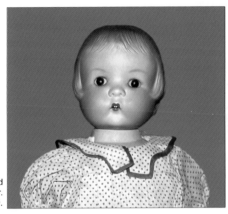

17in (43cm) 127 so-called
Patsy character.
Gloria & Mike Duddlesten.

Marked Character Child
Closed mouth; jointed composition body.
  #127 (so-called Patsy), 17in (43cm) . . . .$2,100-$2,500
  #134, 141, 13-14in (33-36cm) $3,800-4,200
  #140, 15in (38cm) $4,200
  #148, glass eyes, frowning face, 16in (41cm) $6,000
  #149, 16-18in (41-46cm) $8,000
  #154, 166, 169 . . . . .See Kley & Hahn, page 126.

Hertwig & Co.

History Hertwig & Co. porcelain factory, Katzhutte, Thuringia, Germany, 1864-on.

Comment This factory produced an unbelievable quantity of all-bisque dolls and novelties. Earlier items are of better quality than later items, which often were of pink pretinted bisque and did not have fired-in color. Be very careful when buying all-bisque dolls, especially on the internet, as there are fakes and reproductions being sold as all original, many on cards or in boxes.

Mark Incised **Germany**.

Half-Bisque Dolls

1911 on. Bisque one-piece head and body to waist, molded hair, painted features, cloth lower torso, legs and arms, bisque hands and lower legs with molded footwear, appropriate clothes.

    4½ in (11cm) children $175-225
    6½ in (17cm) adults $250-275
    6½-7 in (17-18cm) children $195-225

All-Bisque Children, Painted Eyes

    Boy with molded hair, pouty face,
        4in (10cm) $75-85
    Girl with molded hair, blue bows,
        5in (12cm) $85-95

4in (10cm) shoulder head with molded bonnet. *Howard & Jan Foulke.*

All-Bisque Character Children

Pink bisque, 1920s,
    4in (10cm) $85-95
    5-6in(13-15cm) $125-150
    Girl with downward gaze, molded blue bow
        6in (15cm) $375-425
        8in (20cm) $750
    Girl with downward gaze, glass eyes, wig
        5½in (14cm) $475-525
        7in (18cm) $600-650
    Girl with molded flower wreath, 4¾in (12cm) $150-175
    Mibs ....See page 35.
    Baby Peggy ....See page 36.

All-Bisque Children with Molded Clothes

See the All-Bisque section on page 23.

Bisque Shoulder Head with Molded Bonnet

See the Bisque, German section on page 49.

China Head with Gold Painted Name

See the China section on page 74.

7in (17cm) all-bisque boy. *Howard & Jan Foulke.*

Ernst Heubach

History Ernst Heubach, porcelain factory, Köppelsdorf, Thuringia, Germany. 1887-on.
Comment Called Heubach Koppelsdorf dolls by collectors because of the mark, these children and babies are plentiful. Look for dolls with especially appealing faces. The series of small googlies have particular good faces.
Description Perfect bisque head, glass sleeping eyes, open mouth, nice wig. Kid, cloth or jointed composition child, baby or toddler body. Appropriate clothing.

Mark

Heubach·Köppelsdorf

300-10/0

Germany

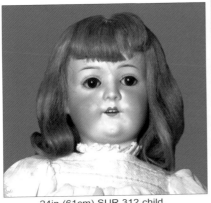

24in (61cm) SUR 312 child.
Kay Jensen Antique Dolls.

11½in (29cm) 267 character baby.
Howard & Jan Foulke.

Heubach Child Doll

Ca. 1888-on.

#275 or horseshoe, kid or cloth body
14in (36cm) $150-175
19-21in (48-53cm) $225-250
24in (61cm) $275-300

#250, 251, composition body
8-9in (20-23cm) five-piece body $195-210
16-18in (41-46cm) $225-250
23-24in (58-61cm) $275-325

#250, 407, painted bisque, 7-8in (18-20cm) $90-110

#312 SUR (for Seyfarth & Reinhard)
19in (48cm) ....$300-$325
28in (71cm) $500
45-46in (113-115cm) ....$3,500°

°Few price samples available.

Character Children

1910-on. Painted eyes, open/closed mouth.
#261, 262, 271 and others. **Bisque shoulder head with molded hair, cloth body with composition lower arms, 12in (31cm)** $250-300
#276, bug on nose, 7½in (19cm) $625
#417, Just Me-type, 12in (31cm) $1,000

Character Baby

1910-on.
#300, 320, 342 and others
    5½-6in (14-15cm) $250-275
    8-10in (20-25cm) $225-250
    14-17in (36-43cm) $275
    19-21in (48-53cm) $300-350
    24-25in (61-64cm) $425-475

Toddler

    9-10in (23-25cm) five-piece body $325-375
    Fully-jointed body
        15-17in (38-43cm) $375-425
        23-25in (58-64cm) $600-700
    Painted Bisque Toddler, **factory original, 11 in (28cm)** $350-400

Infant

Ca. 1925. Perfect bisque head; cloth body.
#349, 339, 350
    10½in (26cm) $325-350
    13-16in (33-41cm) $450-500
#338, 340, 14-16in (36-41cm) ....$725-825°

Gebrüder Heubach

History Gebrüder Heubach, porcelain factory, Licht and Sonneberg, Thuringia, Germany. 1820-on; doll heads, 1910-on.
Comment Gebrüder Heubach produced mainly character dolls that are very popular with collectors because of their expressive faces showing a range of emotions. There is some problem with reproductions, so do look at the bisque carefully.
Description Perfect bisque socket or shoulder head. Kid, cloth or jointed composition body.

Heubach Character Child

Ca. 1910. (For more photographs of Heubach dolls see *Focusing on Dolls*, pages 30-68.)

Marks

#5636, 7663, laughing child, glass eyes
    12-13in (31-33cm) $1,700-1,900
    16-18in (41-46cm) $2,400-2,900
#5689, smiling child,
    26in (66cm) ....$4,000-4,500°
#5730 Santa, 22-24in (56-61cm) $2,000-2,400
#5777 Dolly Dimple
    12in (31cm) $2,200
    19-22in (48-56cm) $3,000-3,200
    Shoulder head, #9355, 17-19in (43-48cm) $850-950

°Few price samples available.

#6969, 6970, 7246, 7347, 7407, 8017, pouty child (must have glass eyes)
    12-13in (31-33cm) $2,000-2,250
    16in (41cm) $2,750-3,000
    18-20in (46-51cm) $3,600-4,000
    24in (61cm) $5,000
    28in (71cm) $8,000
#6969, painted eyes, 16in (41cm) $1,800
#6692 and other shoulder head pouties
    14-16in (36-41cm) $500-550
    20in (51cm) $750-800
#7054 and other smiling shoulder heads
    12-14in (30-36cm) $400-450
    19in (48cm) $700-750
#7407, painted eye, wigged, 16in (41cm) $4,000-5,000
#7604, 7820 and other smiling socket head
    14-16in (36-41cm) $700-800
    20in (51cm) $1,000-1,250
#7602, 6894, 7622 and other socket head pouties,
    16-18in (41-46cm) $800-850
#7660, #7661, squinting eyes, crooked mouth,
    15in (38cm) $7,920
#7665, smiling, 16in (41cm) $1,800
#7679, 8774 Whistler
    10in (25cm) $700-800
    14in (36cm) $1,100
#7684 Screamer
    12in (31cm) $1,500
    16-19in (41-48cm) $2,200-2,500
#7711
    9in (23cm) $750-800
    12-14in (31-36cm) $1,100-1,300
    18in (46cm) at auction $7,700
#7743, big ears, 17in (43cm) $4,500
#7746, grinning boy, 17in (43cm) $6,820
#7764, singing girl, 16in (41cm) $8,000-10,000

21in (53cm) 5636 character girl.
Private Collection.

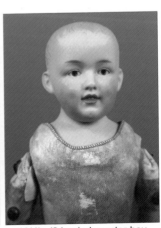

13½in (34cm) character boy.
Howard & Jan Foulke.

°Few price samples available.

#7788, 7850 Coquette
11in (28cm) $850-900
14in (36cm) $1,000-1,100
20in (51cm) $1,300-1,400
Shoulder head, 12in (31cm) $500-600
#7852, shoulder head, molded coiled braids, 16in (41cm) ....$2,200°
#7853, shoulder head, downcast eyes,
14in (36cm) $1,650-1,850
#7911, 8191, grinning
11in (28cm) $650-700
15in (38cm) $900-1,000
#7920, 18in (46cm) ....$2,700°
#7925, 7926, lady
11in (28cm) $1,000-1,100
18-19in (46-48cm) $2,500-2,800
#7956 girl, molded curls, dimples, 19in (48cm) $19,200
#8035, pouty boy, big ears, 17in (43cm) at auction $11,000
#8050, smiling girl with hair bow, 18in (46cm) $10,000-13,000
#8192
9-11in (23-28cm) $275-325
14-16in (36-41cm) $450-500
18-22in (46-56cm) $600-650
#8381 Princess Julianna, 16in (41cm) ....$12,000°
#8413, tongue between teeth, 16in (41cm) $2,200
#8420, pouty with glass eyes
13in (33cm) $1,600-1,750
16in (41cm) $2,000-2,200
#8548 Grumpy, 22in (56cm) ....$17,500°
#8550, molded tongue sticking out,
13in (33cm)
intaglio eyes $750-850
glass eyes $1,000-1,100
#8556, googly-type face ....$11,500°
#9102 Cat, 6in (15cm) ....$1,000-1,150°
#9141 Winker
9in (23cm) glass eye $1,500
7in (18cm) painted eye $850-950
#9617, glass eyes, dimples, 22in (56cm) $6,600
#10532
8½in (21cm) chubby five-piece
toddler, all original ..$600-700
20-22in (51 -56cm) $650-750
28in (71cm) $1,400-1,500
#10586, 10633
12in (30cm) $300-350
18-20in (46-51cm) $475-525
#11173 Tiss Me,
8in (20cm) ....$1,850-2,000°
Baby Bo Kaye, Bonnie Babe,
7-8in (18-20cm) $900-950
#1907 Jumeau
16in (41cm) $1,800-2,000
20-22in (51-56cm) ...$2,400-2,500

14in (36cm) pouty character baby.
*Dr. Carole Stoessel Zvonar
Collection.*

°Few price samples available.

All Bisque

Position Babies and Action Figures, 5in (13cm) $400-450
Girl with bobbed hair, 9in (23cm) $800-900
Girl with headband (Coquette)
    6in (15cm) swivel neck $795-895
    9in (23cm) $900-1,000
Girl with three bows
    6in (15cm) $1,350
    9in (23cm) $1,650
    9in (23cm) swivel neck $2,400
Boy, 8in (20cm) $1,200
Boy or girl, 4½in (11cm) $250-275
Chin Chin, 4½in (11cm) $250-275

Heubach Babies

Ca. 1910.
#6894, 7602, 6898, 7759 and other pouty babies; #7604 laughing
    4½in (12cm) $225
    6in (15cm) $250
    10-12in (25-31cm) $350-450
    14in (36cm) $550-650
    20in (51cm) $1,000
#7877, 7977 Baby Stuart
    Painted eyes
        9in (23cm) $800-850
        13-15in (33-38cm) $1,300-1,500
    Glass eyes, 13in (33cm) ....$2,250°
#8649, blue quilted bonnet,
    12in (31cm) $1,400
#8420, glass eyes,
    14in (36cm) $1,100-1,200
#7959, molded pink cap,
    14in (36cm) ....$4,000°

6in (15cm) all-bisque coquette.
Howard & Jan Foulke.

10½in (26cm) 7850 coquette
character girl.
Howard & Jan Foulke.

°Few price samples available.

Indian Dolls

History Various German factories. Ca 1895-on.
Comment The production of American Indian dolls during this period reflects the interest in different cultures, as bisque Oriental and Black dolls were also popular. The common models are currently in a slow period.
Description Perfect bisque head, wrinkles between wavy eyebrows, set brown glass eyes, black mohair wig. Composition body often with molded shoes. Original Indian-style clothing.

American Indian Doll
Marked "A.M." (Armand Marseille) or unmarked:
   7-8in (18-20cm) \$125-150
   12in (30cm) \$225-250
   15in (38cm) \$350
   18in (46cm) \$550
Bähr & Pröschild 244, closed mouth,
   14-15in (36-38cm) \$1,200-1,300
Gebrüder Heubach 8457, 9467, shoulder head on cloth body,
   14in (36cm) \$2,000-2,500
Simon & Halbig 1303, 15in (38cm) \$3,200-3,500

10in (25cm) American Indian with German bisque head.
Howard & Jan Foulke.

19in (48cm) Jullien Bébé.
James D. Julia, Inc.

Jullien

History Jullien, Jeune of Paris, France. 1875-1904. S.F.B.J., 1904-on.
Comment Jullien produced a lovely *bébé* with a slightly different face from other French makers, but it has never been as popular as the Jumeaus.
Description Perfect bisque head, mohair wig, paperwieght eyes, closed mouth, pierced ears. Jointed wood and composition body. Appropriate vintage clothing.

Jullien Bébé

	Mark Jullien
	9

   17-19in (43-48cm) \$2,800-3,000
   24-26in (61-66cm) \$3,500-4,000
   14in (36cm) factory dress and box, at auction \$3,600
Open mouth
   19-21in (48-53cm) \$1,500-1,600
   29-30in (74-76cm) \$2,200

Jumeau

History Maison Jumeau, Paris, France. 1842-on.
Trademarks Bébé Jumeau (1886), Bébé Prodige (1886), Bébé Français (1896)
Comment Jumeau dolls have a certain cachet and are extremely popular with collectors. The demand keeps the prices stable even though there is a plentiful supply. The most desirable are the early portrait dolls.
Description Perfect bisque head, paperweight eyes, closed mouth, mohair wig, pierced ears. Composition and wood jointed body with Jumeau stamp on rear.

Poupée Peau Fashion Lady
Late 1860s-on. Perfect bisque swivel head on shoulder plate; all-kid body.

> **Mark** On body after 1878
>
> JUMEAU
> MEDAILLE D'OR
> PARIS

    Standard face
        11½-13in (29-33cm) $2,600-3,000*
        17-18in (43-46cm) $3,600-3,800*
        20in (51cm) $4,200-4,600*
    Head and shoulder plate only, size 2 ......$950
    Later face with large eyes
        10½-11in (27-28cm) $2,000-2,500*
        14-15in (36-38cm) $2,800-3,000*

Poupée Bois
    Wood body with bisque limbs, 18in (46cm) $6,500

So-called "Portrait Face"
    19-21in (48-53cm) $7,000-7,250*
    28in (71cm) $10,500
    Wood body (*poupée bois*), 19-21 in (48-53cm) $10,000-11,000

Portrait Face with adult look
    Kid body, 29in (74cm) $34,300
    Wood body, 25in (64cm) $70,400

26in (66cm) Portrait Face *poupée peau*, all original. *Kay Jensen Antique Dolls.*

17in (43cm) *poupée peau. Howard & Jan Foulke.*

Period Clothes for Bébés
    Jumeau shift $400-600
    Jumeau shoes $350-450
    Jumeau dress and hat ....$1,000 up

*Allow up to 50% extra for original clothes.

Portrait Jumeau Bébés

1877-1883. Usually marked with size number only on head, blue stamp on body; skin or other good wig, spiral threaded enamel paperweight eyes, closed mouth, pierced ears; Jumeau jointed composition body with straight wrists and separate ball joints.

Almond-Eyed or First Series

12-14½in (30-37cm)	$13,000-15,000*
16-18½in (41-47cm)	$18,000-22,000*
20in (51cm)	$25,000-30,000*
23in (58cm)	$33,000-38,000*
25in (64cm)	$55,000-65,000*

SIZES
4/0 = 12in (30cm)
3/0 = 13½in (34cm)
2/0 = 14½in (37cm)
0 = 16in (41cm)
1 = 17in (43cm)
2 = 1 8½in (47cm)
3 = 20in (51cm)
4 = 23in (58cm)
5 = 25in (64cm)

Second Series, excellent quality, larger dolls have applied ears.

11-12in (28-31cm)	$5,250-5,750
13-15in (33-38cm)	$6,250
18-20in (46-51cm)	$7,500-8,500
22in (56cm)	$9,500-$10,500
25in (64cm)	$12,000-$13,000
12in (31cm) all original	$18,100

SIZES
4 = 11-12in (28-31cm)
5 = 13-14in (33-36cm)
6 = 15in (38cm)
7 = 16in (41cm)
8 = 18in (46cm)
9 = 20in (51cm)
10 = 22in (56cm)
12 = 25in (64cm)

Premier, Early Unmarked Bébé

Ca. 1880.

9in (23cm) size 0	$6,500-7,500
10-11in (25-28cm) size 1	$8,000
12in (31cm) size 2	$8,500

Incised Jumeau in Cartouche Bébé

12-13in (31-33cm)	$7,500

Long-Face Triste Bébé

1879-1886. Designed by Carrier-Belleuse. Marked with size (9 to 16) number only on head, blue stamp on body, applied pierced ears; Jumeau jointed composition body with straight wrists (separate ball joints on early models).

SIZES
9 = 21in (53cm)
11 = 24in (61cm)
13, 14 = 29-30in (74-76cm)

21-23in (53-58cm)	$20,000-22,500
26-27in (66-69cm)	$25,000
31-33in (79-84cm)	$27,000

E.J. Bébé

1881-1886. Perfect bisque socket head with good wig, paperweight eyes, closed mouth, pierced ears; Jumeau jointed composition body with straight wrists, early models with separate ball joints.

Early Mark

17-18in (43-46cm) size 6	$9,000-10,000
19-21in (48-53cm) size 8	$12,500
23-24in (58-61cm) size 9	$15,000
E.J.A., 25in (64cm)	$20,000-25,000

Early Mark
6
E.J.

Mid to Late Period Mark

9in (23cm)	$8,000-8,500
11in (28cm)	$6,000-6,300
14-16in (36-41cm)	$6,800-7,100
19-21in (48-53cm)	$8,200-8,600
25-26in (64-66cm)	$9,500-10,500
30in (76cm)	$11,500-13,000

Mid to Late Period Mark
DÉPOSÉ
E.10.J

Déposé 9 or 9x, 20-21in (51-53cm)	$6,500-7,500
10x, 22in (56cm)	$9,000-9,500

*Allow extra for unusually large eyes.

23in (58cm) size 4 almond-eyed portrait *bébé*.
Bart Boeckmans.

30in (76cm) long-face or *triste bébé*.
Kay Jensen Antique Dolls.

Incised "Jumeau Déposé" Bébé

1886-1889. Head incised as below, blue stamp on body. Jumeau jointed composition body with straight wrists.

14-15in (36-38cm)	....	$4,800-5,200
18-20in (46-51cm)	....	$6,000-6,500
23-25in (58-64cm)	....	$7,000
14in (36cm) totally original with armband, at auction	....	$24,150

> **Mark** Incised on head
> DÉPOSÉ
> JUMEAU
> 9

APPROXIMATE SIZES OF E.J.S AND TÊTES

1 = 10in (25cm)	6 = 16in (41cm)	11 = 24-25in (61-64cm)
2 = 11in (28cm)	7 = 17in (43cm)	12 = 26-27in (66-69cm)
3 = 12in (31cm)	8 = 19in (48cm)	13 = (29-30in (74-76cm)
4 = 13in (33cm)	9 = 20in (51cm)	
5 = 14-15in (36-38cm)	10 = 21-22in (53-56cm)	

25in (64cm) E.J.A. *bébé*.
Nancy A. Smith.

16in (41cm) E. 6 J. *bébé*.
Howard & Jan Foulke.

Tête Jumeau Bébé

1885-1899, then through S.F.B.J. Red stamp on head as indicated below, blue stamp or "Bébé Jumeau" oval sticker on body. Jointed composition body with jointed or straight wrists.

Mark	DÉPOSÉ
	TÊTE JUMEAU
	Bte SGDG
	10

9-10in (23-25cm) #1	$6,000-7,000*
12-13m (31-33cm)	$4,000-4,200*
15-16in (38-41cm)	$4,600-4,800*
18-20in (46-51cm)	$5,000*
21-23in (53-58cm)	$5,200*
25-27in (64-69cm)	$5,500*
30in (76cm)	$6,500*
34-36in (86-91cm)	$7,500-8,000*
41in (104cm)	$12,000*
Lady body, 20in (51cm)	$6,000-7,000*

Open mouth

14-16in (36-41cm)	$2,000*
20-22in (51-56cm)	$2,400-2,500*
24-25in (61-64cm)	$2,750*
27-29in (69-74cm)	$3,000*
32-34in (81-86cm)	$3,250*

24in (61cm) Tête Jumeau *bébé.*
Howard & Jan Foulke.

30in (76cm) 1907 *bébé.*
Howard & Jan Foulke.

Bébé Phonographe

1894-1899. Open mouth.

24-25in (61-64cm)	$6,500-7,500

Marked E.D. Bébé

Mark used during the Douillet management, 1892-1899. Closed mouth.

| Mark E. 9 D. |

17-19in (43-48cm)	$4,700

Marked B.L. Bébé

1892 on. For the Louvre department store. Closed mouth.

| Mark B. 10 L. |

13in (33cm)	$3,800-4,000
18-21in (46-53cm)	$4,800-5,000

*Allow up to 50% extra for original clothes.

Marked R.R. Bébé

1892 on. Closed mouth.
21 -23in (53-58cm) $5,000
26in (66cm) open mouth $2,900

#230 Character Child

Ca. 1910. Open mouth, set or sleep eyes; jointed composition body.
12in (31cm) $850-950
21-23in (55-58cm) $1,500-1,600

#1907 Jumeau Child

Ca. 1907-on. Sometimes red-stamped "Tête Jumeau." Open mouth.
16in (40cm) $1,800-2,000
19-22in (48-56cm) $2,200
25-27in (64-69cm) $2,800
32-33in (81-84cm) $3,250
Papier-mâché face, 22-24in (56-61cm) $800

DEP Tête Jumeau

See page 77 for details.

SFBJ Tête Jumeau

See page 161 for details.

Jumeau Characters

1892-1899. Perfect bisque head with glass eyes, character expression.
#203, 205 and others . . .$50,000 up
#217, at auction $121,000

#221 Great Ladies

10-11 in (25-28cm),
all original $700-800

23in (58cm) 208 character.
Ruth Covington West.

Princess Elizabeth Jumeau

1938 through S.F.B.J. Highly colored complexion, glass flirty eyes.
18-19in (46-48cm) $1,600-1,800
32-33in (81-84cm) ......$2,700-3,200°

Mark

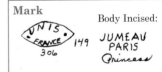

Body Incised:
JUMEAU
PARIS
Princess

Bleuette

First model, incised "1." For further details, see page 56.
10⁵/₈in (27cm) only $4,000-5,000

Kamkins

History Louise R. Kampes Studios, Atlantic City, NJ, 1919-1928 and perhaps longer.
Comment Kamkins dolls were sold on the boardwalk in Atlantic City, NJ. Paint must be original, but may have light wear and soil.
Description Molded mask face with painted features, original mohair wig. Cloth body. Original clothing.

Kamkins
18-20in (46-51cm) $2,500-3,000
Good $1,200-1,500
Fair to good
  condition $850-950
Dirty, face wear,
  naked $500-600
With swivel joints or molded
  derriere $2,500-3,500

Mark Red paper heart on left side of chest.

Also sometimes stamped with black on foot or back of head:
KAMKINS
A DOLLY MADE TO LOVE
PATENTED BY L.R. KAMPES
ATLANTIC CITY, N.J.

19in (48cm) *Kamkins.*
Pat Vallaincourt.

25in (64cm) K & R child.
Howard & Jan Foulke.

Kämmer & Reinhardt

History Kämmer & Reinhardt of Waltershausen, Thuringia, Germany. Bisque heads often by Simon & Halbig. 1886-on.
Comment K & R was one of the leading doll factories of its time, and their dolls are very desired by collectors today, especially the character children. All dolls must have K & R bodies. The character children should be on pink bodies. The numbers 15-100 incised low on the neck are centimeter sizes, not mold numbers. Allow up to 50% extra for all original wig, clothes and shoes. See *Simon & Halbig Dolls* for photographs of dolls not shown here.
Description Perfect bisque socket head, sleeping eyes, open mouth. K & R composition ball-jointed child, toddler or baby body. Most character children have painted eyes and closed mouths. Appropriate vintage clothing.

Mark Size
number is height
in centimeters.
K ☆ R
SIMON&HALBIG
126
Germany
50

Child Doll

1886-1895.

#192

Closed mouth

5in (13cm)

    five-piece body $550

    6-7in (15-18cm) $600-700

    11in (28cm) $800-900

    16-18in

      (41-46cm) $1,600-1,800

    22-24in

      (56-61cm) $2,100-2,300

Open mouth

    7-8in (18-20cm) $550-600

    12in (31cm) $600-700

    14-16in (36-41cm) $500

    20-22in (51-56cm) $600-700

    26-28in (66-71cm) $900-1,000

    9in (23cm) doll in original dressmaker set $2,100

6in (15cm) K & R child,
5-piece body, all original.
Howard & Jan Foulke.

Child Doll

1895-1930s.

#191, 290, 402, 403 or size number only*

Five-piece body

    4½-5in (12-13cm) $450-495

    7-8in (18-20cm) $350-400

    10in (25cm) $450-500

Fully-jointed body

    8-10in (20-25cm) $700-800

    12-14in (31-36cm) $550-600

    16-17in (41-43cm) $400-425

    19-21in (48-43cm) $450-500

    23-25in (58-64cm) $550-650

    28in (71cm) $700-750

    30-31 in (76-79cm) $900-1,100

    33-34in (84-86cm $1,200-1,400

    36in (91cm) $1,800-2,000

    39-42in (99-107cm) $3,200-4,000

Closed mouth, 6in (15cm), five-piece body $500-550

Child Doll

Shoulder head, kid body.

    19-22in (48-56cm) $250-300

*Allow $100 additional for flirty eyes; allow $150 for flapper body; allow $50 for walking body.

Character Babies or Toddlers

1909-on.

#100 Baby

    Painted eyes
        11-12in (28-31cm) $250-300
        14-15in (36-38cm) $350-400
        18-20in (46-51cm) $625-675
        Glass eyes, 16in (41cm) $1,500
    #118A, baby body, 11in (28cm $1,200
    #119, baby body, 24in (61cm),
        at auction $16,000
    #121, 122, baby body
        10-11 in (25-28cm) $375-425
        15-16in (38-41cm) $450-500
        23-24in (58-61cm) $775-875
    #121, 122, toddler body
        10in (25cm)
            five-piece body $1,000-1,100*
        13-14in (33-36cm) $800-900
        20-23in (51-58cm) $1,200-1,300
    #126, 22, baby body
        10-12in (25-31cm) $300-360**
        14-16in (36-41cm) $375**
        18-20in (46-51cm) $425-450**
        22-24in (56-61cm) $500-600**
        28in (71cm) $1,000-1,200
    #126, all-bisque baby
        6-7½in (15-19cm) $750-950
        10in (25cm) at auction $1,650
    #126, all-bisque toddler, 7in (18cm) ....$1,400-1,500°
    #126, 22, five-piece toddler body
        6-7in (15-18cm) $850*
        9-10in (23-25cm) $1,000-1,100*
        15-17in (38-43cm) $425-475
        23in (58cm) $550-650
    #126, toddler, fully-jointed
        12-13in (31-33cm) $550**
        15-17in (38-41cm) $550-650**
        23-25in (58-64cm) $900-1,000**
        28-30in (71-76cm) $1,200-1,500**
    #128, baby body
        15-16in (38-41cm) $500-600**
        20in (51cm) $750-800**
        24in (61cm) $1,000-1,200**
    #128, toddler body,
        16-18in (41-46cm) ......$1,100-1,200°

Composition Heads

    #926, five-piece toddler body,
        18in (46cm) $400-450**
    "Puz" baby, cloth body
        6-17in (41-43cm) $350-400
        23-25in (58-64cm) $500-600

20in (51cm) 100 *Baby*
character.
Howard & Jan Foulke.

13in (33cm) 126
character toddler.
Howard & Jan Foulke.

°Few price samples available.
*With "starfish" hands.
**Allow $50 to $100 additional for flirty eyes.

25in (64cm) 114 character child.
Private Collection.

Character Children
1909-on.

Boxed Set, one doll with four heads, at auction $16,000
#101 (Peter or Marie)
    8-10in (20-25cm) $1,650-1,850
    12in (31cm) $2,450
    14-15in (36-38cm) $3,000
    17in (43cm) $3,500-4,000
    19-20in (48-51cm) $4,500-5,000
    Glass eyes
        15in (38cm) $9,000-10,000
        20in (51cm) $12,500
#101X, flocked hair, 15in (38cm) $5,000-6,000
#102
    12in (31cm) $20,000
    22in (55cm) $75,000
#103, 104, 22in (56cm ....$100,000 up°
#105, 22in (56cm) ....$170,000°
#106, 22in (56cm) ....$145,000°
#107 (Carl)
    12in (30cm) $12,000-14,000
    22in (56cm) $45,000-50,000
#109 (Elise)
    9-10in (23-25cm) $3,000-3,500
    14in (36cm) $7,500-8,500
    17in (43cm) $13,500
    21in (53cm) $18,000-20,000
    Glass eyes, 20in (51cm) $22,500-25,000
#112, 112x
    14in (36cm) $7,500-8,500
    17-18in (43-46cm) $10,000-12,000
    Glass eyes
        16in (41cm) $11,500
        23in (58cm) at auction $15,400
#114 (Hans or Gretchen)
    8-9in (20-23cm) jointed body $1,800-2,200
    12in (31cm) $2,700-3,000
    15-16in (38-41cm) $3,800-4,300
    19-20in (48-51cm) $5,000-5,500

°Few price samples available.

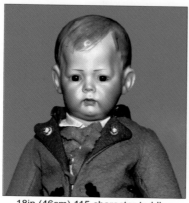

18in (46cm) 115 character toddler.
Linda Kellermann.

15in (38cm) 115a character toddler.
Howard & Jan Foulke.

#114 (Hans or Gretchen) continued

21 -22in (53-56cm)	$5700-6,000
25in (64cm) at auction	$11,500

Glass eyes

15in (38cm)	$7,500-8,000
19in (48cm)	$10,000
24in (61cm)	$15,000-17,000

#115, 15-16in (38-41cm) toddler $4,200-4,600
#115A

Baby

10-12in (25-31cm)	$1,800-2,000
14-16in (36-41cm)	$2,400-2,700

Toddler

15-16in (38-41cm)	$3,200-3,700
19-20in (48-51cm)	$4,400-4,800
23in (58cm)	$5,000-6,000

#116, 16in (41cm) toddler $3,200-3,600
#116A, open/closed mouth

Baby

10-11in (25-28cm)	$1,200-1,300
14-16in (36-41cm)	$1,800-2,200

Toddler

12-13in (31-33cm)	$2,200-2,400
16-18in (41-46cm)	$2,600-3,100

#116A, open mouth

Baby, 14-16in (36-41cm)	$1,000-1,200
Toddler, 16in (41cm)	$1,500-1,600

#117, 117A, closed mouth (may have an H. Handwerck body)

8in (20cm)	$2,200
12in (30cm)	$3,200-3,500
14-16in (36-41cm)	$4,000-4,200
18-20in (46-51cm)	$4,800-5,200
22-24in (56-61cm)	$5,500-5,850
30-32in (76-81cm)	$6,500-7,000

#117n, open mouth

Flirty eyes

14-16in (36-41cm)	$1,100-1,200
20-22in (51-56cm)	$1,600-1,800
28-30in (71-76cm)	$2,000-2,300

Sleep eyes
    14-16in (36-41cm) $850-950
    22-24in (56-61cm) $1,200-1,300
    30-32in (76-81cm) $1,500-1,700
    39in (100cm) $3,500-3,900
    #117, open mouth, 27in (69cm) $3,800-4,000
    #123, 124 (Max & Moritz). Must have special body with
    molded shoes, 17in (43cm) each $15,000-20,000
#127
    Baby
        10in (25cm) $650-700
        14-15in (36-38cm) $900-1,000
        20-22in (51-56cm) $1,100-1,300
    Toddler
        15-16in (38-41cm $1,000-1,100
        20-23in (51-58cm) $1,400-1,500
    #135, child, 14-16in (36-41cm) $1,000-1,200
    #201, 13in (33cm) $1,500-1,800
    #214, 15in (38cm) ....$2,100-2,500°

Infant
1924-on. Cloth body, composition hands.
    #171, 172, 14-15in (36-38cm) ....$3,000-3,500°
    #173, toddler (composition body), 14in (36cm) ....$1,650°
    #175, 11in (28cm) head circumference ....$1,100-1,200°

Cloth Characters
1927. Stockinette faces with needle-sculpted and hand-painted features; straw-filled torso; wire-armature arms and legs, wood feet; all original; excellent condition.
    12in (31cm) $350-400

16in (41cm) 116a character toddler.
Howard & Jan Foulke.

Kestner

History J.D. Kestner, Jr., doll factory, Waltershausen, Thuringia, Germany. Kestner & Co., porcelain factory, Ohrdruf. 1816-on.

Comment Kestner dolls are favorites with collectors because of their appealing faces and fine quality. Although early heads have only a size number, most heads can be identified by the familiar Kestner mold numbers and unique sizing code. Heads must be on Kestner bodies with appropriate markings. See *Kestner, King of Dollmakers* for photographs of mold numbers not shown here.

Description Perfect bisque head, sleeping eyes, closed mouth on early dolls, open mouth on later dolls, mohair wig, plaster dome. Kid or jointed composition child, baby or toddler body. Early child bodies are chunky with straight wrists. Appropriate vintage clothing.

Child Doll, early socket head

Ca. 1880. Kestner composition ball-jointed body. some with straight wrists and elbows. Many marked with size numbers only.

#169, 128, long face and round face with closed mouth; no mold number

7in (18cm)	$1,200-1,500
10in (25cm)	$1,500-1,800
12in (31cm)	$1,800-2,000
14-16in (36-41cm)	$2,000-2,200
19-21in (48-53cm)	$2,300
24-25 in (61-64cm)	$2,750
29in (74cm)	$3,000-3,500
33in (84cm)	$3,500-4,000

Face with square cheeks or white space between lips, closed mouth; no mold number

14-16in (36-41cm)	$1,800-2,000
19-21in (48-53cm)	$2,200-2,400
24-25in (61-64cm)	$2,500-2,600

Very pouty face, closed mouth

7in (18cm)	$1,700-1,900
9in (23cm)	$2,000-2,300
10-12in (25-31cm)	$2,600-2,800
14-16in (36-41cm)	$2,800-3,000
19-21in (48-53cm)	$3,200-3,400
24in (61cm)	$3,800-4,200

#X, 15in (38cm) only	$3,200-3,800
#XI, 16in (41cm) only	$4,200-4,800
#XII, 17in (43cm)	$4,500-5,000
#103, closed mouth, 28-32in (71-78cm)	$3,500-4,500

A.T.-type, closed mouth

17in (43cm)	$8,000
21in (31cm)	$11,000-13,000

Bru-type

Molded teeth, jointed ankles, 17in (43cm)	$3,850-4,250

Open mouth, square cut teeth

12-14in (31-36cm)	$800-1,000
16-18in (41-46cm)	$1,000-1,200
24-25in (61-64cm)	$1,300-1,500

Wax-over papier-mâché head, 11 in (38cm)

all original, at auction	$1,000

24in (61cm) Kestner with very pouty face, incised 15.
Howard & Jan Foulke.

14in (36cm) Kestner with square face, incised 8.
Private Collection.

Child Doll, early shoulder head

Ca. 1880s. Sometimes head is slightly turned; kid body with bisque lower arms; marked with size letters or numbers. (No mold numbers.)

Closed mouth
12in (31cm) $400-450
14-16in (36-41cm) $550-600
20-22in (51 -56cm) $650-700
26in (66cm) $750-800
A.T.-type, closed mouth, 26in (66cm) $17,000
Open/closed mouth, 16-18in (41-46cm) $500-550
Open mouth (turned shoulder head)
16-18in (41-46cm) $325-350
22-24in (56-61cm) $400-450
Open mouth, square cut teeth, 14-16in (36-41cm) $800-1,000

Child Doll, bisque shoulder head, open mouth

Ca. 1892. Kid body, some with rivet joints.
#145, 154, 147, 148, 166, 195
12-13in (31-33cm) $200-225
16-18in (41-46cm) $275-300
20-22in (51 -56cm) $350-375
26-28in (66-71cm) $400-500

Head Mark	Body Mark
154. 10. dep. *F made in Germany.*	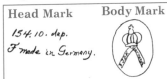

Child Doll, socket head, open mouth

Kestner ball-jointed body.
Mold numbers #142, 144, 146, 164, 167, 168, 171, 214
10-12in (25-31cm) $550-650
14-16in (36-41cm) $600
18-21in (46-43cm) $625-675
24-26in (61-66cm) $700-750
28in (71cm) $800
32-33in (81-84cm) ...$1,000-1,100
36in (91cm) $1,700-2,100
42in (107cm) $3,250-3,750

Head Mark	Body Mark
made in $B\frac{1}{2}$. Germany $6\frac{1}{2}$. 174.	Germany 2½ *or* Excelsior DRP No 70686 Germany

34in (86cm) 241 character child.
Esther Schwartz Collection.

21in (53cm) 181 character child.
Elba Buehler Collection.

16in (41cm) 147 shoulder head, all original.
Howard & Jan Foulke.

19in (48cm) 168 child.
Howard & Jan Foulke.

20in (51cm) 129 child.
Howard & Jan Foulke.

Harder to find molds #128, 129, 149, 152, 156, 160, 161, 173, 174
  10-12in (25-31cm) $700-800
  14-16in (36-41cm) $800-850
  18-21in (46-53cm) $950-1,000
  24-26in (6 1-66cm) $1,100-1,200
#133, five-piece body, 6in (15cm) $350
#155, fully-jointed body
  7-8in (18-20cm) $700-800
  10in (25cm) five-piece body $650-700
#171 Daisy, blonde mohair wig, blue sleep eyes; C½ 7½ head size,
1½ body size
  18in (46cm) only $1,500-1,750
  All-original shift, shoes, socks, wig $2,000-2,250
#196, 215
  18-21in (46-53cm) $500-550
  26-28in (66-71cm) $600
  32in (81cm) $650-700

Character Child

1909-on. Painted or glass eyes; closed, open or open/closed mouth; Kestner
jointed composition body.
  #143 (Pre-1897)
    7-8in (18-20cm) $700-750
    9-10in (23-25cm) $750-800
    12-14in (31-36cm) $800-850
    18-20in (46-51cm) $1,000-1,400
    24-27in (58-69cm) $1,800-2,100
  #177, molded hair, 12in (31cm) at auction $5,500
  #178-190
    Painted eyes
      12in (31cm) $1,800-2,200
      15in (38cm) $3,500-3,800
      18in (46cm) $4,500-5,000
    Glass eyes
      12in (31cm) $3,200-3,500
      15in (38cm) $4,800-5,200
      18in (46cm) $6,000-6,500
    Boxed set, doll with three character heads
    Painted eyes
      12in (31cm) $9,000
      15in (38cm) $12,500
    Glass eyes, 15in (38cm) ....$20,000°
  #206
    12in (31cm) ....$10,000°
    19in (48cm) $20,000-25,000
  #208, painted eyes
    12in (31cm) ....$10,000°
    23-24in (58-61cm) ....$25,000°
  #212, 12in (31cm) at auction ....$8,750°
  #220, toddler
    16in (41cm) $4,500-5,000
    20in (51cm) $5,500-6,000
    27in (69cm) size Q20 ....$7,500-8,500
  #239, toddler, 15-17in (38-43cm) $3,500
  #241, 24-25in (61-61cm) $5,500-6,500

#249
15in (38cm) $600-700
22-24in (56-61cm) $800-900
#260
Toddler, five-piece body, 8-10in (20-25cm) $900-1,000
Jointed body
12-14in (31-36cm) $450-500
18-20in (46-51cm) $600-650
29-30in (74-76cm) $800-900
37in (95cm) at auction $2,800-3,000
42in (107cm) $3,250-3,750

Character Baby
1910-on. Molded hair or mohair wig, sleep eyes, open or open/closed mouth;
Kestner bent-limb body.

#211, 226, 257
11-13in (28-33cm) $400-450
16-18in (41-46cm) $500-550
20-22in (51-56cm) $600-700
25in (64cm) $1,000-1,200
#211, toddler, 14-16in (36-41cm) $750-850
#257, toddler, 8in (20cm) $900-1,000
JDK, solid dome
12-14in (31-36cm) $350-400
17-19in (43-48cm) $450-500
23-25in (58-64cm) $1,000
Painted eyes, 14in (36cm) $325-375

Mark

262.
made in
germany
34.

#262, 263 ....See page 64.
#210, 234, 235, 238 shoulder heads,
13in (33cm) $600-650
Hilda, #237, 245 and solid dome baby 1070
11-13in (28-33cm) $1,800-2,200
16-17in (41-43cm) $2,400-2,600
20-22in (51-56cm) $3,000-3,200
24in (61cm) $3,500-4,000
Toddler
14in (36cm) $3,000-3,200
17-19in (43-48cm) $3,700-4,200
21-23in (53-58cm) $4,500-5,000
27in (69cm) $5,700
#247
14-16in (36-41cm) $1,000-1,200

15in (38cm) solid dome
Hilda 1070 character baby.
Howard & Jan Foulke.

Toddler
15in (38cm) $1,200-1,300
18-20in (46-51cm) $1,500-1,600
#267, molded hair, 22-24in (56-61cm) $3,000-3,300
JDK, solid dome, fat-cheeked (so-called Baby Jean)
12-13in (31-33cm) $600-650
17-18in (43-46cm) $800-900
24in (61cm) $1,500
All-Bisque Baby
Painted eyes, stiff neck, 5-6in (13-15cm) $225-275
Swivel neck, painted eyes
7½in (19cm) $450-500
9in (23cm) $650-750
12in (31cm) $850-950
Glass eyes, swivel neck, 11in (28cm) $1,000-1,200

27in (69cm) 211 character on chubby toddler body, size Q 20, the largest size head Kestner made. *Howard & Jan Foulke.*

5¼in (13cm) all-bisque 150 child. *Howard & Jan Foulke.*

15in (38cm) 257 character toddler. *Howard & Jan Foulke.*

#177, toddler, 8in (20cm) $1,000-1,250
#178, toddler, 6½in (16cm) $850
Immobile position baby, painted features, wig,
    2½in (6cm) $150-165

All-Bisque Child
Perfect all-bisque child, jointed at shoulders and hips; glass eyes; very good quality.
    #130, 150, 160 and 208
        4-5in (10-13cm) $275-325
        6in (15cm) $325-375
        7in (18cm) $425-475
        8in (20cm) $550-600
        9in (23cm) $750-800
        10in (25cm) $900-1,000
        12in (31cm) $1,200
    #184, 208, yellow boots
        4-5in (10-13cm) $400-450
        7in (18cm) $600-650
    #208, swivel neck, yellow boots
        6in (15cm) $750-850
        8in (20cm) $1,250-1,500

#307, #310, yellow stockings
  5-6in (12-15cm) $550-650
  8in (20cm) $1,200-1,400
#620/130 or 208, swivel neck
  Glass eyes
    4in (10cm) $400-425
    5-6in (13-15cm) $550-650
    8in (20cm) $950
  Painted eyes
    4in (10cm) $175-195
    5-6in (13-15cm) $225-275
  #130, 720, painted eyes, 5in (13cm) $225

Early All-Bisque Dolls
See page 25.

Gibson Girl
Ca. 1910. Perfect bisque shoulder head with appropriate wig, closed mouth, up-lifted chin; kid body with bisque lower arms (cloth body with bisque lower limbs on small dolls). Sometimes marked "Gibson Girl" on body.
  #172
    10in (25cm) $700-800
    15in (38cm) $1,300-1,500
    19-21in (48-53cm) $2,300-2,500
    Head only to make a 20in (51cm) doll $825

5½in (14cm) all-bisque 307 child.
Howard & Jan Foulke.

5½in (14cm) all-bisque
620/130 child, all original.
Howard & Jan Foulke.

Lady Doll

Kestner jointed composition body with molded breasts, nipped-in waist, slender arms and legs.

#162

16-18in (41-46cm) $1,600-1,800
Naked, 16-18in (41-46cm) $1,000
All-original clothes,
16-18in (41-46cm) $2,000-2,200

O.I.C. Baby

Perfect bisque solid dome head, wide open mouth with molded tongue; cloth body; dressed; all in good condition. Mold #255.

10in (25cm) head circumference $900-1,100

Siegfried

Perfect bisque head; cloth body with composition hands; dressed; all in good condition. Mold #272.

10in (25cm) ....$1,000°
14in (36cm) ....$1,500°

Marked Century Doll Co. Infant

Ca. 1925. Cloth body. Some with smiling face are mold #277.

16-18in (41-46cm) long $500-550
Double-face ....$2,000-2,500°
Mama doll, bisque shoulder head #281, 21in (53cm) $400-500

Kewpie®

History Designed by Rose O'Neill, 1913. Trademark controlled by George Borgfeldt who licensed it to other manufacturers.

Comment These charming imps took doll form in 1913 and became an instant hit, and are still being made today. Bisque models were made in Germany by J.D. Kestner and other porcelain factories.

Mark Red and gold paper heart or shield on chest and round label on back.

Incised on foot *O'Neill*

All-Bisque

1913-on. Standing, legs together, arms jointed, blue wings. painted features, eyes to side.

2-2½in (5-6cm) $75-85*
4in (10cm) $100-110*
5in (13cm) $125-135*
6in (15cm) $165*
7in (18cm) $200-225*
8in (20cm) $350-400*
9in (23cm) $525*
10in (25cm) $550-600*
12in (3 1cm) $800-1,000*
Jointed hips
4in (10cm) $250-300
6in (15cm) $500
8in (20cm) $700-750

°Few price samples available.
*Allow extra for original clothes.

Perfume bottle, 4½in (11cm) $400-450
Black Hottentot, 5in (13cm) $450-500
Buttonhole, 2in (5cm) $125-135
Pincushion, 2-3in (5-8cm) $225-250
Painted shoes and socks
    4-5in (10-13cm) $400-450
    11in (28cm) $1,200-1,400
With glass eyes and wig, 6in (15cm) $1,000-1,100
With wig, 6in (15cm) $650-700
Shoulder head, 3in (8cm) $165-200

4¼in (11cm) all-bisque *Kewpie*,
all original.
Howard & Jan Foulke.

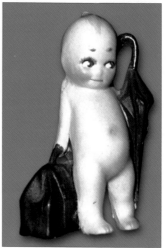

4in (10cm) all-bisque
Kewpie Traveler.
Kay Jensen Antique Dolls.

Action Kewpies (sometimes stamped "©")

Kneeling with outstretched arms, 3¾ in (9cm) $900-1,100
Reclining or sitting, 3-4in (8-10cm) $350-450
Kicking, 4in (10cm) $250-300
Crawling, 4in (10cm) $500-600
Tumbling, 3in (8cm) $450-550
Thinker
    4in (10cm) $175-200
    7in (18cm) $250-275
Kewpie with rabbit, rose, turkey, pumpkin, shamrock or
    other item, 2in (5cm) $350-400
Huggers, 3½in (9cm) $110-125
Sweeper, 4in (10cm) $400-450
Kewpie with cat, 3½in (9cm) $475-525
Guitar Player, 3½in (9cm) $350-400
Guitar Player with Doodle Dog, 4in (10cm) $2600
Traveler, 3½in (9cm) $175-200
Traveler with Doodle Dog, 3½in (9cm) $1350-1650
Place Card Holder, 2in (5cm) $300-350
Kewpie with pen, 3in (8cm) $350-400
Kewpie with pen, on "Kewpish Love" tray, 3in (8cm) $600-650
Kewpie sitting on inkwell, 3½in (9cm) $600-650
Kewpie with basket, 4in (10cm) $500-550

Farmer, **Fireman**, molded hats, 4in (10cm) $550-600
Soldiers
    3½in (9cm) lying Confederate $400-450
    4in (10cm) Hero $600
    5-6in (13-15cm) standing $900-1200
    3½in (9cm) sitting $1,500
Kewpie Hero Soldier with Nurse, 5½ in (14cm) $8,000
Bellhop, 4in (10cm) $600
Kewpie with drum, 3½in (9cm) $600-650
Governor or Mayor, 4in (10cm) $400-500
Doodle Dog
    1½in (4cm) $800
    3in (9cm) $1,500-2,000
    4½in (11cm) $2,500
Kewpie with Doodle Dog on Bench, 3½in (9cm) $3,325
Kewpie on sled, 2½in (6cm) $1,000
Kewpies reading book, 3½in (9cm) 2 standing $750-850
Kewpie with teddy, 4in (10cm) $600-650
Kewpie at tea table, 4½in (11cm) $5,400
Kewpie in bisque swing, 2½in (6cm) $2,500
Kewpie with molded overalls, 4½in (11cm) $2,100
Kewpie with molded suit, 4½in (11cm) $1,500
Kewpie in green chair reading book, 4¾in (12cm) $3,000
Kewpie in bathtub, 3½in (9cm) $1,900
Kewpie with stork, 4¼in (11cm) $3,000
Kewpie Mountain with 17 figures . . . .$17,000 up
Kewpie china shakers, 2in (5cm) set $350-400

Bisque head on chubby jointed composition toddler body, glass eyes
Made by J.D. Kestner.
    10in (25cm) five-piece body $5,000
    12-14in (31-36cm) $6,500-7,500

Mark
"Ges. gesch O'Neill J.D.K."

13in (33cm) composition
Kewpie with label.
Howard & Jan Foulke.

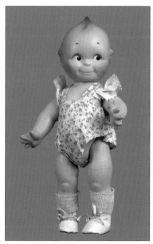

13in (33cm) composition
Kewpie, all original.
Howard & Jan Foulke.

°Few price samples available.

13in (33cm) hard plastic *Kewpie*.
Howard & Jan Foulke.

11½in (29cm) vinyl 1960
Cameo *Kewpie*.
Kay Jensen Antique Dolls.

Bisque head on cloth body

Mold #1377 made by Alt, Beck & Gottschalck.

12in (31cm)
    Glass eyes .... $2,600-2,800°
    Painted eyes .... $1,600-2,000°

Celluloid

Made by Karl Standfuss, Saxony, Germany.
    2½in (6cm) $20-25
    5in (13cm) $40-45
    8in (20cm) $90-100
    12in (31cm) $150
    Black
        2½in (6cm) $75
        5in (13cm) $100
    Kewpie/Billiken double face, **2½in (6cm)** $125
    Made in Japan
        2½in (6cm) bride and groom, pair $30
        4in (10cm) boxed pair $65
        16in (41cm) $135
    Soldier, 3½in (9cm) $35

All-Composition

Made by Cameo Doll Co.. Rex Doll Co. and Mutual Doll Co. All-composition. jointed at shoulders, some at hips; good condition.
    8in (20cm) $95-125
    11-12in (28-31cm) $135-165
    All original, boxed $450-550
    Black, 12-13in (31-33cm) $300-400
    Talcum container, 7in (18cm) $175-200
    Composition head, cloth body, 12in (31cm) $125-150

All-Cloth

Made by Richard G. Krueger, Inc., or King Innovations, Inc., New York. Patent number 1785800. Mask face with fat-shaped cloth body.

10-12in (25-31cm) $175-200
18-22in (46-56cm) $400-450

Hard Plastic

Ca. 1950s.

Standing Kewpie, one-piece with jointed arms, 8in (20cm) ...$85-95
Boxed $150-175
Fully-jointed with sleep eye; all-original clothes,
13in (33cm) $400-500

Vinyl

Ca. 1960s. Cameo Dolls. All original and excellent condition.

12-13in (31-33cm), boxed $50-60
16in (41cm), boxed $75-85
27in (68cm) $150
Black, 12in (31cm) boxed $80-90
Kewpie Baby with hinged body, 16in (41cm) $125-150
Kewpie Gal
    8in (20cm), boxed $50-60
    14in (36cm), boxed $100
Ragsy, molded clothes, 8in (20cm) $25
Jesco Dolls, 1980s. Boxed
    8in (20cm) black $20-25
    12in (31cm) $35
    18in (46cm) $40-50
    24in (61cm) $65-85
Danbury Mint, 1990s. Porcelain, boxed, 12in (31cm) $30-40

Kley & Hahn

History Kley & Hahn, doll factory, Ohrdruf, Thuringia, Germany. Heads by Hertel, Schwab & Co. (100 series), Bähr & Proschild (500 series) and J.D. Kestner (200 series, 680 and Walkure). 1902-on.

Comment Collectors are fond of the high-quality dolls produced by this company. Particularly desirable are the character children.

Description Perfect bisque head, glass sleeping eyes, mohair wig. Character children usually have closed mouths. Composition ball-jointed or baby body. Appropriate clothing.

Mark

>K&H<
546
6
Germany

Trademarks Walküre, Meine Einzige, Special, Dollar Princess.

Character Baby

#138, 158, 160, 167, 176, 458, 525, 531, 680 and others

11-13in (28-33cm) $225-275
18-20in (46-51cm) $350-375
24in (61cm) $500-550
28in (71cm) $1,000-1,200
Toddler
    14-16in (36-41cm) $700-750
    18-20in (46-51cm) $900-1,000
#567, Two-face toddler, 18in (46cm) $2,400
#159, Two-face baby, 11in (28cm) $1,200

Character Child

#520, 526
- 15-16in (38-41cm) $3,500-3,800
- 19-21in (48-53cm) $4,500-5,500

#536, 546, 549
- 15-16in (38-41cm) $4,200-4,800
- 19-21in (48-53cm) $5,200-5,800

#547, 18½in (47cm) at auction . . .$6,825

#548, 568, Toddler,
- 21-23in (53-58cm) $900-1,200

#154, 166, closed mouth, toddler or jointed body
- 14-16in (36-41cm) $1,500-1,600
- 19-20in (48-51cm) $2,000-2,200

#154, 166, open mouth, jointed body
- 13in (33cm) $550-600
- 18-20in (46-51cm) $750-850
- 25in (64cm) $1,000-1,100

Kley & Hahn 546 character child.
James D. Julia, Inc.

#169, closed mouth toddler, 22-23in (56-58cm) $4,500-5,500
#169, open mouth, 23in (58cm) baby $1,000-1,300

Child Doll

#250, 282, or Walküre
- 7½in (19cm) $300-350
- 12-13in (3 1-33cm) $425-450
- 16-18in (41-46cm) $300-350
- 24-25in (61-64cm) $400-450
- 30-31in (76-79cm) $650-700
- 35-36in (89-91cm) $1,000-1,200

Special Dollar Princess, 23-25in (58-64cm) $350-400

12in (31cm) 282 child.
Howard & Jan Foulke.

16in (41cm) 158 character baby.
Howard & Jan Foulke.

Kling

History Kling & Co., porcelain factory, Ohrdruf, Thuringia, Germany. 1870-on.

Comment The Kling factory made high-quality china and bisque doll heads for a long period of time. Many are marked only with a mold and size number, so it's good to become familiar with their mold numbers. The molded hair dolls with glass eyes and decorated shoulder plates are the most beautiful and most desirable to collectors.

Description Perfect china or bisque head. Vintage cloth body, though a few of the "dolly" faces are socket heads for composition bodies. Appropriate vintage clothing.

Mark

166 Ⓚ 3

Bisque shoulder head
Ca. 1880. Molded hair, painted eyes, closed mouth; cloth body with bisque lower limbs. Mold numbers in **100** and **200** Series.

6in (15cm)	$165-185
12-14in (31-36cm)	$250-300
18-20in (46-51cm)	$400-450
23-25in (58-64cm)	$550-600

Glass eyes and molded hair

15-16in (38-41cm)	$500-600*
22in (56cm)	$900-950*

Lady styles with decorated bodice, such as

#135, 144, 170, 21-23in (53-58cm)	$1,500 up

#116, lady with molded blue bonnet,

16in (41cm) at auction	$1,600

China shoulder head
Ca. 1880. Black- or blonde-haired china head with bangs, sometimes with a pink tint; cloth body with china limbs.

#188, 189, 200, 203 and others

13-15in (33-38cm)	$225-275
18-20in (46-51cm)	$325-375
24-25in (61-64cm)	$425-475

Bisque head
Ca. 1890. Perfect bisque head, glass eyes; appropriate body.

#123, closed mouth shoulder head

6½in (17cm)	$200-225

8in (20cm)

all-original pair	$500-600

12in (31cm)

Original costume	$450-550
Re-dressed	$200-225

#152, 166 or 167, closed mouth shoulder head,

16-18in (41-46cm)	$650-750

#182, 190, socket head, closed mouth. composition body,

14in (36cm)	$1,400-1,600

#373, 377, 245, shoulder head, open mouth

13-15in (33-38cm)	$250-300
19-22in (48-56cm)	$325-350

20in (51cm) 123 shoulder head.
Private Collection.

*Allow extra for unusual or elaborate hairdo.

#370, 372, 182, socket head, open mouth
14-16in (36-41cm) $275-300
22-24in (56-61cm) $350-400
27in (69cm) $450-500

All-Bisque
Glass eyes, wig.
#61, 71, pink or blue shirred hose,
5-6in (13-15cm) .... $400-$500*
#94, green shoes, 4in (10cm) $400
#36, 69, 4-5in (10-13cm)
Black boots .... $400-$500*
Yellow boots .... $400-$500*

4¼in (11cm) all-bisque Kling child, all original.
Howard & Jan Foulke.

König & Wernicke

History Konig & Wernicke, doll factory, Waltershausen, Thuringia, Germany. Heads by Hertel Schwab & Co. and Bahr & Pröschild. 1912-on.

Comment Being a late-comer to the doll industry, this company made primarily character babies, but the quality is excellent.

Description Perfect bisque head, open mouth, sleeping eyes, mohair wig. Composition baby or toddler body. Appropriate clothing.

Trademarks Mein Stolz, My Playmate.

Mark
*Made
in
Germany
99/10*

König & Wernicke Character
#98, 99, 100, 1070
10-11in (25-28cm) $225-250**
14-16in (36-41cm) $275-350**
19-21in (48-53cm) $375-400**
24-25in (6 1-64cm) $500-600**
Toddler, fully-jointed body
13-15in (33-38cm) $650-750
19-20in (48-51cm) ... $900-1,100

Child #4711,
Mein Stolz (My Pride)
37in (94cm) $1,300-1,600

12in (30) K & W 99 character baby.
Howard & Jan Foulke.

*Allow extra for swivel neck.
**Allow $50 extra for flirty eyes.

Käthe Kruse

History Käthe Kruse, Bad Kösen, Germany; after World War 11, Donauworth. 1910-on.

Comment This factory, which grew from the vision of one young mother looking for a doll for her child, is still in business producing high-quality dolls that are favorites with collectors. There is a very strong market for Kruse dolls in both Germany and the United States.

Marks On cloth: "Käthe Kruse" on sole of foot, sometimes also "Germany" and a number.

Käthe Kruse
Œ 295

Hard plastic on back: Turtle mark and "Käthe Kruse."

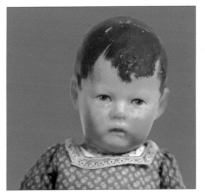

17in (43cm) *Doll I.*
Howard & Jan Foulke.

14in (36cm) *Doll IX,* all original with 1950s E. Germany Bad Kosen mark.
Howard & Jan Foulke.

Cloth Käthe Kruse

Molded muslin head, hand-painted; jointed at shoulders and hips.

Doll I, 1910-1929. 16in (41cm), early model, wide hips

Mint, all original	$5,500-6,500
Very good	$3,200-3,800
Fair	$1,600-2,000
Jointed knees, very good	$6,500 up°

"Frog" hands

Good	$5,000°
Very good, at auction	$10,200

Doll I, 1929-on. 17in (43cm), later model, slim hips

Molded hair, mint	$3,300-3,500
Very good	$2,200-2,600

Doll IH, 1930-on. (wigged)

Mint, all original	$3,000-3,500
Very good	$2,000-2,300
U.S. Zone, all original, excellent, 18in (46cm)	$2,500-2,800

Doll II "Schlenkerchen" Smiling Baby, 1922-1936, 13in (33cm)

Excellent	$8,000

°Few price samples available.

Doll V and VI Babies "Traumerchen," 1925-on. Five-pound weighted "Sand Baby" and Du Mein, unweighted
 Cloth head, 19½-23½in (50-60cm) $4,500-5,000
 Magnesit head, 21in (53cm) $1,600
Doll VII, 1926-1952. 14in (36cm)
 With Doll I head, 1930-on, all original $2,000-2,500
 With Du Mein head (1928-1930), 14in (36cm),
  good condition $2,500-3,000
Doll VIII "German Child," 1929-on. 20½in (52cm) wigged, turning head
 Mint, all original $1,500-1,800
 Good condition, suitably dressed $1,000
Doll IX "Little German Child," 1929-on. Wigged, turning head, 14in (36cm)
 Mint, all original $1,350-1,650
 U.S. Zone, cloth head $1,100-1,300
Doll X, 1930-1952. Turning head
 14in (36cm) all original $2,000-2,500
 U.S. Zone, cloth head $1,100-1,300
Dolls XII and XIII "Hampelchen," 1931-on. With dangling legs
 14in (36cm) $1,400-1,600
 18in (45cm) $2,000-2,500

Hard Plastic (Synthetic) Head

Ca. 1948-on. Hard plastic head with human hair wig, painted eyes; pink muslin body; original clothes; all in excellent condition.
 U.S. Zone
 14in (3 6cm) $600-700
 21in (53cm) $950
 Ca. 1952-1975
 14in (36cm) $375-425
 19-21in (48-53cm) $500-575
 1975-on
 14in (36cm) $225-275
 19-21in (48-53cm) $250-300
 20in (51cm) Du Mein $400-500
Doll XIV Slim Grandchild, 18in (46cm), at auction $1,700

Hanna Kruse Dolls

Däumlinchen 25H, 1957-on. 10in (25cm) with foam rubber
 stuffing $125-150
Rumpumpel Baby or Toddler 32H, 1959-on.
 13in (33cm) $200-250
Doggi, 1964-1967. Vinyl head, 10in (25cm) $150-175
Hard Plastic Baby, 14in (36cm) $90-100

All-Hard Plastic (Celluloid) Käthe Kruse 1955-1961.

Wig or molded hair, sleep or painted eyes; jointed neck, shoulders and hips; original clothes; all in excellent condition. Turtle mark.
 16in (41cm) $300-350
 Re-dressed $175-200
 Vinyl head, 16in (41cm) $200-225

Mannikin Ca. 1950.

 46-52in (116-132cm) $2,500-3,000

Kruse-Type

Bing Art Dolls

Nurnberg, Germany. 1921-1932. Cloth head, molded face, hand-painted features; cloth body with jointed shoulders and hips (some with pinned joints), mitten hands; all-original clothing; very good condition. "Bing" stamped or impressed on sole of shoe.

Cloth head, painted hair
10-12in (25-30cm) $425-475
14in (35cm) $850-950
Cloth head, wigged, 10in (25cm) $400-450
Composition head, wigged, 7in (18cm) $125-135

Heine & Schneider Art Doll

Bad-Kösen, Germany. 1920-1922. All-cloth or head of pressed cardboard covered with cloth, molded hair; cloth body with jointed shoulders and hips (some with cloth-covered composition arms and hands); appropriate or original clothes; all in good condition. Mark stamped on foot.
17-19in (43-48cm) $1,600-1,800

Unmarked Child Dolls

Ca. 1920s.
15-17in (38-43cm) ....$250 up*

16in (41cm) all-celluloid
Gretchen, all original.
Howard & Jan Foulke.

13in (32cm) Rumpumpel 32H
toddlers, all original.
Howard & Jan Foulke.

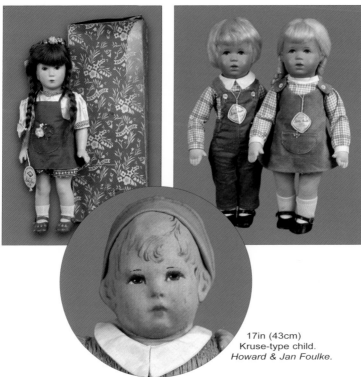

17in (43cm)
Kruse-type child.
Howard & Jan Foulke.

Gebrüder Kuhnlenz

History Gebrüder Kuhnlenz, porcelain factory, Kronach, Bavaria. 1884-on.
Comment There are not a lot of Kuhnlenz dolls available, but they are prized by their followers. The early dolls and all-bisques are excellent quality.

Mark and/or numbers, such as:
41-28   56-18   44-15
The first two digits are mold numbers;
second two are size number.

Gebrüder Kuhnlenz doll with closed mouth

Ca. 1885-on. Perfect bisque socket head (some with closed Belton-type crown), inset glass eyes, closed mouth, round cheeks; jointed composition body.

#28, 31, 32, 39
8-10in (20-25cm) $850-1,100
15-16in (38-41cm) $1,600-1,700
21-23in (53-58cm) $2,400-2,600

#34, Bru-type, French body
15in (38cm) $3,800-4,300
18in (46cm) $5,500-6,000

#38, shoulder head, kid body
12in (31cm) $450-500
16-18in (41-46cm) $600-650
23-24in (58-61cm) $800-900

14in (36cm) 32 child.
Kay Jensen Antique Dolls.

Gebrüder Kuhnlenz Child Doll

Ca. 1890-on. Perfect bisque socket head, sleep or paperweight-type eyes, open mouth, molded teeth; jointed composition body, sometimes French.

#41, 44, 56 (character-type face)
9-10in (23-25cm) $500-600
16-19in (41-48cm) $600-700
24-26in (61-66cm) $800-900

#165
18in (46cm) $275-300
22-24in (56-61cm) $325-350
30-32in (76-81cm) $500-550

#61, 47 shoulder head, 19-22in (48-56cm) $350-400

7in (18cm) all-bisque.
Howard & Jan Foulke.

Gebrüder Kuhnlenz Tiny Dolls

Perfect bisque socket head, wig, stationary glass eyes, open mouth with molded teeth; five-piece composition body with molded shoes and socks; all in good condition. Usually mold #44.

7-8in (18-20cm)
Crude body $165-185
Better body $225-275
Black . . . . .See page 54.
All-Bisque, swivel neck, usually mold #31, 41, 44 or 56
Bootines
7-8in (18-20cm) $2,500-2,800
9½in (24cm) $3,200-3,500
Mary Janes
5in (13cm) $750-850
7in (18cm) $2,150-2,350
8½in (22cm) $3,000
Black . . . . .See page 55.

Lanternier

History A. Lanternier & Cie. Porcelain factory of Limoges, France. 1915-1924.
Comment These are late French dolls, so quality varies, but the character-type faces are interesting.
Description Perfect bisque socket head, glass eyes, pierced ears, good wig. Jointed papier-mâché body. Appropriate clothing.

Mark

Lanternier Child
Ca. 1915.
Cherie, Favorite or La Georgienne
16-18in (41-46cm) $350-400
22-24in (56-61cm) $600-650
28in (71cm) $750

Lorraine Lady
Ca. 1915.
Composition lady body,
16-18in (41-46cm) . . .$650-750*

Characters, "Toto" and others
Ca. 1915.
Smiling character face,
17-19in (43-48cm) $550-600

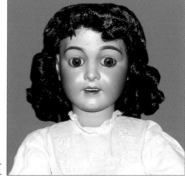

26in (66cm) Lanternier *Favorite.*
Connie Blain.

Lenci

History Enrico & Elana Scavini, Turin, Italy. 1920-on.

Comment Lenci is the top name in cloth art dolls. Mint examples of rare dolls will bring higher prices. To bring the prices quoted, dolls must be clean with good color and no moth holes. Faded and dirty dolls will bring only one-quarter to one-third of these prices.

Lenci

All-felt (sometimes cloth torso); pressed felt head, painted features, eyes usually side-glancing; jointed shoulders and hips; original clothes, often of felt or organdy; in excellent condition.

Mark "LENCI" on cloth and various paper tags; sometimes stamped on bottom of foot.

Lenci

Miniatures and Mascottes

8-9in (20-23cm) Regionals	$275-325
Children or unusual costumes	$400-450
Jackie Coogan with cigarette	$1,800
Purse	$250-300
Bookmark	$125-165

Children #300, 109, 149, 159, 111

13in (33cm)	$850-1,000
17in (43cm)	$1,500-2,000
19-22in (48-56cm)	$1,600-2,200
Black Hottentot, 15in (38cm)	$2,500-3,000
Clown, red felt hair, 18in (46cm)	$2,700
Indian Chief, 20in (51cm)	$3,500
#1500 scowling face, 17-19in (43-48cm)	$2,250-2,750
#500, 21in (53cm)	$1,650-1,850
Baby, 18-21in (46-53cm)	$2,500-3,000

1930s Children

"Lucia" face, 14in (36cm)	
Child clothes	$800-1,200
Regional outfits	$600-800
"Laura" face,	
16in (41cm)	$1,000-1,200
"Mariuccia" face,	
17in (43cm)	$1,200-1,500
"Benedetta" face,	
9in (48cm)	$1,500-1,600
"Henriette" face,	
25in (63cm)	$1,700-2,200
Teen Age, slender legs,	
16in (41cm)	$1,800-2,000

1935 Round face

11-12in (28-31cm)	$750-850
20in (51cm)	$1,250

Becassine

11in (28cm)	$950
20in (51cm) glass eyes	$3,000

Ladies and long-limbed novelty dolls

24-28in (61-71cm)	$1,500-2,500
40in (102cm),	
faded color	$1,000-1,250

17in (43cm) 300 boy, all original. *Howard & Jan Foulke.*

8in (20cm) *Little Orphant Annie,*
all original.
Howard & Jan Foulke.

14in (36cm) Tyrolean Pair with
Lucia face, all original.
Howard & Jan Foulke.

Pierrot (Dudovich), ...$3,000-3,500
Opium Smoker, 20in (51cm) $3,200
Valentino, 29in (74cm) $15,400
Glass Eyes, 20in (51cm), Valentine, Widow Allegra
    and others $3,000-4,000
"Surprised Eye" (round painted eyes), fancy clothes
    20in (51cm) $2,200-2,600
Hand Puppet $400-500
Winkers
    12in (31cm) $750-950
    Black Bellhop, at auction $2,500
Wood head, 6in (15cm) $40-60
Mask face, disc eyes, 23in (58cm) $600-700
Flocked hard plastic, 11 in (28cm) $150-175
Celluloid-type, 6in (15cm) $65-75
Catalogs $450-750
1950 Characters ....$300 up
Modern Series, 1979 on
    13in (28cm) $85-110
    22-21in (51-53cm) $175-200
    22in (56cm) surprised eyes $250-275
    26in (66cm) lady $200-225
    27-28in (69-71cm) long gown $225-250

Lenci-Type

Vintage Felt or Cloth Doll
Mohair wig, painted features; stuffed cloth body; original clothes or costume;
excellent condition.
    Child dolls
        16-18in (41-46cm) depending upon quality, up to $750
        Regional costume, very good quality
            7½-8½in (19-22cm) $30-40
            12in (31cm) $75-85

8in (20cm) Ronnaug Petterssen pair,
all original.
Jean Grout.

13in (33cm) and 14in (36cm) Italian pair,
all original.
Howard & Jan Foulke.

Alma, Turin, Italy
    11in (28cm) $200-250
    16in (41cm) $400-500
Dean's Rag Book Company, England
    14-16in (36-41cm) $300-400
    Composition face, 18in (46cm) $500-600
    Dancing Dolls, 12in (31cm) $150-175
Ronnaug Pettersen, Norway. All-original Norwegian costume
    8in (20cm) $60-75
    15in (38cm) $800-1,000
    17-18in (43-46cm) $1,500-1,800
Vecchiotti, Milano. Italy, 9½in (24cm) all original $100-125
Baitz, Austria, 9in (23cm) all original $25
Farnell's Alpha Toys, London, England
    Child, 14in (36cm) $225-250
    Black character, 14in (36cm) $275-300
    King George VI, 1937, 16in (41cm) $400-450
Allwin Nightdress Case,
    20in (51cm) $400
    Shirley Temple,
    20in (51cm) at auction $2,200
Eugene Poir, Gre-Poir French doll
makers. Paris and New York.
    16-18in (41-46cm)
        Cloth face $300-350
        Felt face $450-550
Raynal, Venus, Marina, Clelia, Paris,
France, 17-18in (43-46cm)
    mint $1,000-1,200
Poupées Nicette, 14in (36cm),
    regional costumes $250-300
Poupées Gerb, 21in (53cm) $450
Goodchild Toys, Australia,
    17in (43cm) $165

17in (43cm) Goodchild Toys, Australia, all felt child.
Howard & Jan Foulke.

Liberty of London

History Liberty & Co. of London, England. 1906-on.
Comment These interesting dolls are very well made and have a following of collectors who avidly seek them.

Mark Cloth label or paper tag "Liberty of London."

Liberty of London *King George VI.*
Howard & Jan Foulke.

British Coronation Dolls

1939. All-cloth with painted and needle-sculpted faces; original clothes; excellent condition.

The Royal Family and Coronation Participants
    9-9½in (23-24cm) $175-200
    1935 George V Silver Jubilee, at auction $785
    Queen Mary Silver Jubilee at auction $715
English Historical and Ceremonial Characters
    9-10in (23-25cm) $150-195
    Beefeater (Tower Guard) $85

Armand Marseille (A.M.)

History Armand Marseille of Koppelsdorf, Thuringia, Germany (porcelain and doll factory). 1885-on.
Comment Collectors refer to these dolls as A.M.s. This factory was one of the largest doll establishments in the world. The quality of the early dolls is very good, especially the 1894 models; later dolls are not as well made, so choose carefully. Some of the A.M. character dolls are very rare and desirable. The *Just Me* model, though not rare, is very popular.
Description Perfect bisque socket head, sleeping glass eyes, open mouth, mohair wig or molded hair. Some character dolls have painted eyes and closed mouths. Kid, cloth or composition child, toddler or baby body. Appropriate clothing.

Marks

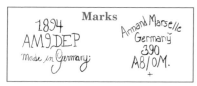

9½in (24cm) 390 child,
all original.
Howard & Jan Foulke.

Child Doll

1890-on. Composition ball-jointed body.
**#390 (larger sizes marked only "A. [size]
M."), Florodora, 1894**

> 9-10in (23-25cm) $200-225
> 12-14in (31-36cm) $175
> 16-18in (41-46cm) $200-225
> 20in (51cm) $225-250
> 23-24in (58-61cm) $275-300
> 28-29in (71-74cm) $400-450
> 30-32in (76-81cm) $500
> 35-36in (89-91cm) $650-750
> 38in (96cm) $900-1,100
> 40-42in (102-107cm) $1,500-2,000
> 15-18in (38-46cm) all-original
>   factory clothes $500-600
> **Five-piece composition body,
> (excellent quality body)**
> 6-7in (15-18cm) $175-200
> 9-10in (23-25cm) $225-250
> **Closed mouth,**
> 5-5½in (12-14cm) $225-250

Cardboard and stick leg body

> 9-10in (23-25cm) $100-125
> 12-14in (31-36cm) $125-135
>   All-original factory clothes $300-350
> 16-18in (41-46cm) $150-175

#1894 (composition body; early pale bisque)

> 14-16in (36-41cm) $300-350
> 21-23in (53-58cm) $450-500
> 26in (66cm) $600-650

**#370, 3200, 1894, Florodora, Anchor 2015, Rosebud, Lily, Alma, Mabel,
Darling, Beauty, Princess, shoulder heads on kid or cloth bodies.**

> 11-12in (28-31cm) $100-110
> 14-16in (36-41cm) $135-150
> 22-24in (56-61cm) $200-225
> 25-26in (64-66cm) $250

#2000, 14in (36cm) . . . .$800-900°

Queen Louise, Rosebud (composition body)

> 12in (31cm) $225-250
> 23-25in (58-64cm) $300-350
> 28-29in (71-74cm) $400-450

Baby Betty

> 14-16in (36-41cm) composition
>   body $325-375
> 19-21in (48-53cm) kid body . .$275-325

**#1894, 1892, 1896, 1897 shoulder heads
(excellent quality),**

> 19-22in (48-56cm) $300-325

14in (36cm) 1894 child,
all original.
Howard & Jan Foulke.

Character Children

1910-on. Glass or painted eyes, open or closed
mouth; composition body.

#230 Fany (molded hair)

> 15-16in (38-41cm) $6,000-7,000
> 18in (46cm) $8,500-9,500

#231 Fany (wigged)
  13-14in (33-36cm) . . .$5,000-5,500
  16in (41cm) $6,500
#250, 11-13in (28-33cm) $400-500
#251/248 (open/closed mouth)
  12in (31cm) $1,000-1,200
  16-18in (41-46cm) . . .$1,800-2,000
#340, 13in (33cm) . . . .$2,500°
#345 (wig, intaglio eyes),
  12in (31cm) at auction . . .$2,800
#372 Kiddiejoy, shoulder head, "mama"
  body, 19in (48cm) $450-500
#400 (child body)
  13in (33cm) . . . . . .$1,600-1,800°
  17in (43cm) . . . . . .$2,600-2,800°
#500, 600, 13-15in (33-38cm) .$400-500
#550 (glass eyes)
  12in (31cm) $1,500-1,800
  18-20in (46-51cm) . . .$2,600-2,800
#560, 11-13in (28-33cm) $400-500
#590 (open/closed mouth),
  15-16in (38-41cm) $700-800
#620, shoulder head,
  16in (41cm) $500

10in (25cm) 3200 child, all original.
Howard & Jan Foulke.

#640, shoulder head (same face as 550 socket),
  20in (51cm) $500-600
#700
  11 in (28cm) painted eyes . . . .$2,100°
  14in (36cm) glass eyes . . . .$3,500-4,000°
A.M. (intaglio eyes)
  16-17in (41-43cm) $6,000-6,800

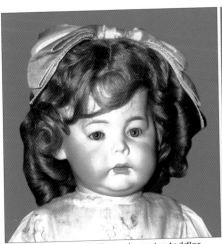

19in (48cm) 231 *Fany* character toddler.
Kay Jensen Antique Dolls.

12½in (32cm) 248/251
character child.
Howard & Jan Foulke.

°Few price samples available.

Character Babies and Toddlers

1910-on. Sleep eyes, open mouth, some with teeth; composition bent-limb body.

Mold #990, 985, 971, 996, 1330, 326, (solid dome), 980, 991, 327, 329, 259 and others

10-11 in (25-28cm)	$175-200
13-15in (33-38cm)	$225-250
18-20in (46-51cm)	$300-350
22in (56cm)	$400
24-25in (61-64cm)	$450-500

#233

13-15in (33-38cm)	$400-450
20in (51cm)	$600-650

#251/248 (open/closed mouth), 11-12in (28-31 cm) $500-600
#251/248 (open mouth), 12-14in (31-36cm) $450-450
#410 (two rows of teeth), 12in (31cm) $600-700
#518

16-18in (41-46cm)	$400-450
25in (64cm)	$700-800

#560A

10-12in (25-31cm)	$275-300
15-17in (38-43cm)	$375-425

#580, 590 (open/closed mouth)

9in (23cm)	$375-425
15-16in (38-41cm)	$900-950

#590 (open mouth)

12in (31cm)	$375-425
16-18in (41-46cm)	$550-600

#920, shoulder head, "mama" body, 21in (53cm) .... $450-500°
Melitta, 19in (48cm) toddler $800-900

Marks

640
A.4/0M
Germany

560
Germany
A.2/0M. D.R.G.M.

Infant

1924-on. Sleep eyes; hard-stuffed jointed cloth body or soft-stuffed cloth body.

#351, 341, Kiddiejoy and Our Pet

Mark

A.M.
Germany
341.73.

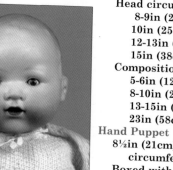

20in (51cm) 351 infant.
Howard & Jan Foulke.

Head circumference

8-9in (20-23cm)	$135-165
10in (25 cm)	$175-195
12-13in (31-33cm)	$225-250
15in (38cm)	$300-350

Composition body (length)

5-6in (12-15cm)	$185-210
8-10in (21-25cm)	$225-235
13-15in (33-38cm)	$250-265
23in (58cm)	$400-500

Hand Puppet

8½in (21cm) head circumference	$225
Boxed with label	$350-400

#352, 17-20in
(43-51 cm) long $350-400

#347, head circumference, 12-13in (31-33cm) $300-350
Baby Phyllis, head circumference
   9in (23cm) black $225-250
   12-13in (31-33cm) $225-250
Baby Gloria, RBL, New York
   12in (31cm) $300-350
   15-16in (38-41cm) $500

9in (23cm) *Just Me.*
Howard & Jan Foulke.

Marked "Just Me" Character

Ca. 1925. Perfect bisque socket head, curly wig, glass eyes to side, closed mouth; composition body: dressed. Some of these dolls, particularly the painted bisque ones, were used by the Vogue Doll Company in the 1930s and will be found with original Vogue labeled clothes.

Mark
Just ME Registered Germany 310/11/0M

7½-8in (19-20cm) $1,450-1,650
9-10in (23-25cm) $2,250-2,450
11in (28cm) $3,000
13in (33cm) $4,000
Painted bisque
   7-8in (18-20cm) all original ...$1,250
   10in (25cm)
      all original $1,300-1,400

Lady

1910-1930. Bisque head with mature face, mohair wig, sleep eyes, open or closed mouth; composition lady body with molded bust, long slender arms and legs..

#401 and 400 (slim body), 14in (36cm)
   Open mouth $1,500-1,600
   Closed mouth $2,250-2,500
   Painted bisque $900-1,000
#300 (M.H.)
   9in (23cm) ......$1,400-1,500°
   All original ....$1,650°
#400, flapper body,
   16-19in (41-48cm) $2,250-2,750

14in (36cm) 401 flapper.
Private Collection.

°Few price samples available.

Metal Dolls

German Metal Head Child
Ca. 1888-on. Marked Minerva, Juno and Diana or unmarked. Metal shoulder head on cloth or kid body; dressed; very good condition, not repainted.

Molded hair, painted eyes
12-14in (31-36cm) $100-125
20-22in (51-56cm) $125-150

Molded hair or wig, glass eyes
12-14in (31-36cm) $140-160
20-22in (51-56cm) $210-235

American All-Metal Child
Ca. 1917-on. Giebeler-Falk. Atlas Doll & Toy Co. and others. Wig. sleep eyes; fully-jointed body; dressed; all in good condition, not repainted.

16-20in (41-51cm) $200-250
All-Metal Baby, 11-13in (28-33cm) $75-100

Missionary Ragbabies

History Julia Beecher, Elmira, NY, designer and maker. 1893-1910. The sale of the dolls benefited her church missionary fund, hence the name Missionary Ragbabies.

Comment A very desirable American cloth doll, some wear is acceptable, but no repainting.

Description All stockinet with needle-sculpted and hand-painted features, applied ears, looped wool hair. Vintage clothing. Sizes, 16-23in (41-58cm).

Mark None.

Beecher Baby
21-23in (53-59cm) $3,500-4,000
Excellent $5,000
Fair $1,800-2,000

Moravian

History Ladies Sewing Society of Central Moravian Church. 1872-on.
Comment Polly Heckewelder is still being produced by the Moravian Church ladies in Bethlehem, PA. New dolls are easily distinguishable, but some study is required to determine the approximate age of many of the older dolls.
Mark None.

Moravian Cloth *Polly Heckewelder*
Bethlehm, PA. All-cloth with flat face, hand-painted hair and features, stitch-jointed limbs, mitten hands with stitched fingers and separate thumbs; original 1870s style clothes: blue or pink checked cotton dress with lace-trimmed white apron, lace edging and crocheted outer bonnet with bow in color to match dress, black shoes and white stockings.

16-18in (41-46cm) early model $2,500-3,800
1930s to 1940s model $1,500-2,000
Recent $150-250

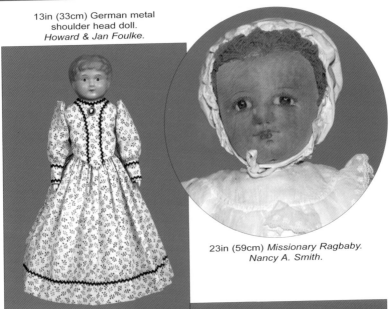

13in (33cm) German metal
shoulder head doll.
Howard & Jan Foulke.

23in (59cm) *Missionary Ragbaby.*
Nancy A. Smith.

18in (41cm) *Polly*
Heckewelder, all original.
Connie Blain Collection.

Moravian Cloth *Benigna*

1943. Bethlehem, PA. All-cloth with painted features, depicting Moravian
females with different colored caps designating their position. Each doll carried a drawstring reticule containing a paper identifying her.

    4-5in (10-12cm) $250

Maggie Bessie

Named for the Salem, NC sisters who made her. All cloth with flat face, hand-
painted hair and features, stitch-jointed and oil-painted limbs, detailed fingers. Appropriate vintage clothing. No repaint.

    15in (38cm) $16,500

Multi-Faced Dolls

> **History** Various German, French and American companies. 1888 and perhaps earlier.

Marked C.B. Doll

Carl Bergner. Sonneberg, Germany. Perfect bisque head with two or three different faces, usually sleeping, laughing and crying; papier-mâché hood hides the unwanted face(s); a ring through the top of the hood attached to a dowel turns the faces; cloth torso, composition limbs or jointed composition body; dressed; all in good condition.

Two or three faces, 12-13in (31-33cm) $1,350-1,450
#202 dep, two-faced black and white, 13in (33cm) $2,500-3,000
Red Riding Hood, Grandmother and Wolf,
    13in (33cm) ....$5,000-6,000°

German Character Babies

Ca. 1910. Perfect bisque head with two faces, usually crying, sleeping or smiling; swivel neck; composition or cloth body; dressed; all in good condition. Some have papier-mâché hoods to cover unwanted faces, while some use cloth bonnets.

HvB (von Berg) two-faced baby, 17in (43cm) $1,000-1,200
Gebrüder Heubach three-faced baby, 13in (33cm) $1,600-1,800

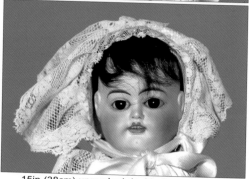

15in (38cm) unmarked double-face child doll.
Kay Jensen Antique Dolls.

°Few price samples available.

Kley & Hahn two-faced baby, 13in (33cm) $1,200-1,400
Max Schelhorn two-faced baby, 9in (23cm) $500-600
Herm Steiner topsy-turvy baby, 8in (20cm) $400-500

American Composition Dolls

Trudy, 3-in-1 Doll Corp., New York; sleeping, crying,
  smiling, all original, 14in (36cm) $175-225
Johnny Tu-Face, Effanbee, New York; crying and smiling,
  16in (41cm) $400-450

Munich Art Dolls

History Marion Bertha Kaulitz, Munich, Germany. 1908-1912. Doll heads designed by Paul Vogelsanger, Josef Wackerle and Marie Marc-Schnur.
Comment Dolls were part of the Puppen Reform movement which advocated dolls with faces and clothing made to look like real children, particularly the peasant children from the country who came to visit the city markets.

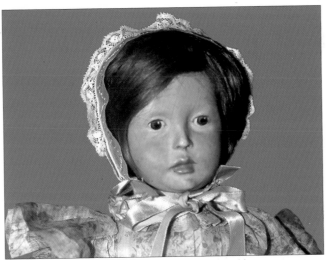

17in (43cm) Munich Art character girl.
Kay Jensen Antique Dolls.

Munich Art Dolls

Molded composition character heads with hand-painted features; fully-jointed composition bodies; appropriate regional or "country style" clothes; all in good condition.
  13-14in (33-36cm) $4,000-5,000
  18-19in (46-48cm) $8,000-11,000

Ohlhaver

History Gebrüder Ohlhaver, doll factory, Sonneberg, Thuringia, Germany. Heads made by Gebrüder Heuhach, Ernst Heubach and Porzellanfabrik Mengersgereuth. 1912-on.

Comment The Revalo child has a distinctive face that is a favorite with collectors. Look for an example that still retains her original hair eyelashes.

Description Perfect bisque head, sleeping eyes, open mouth, appropriate wig. Composition child, baby or toddler body. Appropriate clothing.

Trademark Revalo.

Mark
Germany
Revalo
22-3

Revalo Character Baby or Toddler
#22

15-17in (38-41cm)	$300-350
22in (56cm)	$450-500
Toddler, 22in (56cm)	$650-750

Revalo Child Doll
Mold #150 or #10727

14-15in (36 38cm)	$300-350
18-20in (46-51cm)	$375-425
24-25in (61-64cm)	$475-525
28in (71cm)	$650-750
Shoulder head,	
22-25in (56-64cm)	$400-450

Revalo Character Doll
Bisque head with molded hair, painted eyes, open/closed mouth; composition body.

Coquette, 12-13in (31-33cm)	$550-650
Coquette with hair bows, 13-14in (33-36cm)	$750-800

15in (38cm) *Revalo* 22 character baby.
Howard & Jan Foulke.

Oriental Dolls

Japanese Traditional Dolls, Ichimatsu (play doll)

1868-on. Papier-mâché swivel head on shoulder plate, hips, lower legs and feet (early ones have jointed wrists and ankles); cloth midsection, cloth (floating) upper arms and legs; hair wig, dark glass eyes, pierced ears and nostrils; original clothes; all in very good condition.

Meiji Era (1868-1912)

3-5in (8-13cm)	$250-300
12-14in (31-36cm)	$500-550
18-20in (46-51cm)	$750-800
24-26in (61-66cm)	$1,600-1,800
Early three-bend body (Mitsuore),	
14-16in (36-41cm)	$2,000 up
Ca. 1920s and 1930s	
13-15in (33-38cm)	$300-350
17-18in (43-46cm)	$500-550
24in (61cm)	$700-750

Ca. 1940s
   10-12in (25-31cm) $60-75
   14-16in (36-41cm) $100-115
   20in (51cm) $150-175
Gosho Ningyo, Ca. 1900. Chubby immobile baby in various poses
   with accessory, 7in (18cm) $400-500
Traditional Lady (Kyoto or Fashion Doll)
   Ca. 1900, 12in (31cm) $350-400
   1920s
      10-12in (25-31cm) $100-125
      16in (41cm) $175-200
   1940s
      12-14in (31-36cm) $55-65
      6½in (16cm) Geisha with six wigs, boxed $80-90
Traditional Warrior
   1880s, 16-18in (41-46cm) $500-600
   1920s, 11-12in (28-31cm) $150-175

16in (41cm) *Ichimatsu*, all original.
Private Collection.

10½in (26cm) warrior.
Private Collection.

Royal Personages
   Ca. 1890, 10in (25cm) $500-600
   1920s-1930
      4-6in (10-15cm) $65-85
      12in (31cm) $250-275
Baby with bent limbs
   Ca. 1910, 11in (28cm) $200-250
   Ca. 1930s, souvenir dolls
      8-10in (20-25cm) $50-60
      16in (41cm) $100-125
Carved Ivory, Ca. 1890
   2-3in (5-8cm) fully-jointed, exquisite carving $350
   Lesser quality $225
Chinese Papier-mâché, Ca 1930-1940
   Opera Doll, all original
      8in (20cm) $110-135
      26in (66cm) $500-600
   Child Doll, papier-maché head, hands and feet,
      cloth body; all original, 9-10in (23-25cm) $25-35

17in (43cm) S & H 1329 oriental lady.
Howard & Jan Foulke.

13in (33cm) JDK 243 oriental baby.
Kay Jensen Antique Dolls.

Oriental Bisque Dolls

Ca. 1900-on. Made by French and German firms. Bisque head tinted yellow; matching ball-jointed or baby body; original or appropriate clothes.

B.P. #220
    11in (33cm) $2,000-2,300
    16-17in (41-43cm) $2,800-3,200
Belton-type, 12in (31cm) $1,250-1,450
BSW #500
    11in (28cm) $1,000-1,100
    14-15in (36-38cm) $1,800-2,000
Bru Jne, 20in (51cm) $24,000-26,000
E.B. *Poupée*, 15in (38cm) $9,000
Jumeau
    Closed mouth, 19-20in (48-51cm) .... $48,000-62,000°
    Open mouth, 18in (46cm) $6,500
French *Poupée*, wood body, 15in (38cm) $10,000
JDK 243
    13-14in (33-36cm) $4,300-4,800
    16-18in (41-46cm) $5,300-5,800
A.M. 353
    9½ (24cm) $650-750
    12in (31cm) $750-850
    15-16in (38-41cm) $1,000-1,200
    10in (25cm) cloth body $600
A.M. Girl, 8-9in (20-23cm) $450-550
S&H 1329
    14-15in (36-38cm) $1,400-1,600*
    18-19in (46-48cm) $2,000-2,200*
    24in (61cm) $3,000-3,200*
8&H 1099, 1129, and 1199
    9-10in (23-25cm) $1,200-1,300*
    12in (31cm) $1,700-1,900*
    15-16in (38-41cm) $2,300-2,600*
    24in (61cm) $4,000-4,250
S PB H
    9in (23cm) $450-550
    16in (41cm) $1,200-1,400

°Few price samples available.
*Allow extra for elaborate original outfits.

#164, 16-17in (41-43cm) $1,650-1,850
Unmarked
    4½in (12cm) painted eyes $175-195
    4¾in (12cm) glass eyes $400
    11-12in (28-31cm) glass eyes $650-700

All-Bisque Dolls

JDK Baby, 7in (18cm) ....$2,200°
Heubach Chin Chin, 4in (10cm) $250-275
S&H Child
    4½in (12cm) $550-600
    5½in (14cm) $650-700
    7in (18cm) $800-850
Man with molded hat and mustache, 3½in (6cm) $330

Bisque Heads of Unknown Origin

Lady with molded hair or hat, wood jointed body,
    13in (33cm) ....$750-850°
Character man with molded mustache, jointed body,
    11in (28cm ....$1,100°

German Papier-mâché

Ca. 1925.
August Möller, 14in (36cm) all original, boxed, at auction $650
#419, Papier-mâché man, molded hat and mustache,
    cloth body, 13in (33cm) $300-350

American Cloth

Oil painted stockinette in the Chase manner; original
    clothes, 16in (41cm) $800-1,000

Ada Lum

1920-1950. Hong Kong. All cloth with embroidered face.
    15in (38cm) $50-60
    28in (71cm) $150

20in (51cm) oriental Bru.
Kay Jensen Antique Dolls.

°Few price samples available.

Papier-mâché
So-Called French-type

History Heads by German firms such as Johann Müller of Sonneberg and Andreas Voit of Hildburghausen, were sold to French and other doll makers. 1835-1850.

Comment Due to their age, some wear and crazing is acceptable on this type of doll, but be careful of any repaint and repair which can substantially reduce the value. Dolls with original clothing would bring a premium price.

Description Shoulder head with painted black pate, brush marks around face, nailed-on human hair wig (often missing), set-in glass eyes, closed or open mouth with bamboo teeth, pierced nose; French pink kid body with stiff arms and legs; appropriate old clothes.

Mark None

French-type Papier-mâché

14-16in (36-41cm)	$1,800-2,200
19-21in (48-51cm)	$2,500-2,600
24-26in (6 1-66cm)	$2,800-3,000
32in (81cm)	$3,500-3,800
Painted eyes	
6-8 in (15-20cm)	$550-600
14-16in (36-41cm)	$1,200-1,500
Wood-jointed body,	
6in (15cm)	$750-800
Shell decoration	
8in (20cm) pair	$1,100-1,300
18in (46cm) pair	$2,500
Poupard, molded bonnet and	
clothes, 12in (31cm)	$350-400

14in (36cm) French papier-mâché fashion with original wig. *Howard & Jan Foulke.*

21in (53cm) German papier-mâché with bun hairdo. *Private Collection.*

German

Comment The models from the 1820s and 1830 represent the early production period and the beginning of the German doll industry. Hence, they are very important historically. Some wear and crazing is acceptable, but avoid dolls with repaint and repair. Dolls with original clothing would bring a premium price.

Papier-mâché Shoulder Head

Ca. 1840s-1860s. Johann Müller and others. Unretouched shoulder head, molded black hair, painted eyes; some wear and crazing; cloth or kid body; original or appropriate old clothing; entire doll in fair condition.

16-18in (41-46cm)	$900-1,000*
22-24in (56-61cm)	$1,100-1,300*
32in (81cm)	$1,900-2,200*
18½in (47cm) all original, exceptional model and condition	$5,000
Long curls, 19in (48cm)	$2,300

Glass eyes, short hair

19in (48cm)	$1,650-1,850
24in (6 1cm)	$2,400
21in (53cm) all-original provincial costume	$2,600
Glass eyes, long hair, 22in (56cm)	$1,700-2,000
Glass eyes, bun and exposed cars, 20-22in (51-56cm)	$4,000-5,000
Flirty eyes. long hair, 23in (58cm)	$2,700-3,000

Unmarked So-called Pre-Greiner

Ca. 1850. Unknown makers, some may be American. Papier-mâché shoulder head; molded and painted black hair, pupil-less black glass eyes; stuffed cloth body, mostly homemade, wood, leather or cloth extremities; dressed in good old or original clothes; all in good condition, showing some wear.

18-22in (46-56cm)	$1,200-1,500
28-32in (71-81cm)	$2,200-2,700
Fair condition, much wear, 20-24in (51-61cm)	$700-800
Flirty eye, 30in (76cm)	$3,000-3,500

Molded Hair Papier-mâché: So-called Milliners' Model

1820s-1860s. Unretouched shoulder head, various molded black hairdos, blue, black or brown eyes, painted features; original kid body, wooden arms and legs; original or very old handmade clothing; entire doll in fair condition.

Long curls

9in (23cm)	$550**
13in (33cm)	$675-725**
23in (58cm)	$1,400-1,500**

Covered wagon hairdo

7in (18cm)	$275-325**
11in (28cm)	$500-550
15in (38cm)	$675-775**

Side curls with braided bun

9-10in (23-25cm)	$900-1,000**
16in (41cm)	$1,650

*Allow extra for unusual models.
**Allow extra for excellent condition and original clothes.

Center part with molded bun
   7-8in (18-20cm) $575-650
   11in (28cm) $1,100-1,200**
   Wood-jointed body $1,500
Side curls with high beehive (Apollo knot)
   11-12in (28-31cm) $1,100-1,300**
   18in (46cm) $2,000-2,250**
Coiled braids at ears, braided bun
   10-11 in (25-28cm) $1,000-1,100**
   20in (51cm) $2,000-2,200*
Braided coronet
   11in (28cm) $1,250-1,450**
   17-18in (43-46cm) $3,200-3,500
Short wind-blown hair
   11in (28cm) $1,100**
   18in (46cm) $1,750**
Molded bonnet, Tyrol hat, 16in (41cm) $1,650

Sonneberg Täufling So-called Motschmann Baby***

Ca. 1850-on. Heinrich Stier and other Sonneberg factories. Papier-mâché or wax-over-composition head with painted hair, dark pupil-less glass eyes; composition lower torso, composition and wood arms and legs, jointed at the ankles and wrists, cloth-covered midsection with voice box, cloth-covered upper arms and legs, called floating joints; dressed in shift and bonnet.

Very good condition
   6in (15cm) $800-900
   12-14in (31 -36cm) $1,000-1,200
   18-20in (46-51cm) $1,800-2,300
   24-26in (61-66cm) $3,000-3,250
Fair condition, with wear
   12-14in (31-36cm) $600-750
   18-20in (46-51cm) $1,200-1,300

8½in (21cm) patent washable, all original.
Howard & Jan Foulke.

Patent Washable Dolls

1880-1915. F.M. Schilling and other Sonneberg factories. Composition shoulder head with mohair or skin wig, glass eyes, closed or open mouth; cloth body with composition arms and lower legs, sometimes with molded boots; appropriately dressed; all in good condition.

Superior Quality
   12-14in (31-36cm) $450-500
   16-18in (41-46cm) $650-700
   22-24in (56-61cm) $800-850
   30in (76cm) $1,000-1,200
Standard Quality
   11-12in (28-31cm) $150-175
   14-16in (36-41cm) $225-250
   22-24in (56-61cm) $350-375
   30-33in (76-84cm) $450-500
   38in (97cm) $600-700
Lady, 13-16in (33-41cm) $750-850
Oriental, 12in (31cm) $250

**Allow extra for excellent condition and original clothes.
***Some are found stamped "Ch. Motschmann" but he was the holder of the patent for the voice boxes, not the manufacturer of the dolls.

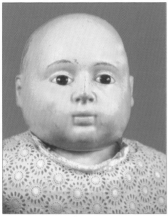

26½in (67cm) Sonneberg taufling.
Howard & Jan Foulke.

12in (30cm) Sonneberg-type
papier-mâché doll, all original.
Howard & Jan Foulke.

Sonneberg-type Papier-mâché

Ca. 1880-1910. Muller & Strasburger, A. Wislizenus, Cuno & Otto Dressel and other Sonneberg factories. Shoulder head with molded and painted black or blonde hair, painted eyes, closed mouth; cloth body, sometimes with leather arms; old or appropriate clothes; all in good condition, showing some wear.

13-15in (33-38cm)	$250-350
18-19in (46-48cm)	$400-450
23-25in (58-64cm)	$550-600
Glass eyes, 18in (46cm)	$550
Topsy-Turvy, 7½in (19cm) all original	$300

Papier-mâché child

Ca. 1920-on. Papier-mâché head, good wig, painted features; hard stuffed body; original clothes, all in good condition.

10-12in (25-31cm)	$50-60

Parian-type (Untinted Bisque)

History Various German firms. Ca. 1860s through 1870s.

Comment When studying these beautiful fancy heads, it is easy to see how the idea of making doll heads of bisque evolved from the production of figurines. Examples with elaborate hairdos featuring beads, feathers, flowers and ribbons, decorated shoulder plates with molded or applied collars, necklaces and ribbons, pierced ears and glass eyes bring the highest prices. Be especially careful to closely check the applied decorations for possible damage.

Description Pale or untinted shoulder head, sometimes with molded blouse, beautifully molded hairdo (may have ribbons, beads, comb or other decoration), painted eyes, closed mouth; cloth body; lovely clothes; entire doll in fine condition.

Mark Usually none, sometimes numbers.

Unmarked Parian

Common, plain style
    8-10in (20-25cm) $110-125
    14-16in (36-41cm) $250-300
    22-24in (56-61cm) $425-475
Swivel neck, 17½in (45cm) $600-650
Glass eyes, 23in (58cm) $600-650
Exaggerated eye painting, 20in (51cm) $600-650
Molded white blouse, blue scarf, 22in (56cm) $550-600
Pretty hairdo, may have simple ribbon, comb or snood
    14-15in (36-38cm) $650-750
    21-23in (53-58cm) $1,200-1,300
Head only, braided coronet, 6in (15cm) $750
Decorated shoulder plate
    14in (36cm) $1,500-1,800
    22-24in (56-61cm) $2,200-2,400
    Head only, 4½in (11cm) $900
Fancy hairdo
    Painted eyes
        14-16in (36-41cm) $900-1,000
        20-22in (51-56cm) $1,300-1,500
    Glass eyes
        11-12in (24-31cm) $1,000-1,200
        21-23in (53-58cm) $1,900-2,100
Detachable cluster of curls,
    17-19in (43-48cm) $4,500-5,000
Alice hairdo
    11-14in (24 36cm) $450-500
    21in (53cm) $650-750
"Augusta Victoria" (blonde hair, molded blouse),
    18in (46cm) $1,200-1,300
"Countess Dagmar," 22in (56cm) $1,150-1,250
"Dolly Madison," glass eyes, swivel neck
    20in (51cm) $800-900
    Decorated plate, 17in (43cm) $1,250-1,350
"Empress Eugenie," pink lustre hat and snood,
    13-15in (33-38cm) $1,100-1,200
    21-23in (53-58cm) $2,000-2,400

19in (48cm) parian child
with glass eyes.
Howard & Jan Foulke.

10in (25cm) parian lady
with glass eyes.
Connie & Jay Lowe.

"Irish Queen," Limbach 8552,
16in (41cm) $600-700
"Miss Liberty," gold crown,
24in (61cm) $1,200-1,500
Child, short blonde hair,
15-16in (38-41cm) $600-700
Child, glass eyes, molded blonde curls,
14-16in (36-41cm) $950-1,250
Boy, molded hat and shoulder plate,
glass eyes, 18in (46cm) $3,000
Man, molded collar and tie,
16-17in (41-43cm) $650-750
All-parian, pink lustre boots, fine
quality, 5½in (14cm) $250-275

3½in (9cm) parian shoulder head.
Howard & Jan Foulke.

Philadelphia Baby

History J.B. Sheppard & Co., Philadelphia, PA, U.S.A. Ca. 1900. All-cloth.
Comment The maker of these dolls sold by the Philadelphia Sheppard store remains a mystery. Some paint wear is acceptable, but no repaint.
Description All stockinet with oil-painted features and hair, well-modeled facial features and ears, painted lower limbs with bare feet. Appropriate vintage clothing.
Mark None.

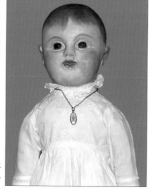

21in (53cm) *Philadelphia Baby.*
Nancy A. Smith.

Philadelphia Baby
18-22in (46-56cm) $4,200-4,500
Fair, showing wear $1,600-1,800
Rare style face at auction $9,350

Rabery & Delphieu

History Rabery & Delphieu of Paris, France. 1856(founded)-1899, then with S.F.B.J.
Comment The early models with the very strong, well-modeled faces are the most sought-after of the R.D. dolls.
Description Perfect bisque head, lovely wig, paperweight eyes. closed mouth; jointed composition body.

Mark R. 1. D.

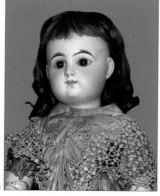

21in (53cm) *Bébé Rabery.*
Bart Boeckmans

R.D. Bébé
Ca. 1880s.

12-14in (31 -36cm)	$2,700-2,900*
18-19in (46-48cm)	$3,200-3,500*
24-25in (61-64cm)	$3,800-4,200*
28in (71cm)	$4,750-5,000*
Open mouth, 19-22in (48-56cm)	$1,650-1,850

Raggedy Ann and Andy

History Various makers. 1915 to present.
Comment Raggedy Ann, created by Johnny B. Gruelle, is the most well-known and well-loved doll ever made. She has been in continuous production for nearly 100 years. Older dolls may have some wear and fading, but newer dolls must be excellent with no wear and fading to bring book prices.

Early Raggedy Ann or Andy
Volland Co. 1918-1934. All-cloth with movable arms and legs; brown yarn hair, button eyes, painted features; legs of striped fabric for hose and black for shoes; original clothes; all in good condition.

Mark PATENTED SEPT. 7, 1915.

Early face Ann	$2,200
Single eyelash	$3,000-3,500
Early face Andy	$1,650
Printed face Ann	$1,200-1,500
Printed face Andy	$1,000-1,250
Wear, stains, not original clothes	$800-900
Characters	$2,500
Beloved Belindy	$2,500-3,000

Mollye's Raggedy Ann or Andy
1935-1938. Manufactured by Mollye's Doll Outfitters. Red hair and printed features; original clothes; all in good condition, bright color.

Mark Raggedy Ann and Raggedy Andy Dolls. Manufactured by Mollye's Doll Outfitters [printed writing in black on front torso].

18-22in (46-56cm) each	$1,250-1,500
Babies, 14in (36cm) pair	$4,000-5,000

17in (43cm) Volland *Raggedy Ann* with early face.
Howard & Jan Foulke.

16in (41cm) early dot lash Volland *Raggedy Ann.*
Howard & Jan Foulke.

*Allow extra for modeling and decoration.

19in (48cm) Georgene *Raggedy Ann & Andy*
with black outline noses, all original.
Nancy A. Smith

Exposition Doll & Toy Co.
Late 1934 to mid 1935. Very distinctive look.
  18in (46cm) $5,500-6,500

Georgene Raggedy Ann or Andy
1938-1963. Manufactured by Georgene Novelties. Inc. Red hair, black button eyes; original clothes; all in good condition, light wear and fading acceptable.
Mark Various cloth labels sewn in side seam of body.
  Black Outline Nose, Ca. 1938-1944
    19-20in (48-51cm) $1,100-1,200
    32in (81cm) $2,300-2,500
  Asleep/Awake, Black Outline Nose, 13in (33cm) pair $1,800
  Asleep/Awake, plain nose, 12in (30cm) $800
  Face #2, long nose, ca. 1944-1946, 19in (48cm) $1,000
  Silsby Label. 1946. bright color
    15in (38cm) $450-550
    20in (51cm) pair $1,250
  Blue-striped legs, red-checked legs, vertical-striped legs,
    flowered feet, 19in (48cm) $550-650
  Small nose, curved sides, bright color, excellent condition
    15in (38cm) $225-275
      Boxed $400-450
    19-20in (48-51cm) $350-400
      Boxed $500
    23in (58cm) $450-550
  Small nose, worn, faded, all original
    15in (38cm) $150-175
    19in (48cm) $225
  Camel with Wrinkled Knees, at auction $2,638
  Beloved Belindy, 19in (48cm) $1,500

Handmade Raggedy Ann or Andy
1930-1940.
  15-19in (38-48cm) $150-200

Knickerbocker Toy Co. Raggedy Ann or Andy

1963-1982. Bright color, excellent condition.

Early, 1964. 15in (38cm) boxed
 with clouds $250-300
Various print dresses
 15in (38cm) $150-175
 19in (48cm) $200-250
Common print dress
 15in (38cm) $55-65
 19in (48cm) $75-85
  Boxed $110-125
 32-35in (81-86cm) pair ...$275-300
Beloved Belindy,
 15in (38cm) $650-750
Camel with Wrinkled Knees,
 15in (38cm) $200-250
Musical, 1966. 15in (38cm)
 boxed $200-225
Teach N Play ("Dress Me"), 1971.
 18in (46cm) $85-95
Embraceables, 1973.
 7in (18cm) pair $25-30
  Boxed $50-60

15in (38cm) Knickerbocker
Beloved Belindy, all original.
Howard & Jan Foulke.

Talking, 1973. 18in (46cm) boxed $200-225
Hand Puppets, 1973. 9½in (24cm) pair $15-20
Pajama Bag, 25in (64cm) $85-90
Marionette, 12in (31cm) boxed $40-50

15in (38cm) Georgene
Raggedy Andy, all original.
Howard & Jan Foulke.

Applause

1981-on.
Embroidered eyes
 9in (23cm) $8-10
 12in (3 1cm) $11-13
 17in (43cm) $14-16
 24in (61cm) pair $50-60
 36in (91cm) pair $75-85
Classic model, button eyes
 17-20in (43-51cm) $15-20
 25in (63cm) $25-30
Talking, 16in (41cm) boxed $25
Dance With Me, 45in (115cm) $25
Musical, 6½in (17cm) $30-35
1992 75th Anniversary Ann or Andy,
 19in (48cm) boxed $40-50
1993 Molly-E Baby Raggedy Ann,
 13in (33cm) $40-50
1994 Raggedy Ann or Andy
 13in (33cm) boxed $40-50
 Camel with Wrinkled Knees ..$55
1995 Raggedy Ann, U.S. Patent, 17in (43cm) $65-75
1997 Stamp Doll, 17in (43cm) boxed $35
1998 Stars & Stripes, 17in (43cm) boxed $60-65
1998 Rags, 18in (46cm) $60-65

Hasbro, Inc.

1983-on.
 12in (31cm), boxed pair $15-18
 18in (46cm), boxed pair $22-25

24in (61cm) $20
Baby, 9in (23cm) pair, boxed $20-22
80th Anniversary Ann,
   18in (46cm) boxed $15-20
1996 Anniversary pair,
   11in (28cm) boxed $20-25

Playskool
1989-on.
1992 Boxed pair, 14in (36cm) $22
1990 Christmas Ann & Andy pair,
   12in (31cm) pair $15
1989 Baby Ann or Andy, 10in (25cm) ...$7-8
1991 Dress Me Raggedy Ann,
   14in (35cm) boxed $15

Alexander
1993 Mop Top Wendy & Billy
   pair $25-35

15in (38cm) Georgene
1951 label *Raggedy Ann*,
all original.
Howard & Jan Foulke.

Recknagel

History Th. Recknagel, porcelain factory, Alexandrienthal, Thuringia, Germany. 1886-on.

Comment This factory specialized in making small character heads with a wide variety of expressions. A group of them makes a fun collection.

Description Perfect bisque head, painted or glass sleeping eyes, molded hair or mohair wig. Composition body may have molded shoes or socks. Some babies are on cloth bodies. Appropriate clothing.

Mark
R A
22-12/0

8in (20cm) R.A. 45 character.
Howard & Jan Foulke.

R.A. Child
Ca. 1890s-World War 1.
1907, 1909, 1914
   8-9in (20-23cm)
      five-piece body $125-150
   16-18in (41-46cm) $225-250
   24in (61cm) $300-350

R.A. Character Baby
1909-World War 1.
#121, 126, 127, 1924 infants,
   8-9in (20-23cm) long $175-185
#23 character babies,
   7-8in (18-20cm) $200-225
#22, 28 and 44 bonnet babies
   8-9in (20-23cm) $400-450
   11-12in (28-31cm) $600-650

Character Children
6-8in (15-20cm) composition body $225-250
   18in (46cm) smiling face, at auction $1,700
#31 Max and #32 Moritz, molded hair, painted features,
   8in (20cm) $650-700
#45, 46 and 50 googlies, 7in (18cm) $325-375
$43, 44 googlies with molded hats, 7in (18cm) $500-550
#57, laughing, 9½in (24cm) $600

Grace Corry Rockwell

14in (36cm) *Pretty Peggy*
with bisque head.
Howard & Jan Foulke.

History Heads designed by Grace Corry Rockwell, 1920s.
Comment The bisque Rockwell dolls are very rare and very desirable. Heads were made in Germany by Alt, Beck & Gottschalck. Molded hair model is #1391.

Grace Corry Rockwell Child

1926-1928. **Pretty Peggy**, George Borgfeldt & Co. Perfect bisque head with molded hair or wig; sleep eyes, closed mouth; cloth body with composition limbs; appropriate vintage clothes; all in excellent condition.

Mark
Copr. By
Grace C. Rockwell
Germany
1391/30

14in (36cm) $3,500-4,000
18in (46cm) $5,500-6,000

Grace Corry Child

1927. **Little Brother** and **Little Sister**, Averill Mfg. Co. Smiling composition face, molded hair, sometimes covered with a wig, painted eyes, closed mouth; cloth body with composition limbs; appropriate or original clothes, some with Madame Hendren labels; all in very good condition.

Head Mark	Body Mark
©	**Genuine**
By	**Madame Hendren**
Grace Corry	**Doll**

14in (36cm) $325-425

Rollinson Doll

History Utley Doll Co., Holyoke, MA, U.S.A. 1916-on. Designed by Gertrude F. Rollinson.
Comment Rollinson dolls are similar to the Chase dolls, but much more rare. The wigged dolls are seldom found. Dolls may have some wear and aging, but no repaint or restoration.
Description All cloth with stockinet head, lower arms and legs; oil-painted hair (a few with wigs) and features; sateen body, jointed elbows and knees. Appropriate vintage clothing.

Marked Rollinson Doll

Child with painted hair, 18-22in (46-51cm) $800-1,200
Child with wig
    16in (41cm) $800-1,200
    26in (66cm) $1,500-2,000

14in (36cm) *Little Sister* with composition head. *Howard & Jan Foulke.*

Rollinson with pierced nose. *Nancy A. Smith.*

S.F.B.J.

History Société Française de Fabrication de Bébés & Jouets, Paris, France. 1899-on.

Comment Many of the French doll makers joined together in an attempt to cut down costs and produce dolls more economically to better compete with the cheaper German products. This company is the "swan song" of the French doll trade. Although many of the dolls are charming, the quality varies, so choose carefully.

Description Perfect bisque socket head, human hair wig, some characters with molded hair, glass sleeping eyes, open or open/closed mouth. Jointed composition child, baby or toddler body. Appropriate clothing.

Marks
```
SF.B.J.
  301
PARIS
 -5-

  7
DEPOSE
S.F.B.J.
  8
```

Child Doll

1899-on.

Jumeau-type, paperweight eyes (no mold numher), 1899-1910

18-20in (46-51cm)	$1,000-1,100
25in (64cm)	$1,250-1,350
30in (76cm)	$1,650-1,750

#301 (some stamped "Tête Jumeau" on labeled Jumeau body)

8in (20cm)	$650
10in (25cm)	$750-850
12-14in (31-36cm)	$550-650
18-21in (46-53cm)	$500-600
28-30in (71-76cm)	$700-800
15in (38cm) original box and trousseau	$2,000
22in (56cm) lady body	$850

#60, end of World War 1 on

7½in (19cm) with Jumeau tag	$425-450
12-14in (31-36cm)	$425-475
19-21in (48-53cm)	$450-500
28in (71cm)	$650-700
Walking, kissing and flirting, 22in (56cm)	$1,600-1,800

Papier-mâché head #60, fully-jointed body
17in (43cm) $225-250
22in (56cm) $325-350
Bleuette #60 or 301, 10½-11in (27-29cm) ....See page 56.

Character Dolls

1910-on. Molded, sometimes flocked hair on mold numbers 266, 227 and 235, sleep eyes; composition body.

Mark
.21.
S.F.B.J.
236
PARIS
.L.

#226, 17-19in (43-48cm) $1,700-1,900
#227, 17in (43cm) $1,750-1,850
#229, 16in (41cm) $2,000-2,200
#230, (sometimes Jumeau)
    12-14in (30-36cm) $850-950
    20-23in (51-58cm) $1,400-1,600
#233
    16in (41cm) $2,500-2,750
    20in (51cm) $3,200-3,500
#234, 15in (38cm) baby $2,500-3,000

14in (35cm) 233
character boy.
*Mary Barnes Kelley
Collection.*

    #235, 16in (41cm) child $1,250-1,400
    #236
    Baby
        12-13in (31-33cm) $500-600
        15-17in (38-43cm) $700-800
        20-22in (51-56cm) $950-1,150
        25in (64cm) $1,300-1,500
    Toddler
        15-16in (38-41cm) $1,000
        24in (61cm) $1,500
    #237, 18-19in (46-48cm) $2,600-3,200
    #238, child, 17-18in (43-46cm) $2,200-2,500
    Lady, 18-19in (46-48cm) $3,000
    #239, 13in (33cm) Poulbot,
        all original pair $12,500
    #242, nursing baby,
        13-14in (33-35cm) ....$3,250°
    #245 Googly ....See page 91.
    #246, 16½in (42cm) ....$3,100°

35in (89cm) SFBJ 16 *bébé.*
Howard & Jan Foulke.

18in (46cm) SFBJ *bébé,*
Jumeau mold.
Howard & Jan Foulke.

°Few price samples available.

#247

  Toddler

   12-14in (31-36cm) $1,500-1,700

   20in (51cm) $2,000-2,250

   Baby, 7in (18cm) in original presentation basket, ...$2,200

#248, 10-12in (25-30cm $6,500-7,500

#250, 19-20in (48-51cm) $3,250-3,500

#251, toddler

   8in (20cm) $1,400-1,600

   14-15in (36-38cm) $1,100-1,300

   21-23in (53-58cm) $1,700-1,900

#252

  Baby

   7-8in (18-20cm) $1,600-2,000

   12in (31cm) $3,200

  Toddler

   13in (33cm) $4,800-5,500

   20in (51cm) $6,500-7,500

   23in (58cm) $11,000

Boxed set, 12in (30cm) baby with three

   character heads ....$7,500-8,500°

15in (38cm) 236 character baby.
Howard & Jan Foulke.

20in (52cm) 251 character toddler.
Private Collection.

Bruno Schmidt

History Bruno Schmidt, doll factory, Waltershausen, Thuringia, Germany. Heads by Bähr & Pröschild, Ohrdruf, Thuringia, Germany. 1898-on.

Comment "Wendy" mold 2033/537 is the most desirable of this company's character dolls.

Description Perfect bisque socket head, good wig or molded and painted hair, glass sleeping eyes. Jointed composition child, baby or toddler body. Appropriate clothing.

Mark

Made in Germany

Marked B.S.W. Child Doll

Ca. 1898-on.

  18-20in (46-51cm) $300-325*

  24-26in (61-66cm) $375-425*

°Few price samples available.   *Allow $50 extra for flirty eyes.

Marked B.S.W. Character Dolls

#2048, 2094, 2096, (so-called"Tommy Tucker"), molded hair, open mouth
- 13-14in (33-36cm) $650-750
- 19-21in (48-53cm) $850-950
- 25-26in (64-66cm) $1,200-1,300

#2042 (molded hair, painted eyes),
- 16in (41cm) toddler $1,650

#2048, (closed mouth) toddler,
- 16-18in (41-46cm) $2,200-2,500

#2972, 19in (48cm) toddler $2,800-3,000

#2033 (so-called Wendy) (537)
- 12-13in (30-33cm) $12,500
- 15-17in (38-43cm) $23,500
- 20in (51cm) $30,000

BSW 2033/537 so-called *Wendy*.
James D. Julia, Inc.

24in (61cm) BSW child.
Howard & Jan Foulke.

#2023 (539), 24in (61cm) $3,000

#2025 (529), closed mouth, wigged,
- 22in (56cm) ....$6,500-7,000°

#2097, #692, character baby, open mouth
- 13-14in (33-36cm) $275-325
- 18in (46cm) $400-425
- 24in (61cm) $550-600

#2097, toddler, 17in (43cm) $650-750

#425, all-bisque baby, 5½-6in (13-15cm) $300-350

#426, all-bisque toddler, 9½in (24cm) ....$1,200°

Franz Schmidt

History Franz Schmidt & Co., doll factory, Georgenthal near Waltershausen, Thuringia, Germany. Heads by Simon & Halbig, Gräfenhain, Thuringia, Germany. 1890-on.

Comment This company produced high quality dolls. A few of their character dolls are very rare and very desirable.

Description Perfect bisque socket head, good wig or molded and painted hair, glass sleeping eyes. Jointed composition child, baby or toddler body. Appropriate clothing.

°Few price samples available.

Marked S & C Child Doll
Ca. 1890-on. Some #293 or 269.

6-7in (15-18cm) five-piece body	....$300-350
11in (28cm)	.....................$550-600
16-18in (41-46cm)	...............$275-300
22-24in (56-61cm)	...............$350-400
29-30in (74-76cm)	...............$500-600

Flapper

20in (51cm), flirty eyes	.......$450-500
42in (107cm)	..................$2,500

Shoulder head, kid body,
  24-26in (61-66cm) $300-350

Mark

F.S.Cᵉ.
1272/35Ƶ
Deponiert

Marked F.S. & Co. Character Baby
Ca. 1910.

#1271, 1272, 1295, 1296, 1297, 1310

Baby

12-14in (31-36cm)	..........$300-325
20-21in (51-53cm)	..........$400-500
26-27in (66-69cm)	...........$750-850

Toddler

7-8in (18-20cm)	.............$850-950
13-15in (33-38cm)	..........$550-650
19-21in (48-53cm)	..........$750-850

#1266, bald head, painted eyes, closed mouth,
  16-17in (41-43cm) ....$3,590-3,900°
#1267, open/closed mouth, painted eyes
  12in (31cm) baby ....$1,450°
  23in (58cm) $2,100
#1270, 11in (28cm) baby ....$1,200°
#1286, molded hair with blue ribbon, glass
  eyes, open smiling mouth,
  16in (41cm) toddler ....$4,000°

Mark   *S & C*

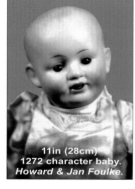

11in (28cm)
1272 character baby.
Howard & Jan Foulke.

9in (23cm) 1295
character toddler.
Howard & Jan Foulke.

Schmitt

History Schmitt & Fils, Paris, France, 1854-1891.
Comment Schmitt made premium dolls, very desirable to collectors. Be sure that the body is stamped on the flat bottom edge with the Schmitt trademark.
Description Perfect bisque socket head with skin or mohair wig, large paperweight eyes, closed mouth, pierced ears. Marked Schmitt composition body with flat bottom edge. Vintage clothing.

Marked Schmitt Bébé
Ca. 1879.

Long face

16-18in (41-46cm)	..................$13,000-15,000
23-25in (58-64cm)	..................$18,000-20,000
30in (76cm)	...........................$25,000

Mark

°Few price samples available.

Short face (parted lips)
11in (28cm) $13,000
14-16in (36-41cm) . .$12,000-14,000
Oval/round face
13-14in (33-36cm) . .$10,000-12,000
17-18in (43-46cm) . .$13,000-$15,000
Cup and saucer neck,
17in (43cm) . . . .$17,000°
Open/closed mouth, two rows of teeth,
24in (61cm) . . . .$25,000°
Wax-over papier-mâché head,
16in (41cm) . . . .$2,750-3,000°

18in (46cm) *Bébé Schmit,* with short face.
Kay Jensen Antique Dolls.

Schoenau & Hoffmeister

History Schoenau & Hoffmeister, Porzellanfabrik Burggrub, Burggrub, Bavaria, Germany, porcelain factory, 1901-on. Arthur Schoenau also owned a doll factory. 1884-on.

Comment Though dolls by this factory are plentiful except for several of the characters, collectors seem to like their faces as they have a hint of distinction to them.

Description Perfect bisque head, good wig, open mouth, glass sleeping eyes. Composition child, baby or toddler body. Appropriate clothing.

Trademarks Hanna, Burggrub Baby, Bébé Carmencita, Viola, Künstlerkopf, Das Lachende Baby.

Mark

S P.B H
Hanna
2/0

Child Doll

#1906, 1909, 5700, 5800
14-16in (36-41cm) $225-250
21-23in (53-58cm) $300-350
28-30in (71-76cm) $400-450
33in (84cm) $650
39in (99cm) $1,500-1,800
#4000, 4600, 5000, 5500
15-17in (38-43cm) $325-350
22in (56cm) $375-425
26in (66cm) $600-700
35in (89cm) $950
Künstlerkopf
24-26in (61-66cm) . . . .$850-950°
Shoulder head, kid body
18-20in (46-51cm) . . .$175-225
13-15in (33-38cm) hinged
pink kid body $350-375

25in (63cm) *Bébé Carmencita,* all original.
Kay Jensen Antique Dolls.

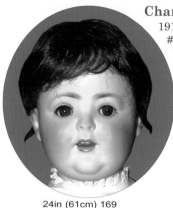

Character Baby
1910-on.
#169, 769 "Burggrub Baby" or "Porzellanfabrik Burggrub"

13-15in (33-38cm) $225-250
18-20in (46-51cm) $300-350
23-24in (58-61cm) $400-450
28in (71cm) $650-750
Painted bisque, 14in (36cm) toddler,
factory original $325-350

Hanna
Baby
14-16in (36-41cm) $350-400
20-22in (51-56cm) $600-650
Toddler,
14-16in (36-41cm) $550-650
Brown . . . . .See page 54.
OX, 17in (43cm) toddler $1,800-2,000

24in (61cm) 169 character baby.
Kay Jensen Antique Dolls.

Das Lachende Baby, 1930. 23-24in (58-61cm) . . . .$2,200-2,500°

Princess Elizabeth
1929.
Chubby five-piece body
17in (43cm) $1,700-1,900
20-23in (51-58cm) $2,000-2,200

Pouty Baby
Ca. 1925. Closed pouty mouth; cloth body with composition arms and legs.
11-12in (28-31cm) $400-500

Schoenhut

History Albert Schoenhut & Co., Philadelphia, PA. Early dolls designed by Adolph Graziana and Mr. Leslie; later dolls by Harry E. Schoenhut. 1872-on.

Comment These American dolls were truly innovative and unique. No other company copied them. Collectors prefer the character faces, particularly those with carved hair, over the baby or dolly faces. Prices are for dolls with original paint, though they may have some wear. Dolls with deep wear and repainting sell for 50% or less.

Description All wood with socket head and metal spring-jointed body, holes in feet to accommodate a stand and allow the doll to be posed; original mohair wig or carved hair, painted eyes, usually intaglio style. Appropriate vintage clothing.

> **Mark** Oval paper label or incised
> **SCHOENHUT DOLL**
> **PAT. JAN. 17, '11. U.S.A.**
> **& FOREIGN COUNTRIES**

Salesman's Cutaway Sample $800-1,000
Original Stand $75-100
Original Shoes, **very good condition** $100-200

°Few price samples available.

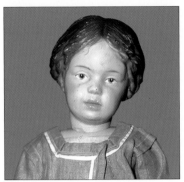

16in (41cm) carved hair
character girl #102.
Kay Jensen Antique Dolls.

16in (41cm) #300 character girl.
Howard & Jan Foulke.

Character

1911-1930. Original mohair wig, brown or blue intaglio eyes, open/closed mouth with painted teeth or closed mouth.

14-21in (36-53cm)
> Excellent condition $1,900-2,200*
> Very good, some wear $1,200-1,400*
> Fading, wear, crazing $700-900
> Pouty face, based on K & R 114, exceptional and all-original
> condition, at auction $4,125

Character with carved hair

Ca. 1911-1930. Carved hair, comb marks, possibly a ribbon or bow, intaglio eyes, mouth usually closed.

14-21in (36-53cm)
> Excellent condition $2,800-3,100
> Very good, some wear $1,600-1,800
> Fading, wear, crazing $900-1,100
> Early style, 16in (41cm) $5,000-8,000
> Tootsie Wootsie, 15in (38cm) at auction $4,900
> Snickelfritz, 15in (38cm) with moderate wear ....$3,800°
> Carved Bonnet $6,500-7,500
> Mannekin Man, 20in (51cm) ....$2,500°

Baby Face

Ca. 1913-1930. Fully-jointed toddler or bent-limb baby body, painted hair or mohair wig, painted eyes, open or closed mouth..

Baby
> 12in (31cm) $300-350
> 15-16in (38-41cm) $500-550

Toddler
> 11in (28cm) $500-600
> 14-16in (36-41cm) $450-550

Mark
Round paper label
H.E. Schoenhut
©
1913

Mama Doll

1924-1927.
> **Wood head and hands, cloth body, 14-17in (36-43cm)** $650-750

°Few price samples available.
*Allow extra for rare faces and exceptional original condition.

Walker

Ca. 1919-1930. "Baby face," curved arms, straight legs with "walker" joint at hip, no holes in bottom of feet.

13-17in (33-43cm) $500-600*

Miss Dolly

Ca. 1915-1930. Original mohair wig, decal eyes; open/closed mouth with painted teeth.

14-21in (36-53cm)
    Excellent condition $700-750
    Good condition, some wear $500-600
    Mint, all original $1,000-1,250
    Sleep Eyes, good condition, some wear $500-600

All-Composition

Ca. 1924. Molded blonde curly hair, painted eyes, tiny closed mouth; original or appropriate clothing; in good condition.

13in (33cm) ....$500-600°

19in (48cm) #308 character girl.
Howard & Jan Foulke.

13in (33cm) bald head baby.
Howard & Jan Foulke.

Schuetzmeister & Quendt

History Schuetzmeister & Quendt, porcelain factory, Boilstadt, Thuringia, Germany. Made heads for various doll factories, including Welsch, K & R, and Wolf & Co. 1889 on.

Description Child or character baby with perfect bisque socket head, jointed composition body, open mouth, sleeping eyes, appropriate clothes and wig.

Child Doll

Ca. 1889 on.
    #101, Jeanette
        15-17in (38-43cm) $200-250
        22-23in (56-58cm) $275-325

Mark
S & Q
101
Dep.

°Few price samples available.
*Allow $100 additional for original shoes with "wedge" sole.

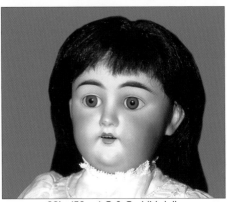

22in (56cm) S & Q child doll.
Kay Jensen Antique Dolls.

Character Baby

Ca. 1910.

#201, 301

			Mark
13-15in (33-38cm)	....	$225-275	301
23-24in (58-61cm)	....	$400-500	S & Q [entwined]
			Germany

Simon & Halbig

History Simon & Halbig, porcelain factory, Gräfenhain, Thuringia, Germany, purchased by Kämmer & Reinhardt in 1920. 1869-on.

Comment S & H made high quality bisque heads and parts over a long period of time, from molded-hair shoulder heads of the 1870s to the infants of the 1920s. Their early dolls, all-bisques and characters are outstanding. See *Simon & Halbig Dolls* for photographs of mold numbers not shown here.

Description Perfect bisque head, glass sleeping eyes, mohair wig, pierced ears. Kid body or composition child, toddler, lady or baby body. Appropriate vintage clothing.

Marks

SIMON & HALBIG
Germany
1329   S & H

Shoulder head with molded hair

1870s. Painted or glass eyes, closed mouth, molded hair; cloth body, bisque lower arms.

			Mark On front
13-15in (33-38cm)	....	$1,100-1,200	shoulder plate
17-18in (43-46cm)	....	$1,400-1,600	S 9 H
23in (58cm)	....	$2,200-2,400	

Swivel neck

9in (23cm)	....	$1,250
12in (31cm)	....	$1,500

Fashion Doll (*Poupée*)

Ca. 1870s. Mohair wig or molded blonde hair, glass eyes; closed mouth; gusseted kid lady body.

15-17in (38-43cm) $3,000-3500

Twill over wood body

9-10in (23-25cm) $3,500-4,000

15-16in (38-41cm) $5,500-6,500

Child doll with closed mouth

Ca. 1879. Ball-jointed wood and composition body; good wig, glass set or sleep eyes, closed mouth, pierced ears.

#719

12in (31cm) $3,250-3,750

20-23in (51 -58cm) $5,500-6,500

#749, 20-22in (51-56cm) ....$3,800°

#905, 908, 14-17in (36-43cm) ....$3,500-4,500°

#929, 17-18in (43-46cm) ....$3,800-4,200°

#939

14-15in (36-38cm) $2,200-2,500

26in (66cm) $3,000-3,500

#949

10in (25cm) $2,5000

14-15in (36-38cm) $1,900-2,200

22-23in (56-58cm) $2,900-3,100

27-28in (69-71cm) $3,800-4,200

#979, 15-16in (38-41cm) ....$3,000°

Kid or Cloth Body

#720, 740, 940, 950

9-10in (23-25cm) $550-650

16-18in (41-46cm) $900-1,100

22in (56cm) $1,300-1,500

#949, 18-21in(46-53cm $1,200-1,400

#920, 18-20in (46-51cm) $1.800-2,000

#919, 16in (41cm) at auction $3,630

9½in (24cm) early shoulder head with closed mouth.
Howard & Jan Foulke.

24½in (62cm) 939 open-mouth child.
Richard Saxman Antiques.

°Few price samples available.

All-Bisque Child

1880-on. All-bisque child with swivel neck, pegged shoulders and hips; appropriate mohair wig, glass eyes, open or closed mouth; molded stockings and shoes.

#886, over-the-knee black or blue stockings, low orange or blue stockings; open mouth

4½in (11cm)	.........$750-800*
5½-6in (14-15cm)	...$1,100-1,300*
7-7½in (18-19cm)	...$1,600-2,000*
8½-9in (22-23cm)	...$2,500-3,200*

#886, five-strap boots,

7½in (19cm)	.......$2,500-2,750

#890, over-the knee black stockings; open mouth

3¾in (9cm)	...........$550-600
5-5½in (13-14cm)	......$800-900
7-7½in (18 19cm)	....$1,100-1,250

Closed mouth, round face

6-6½in(15-16cm)	.... $2,000-2,350
Jointed knees	..........$5,500°

Closed mouth, five-strap bootines,

7½-8in (19-21cm)	...$3,600-4,400°

9in (23cm) 886
all-bisque child.
Howard & Jan Foulke.

Child doll with open mouth and composition body

Ca. 1889 to 1930s. Ball-jointed composition body (may be French).

#719, 739, 749, 759, 769, 939, 979

17-19in (43-45cm)	...........................$1,900-2,100
22-23in (56-58cm)	...........................$2,500-2,800

#719, 23in (58cm) Edison, operating $5,200

#905, 908, 14-16in (36-41cm) $1,700-1,800

#929, 23in (58cm) ....$3,800°

#949

17-18in (43-46cm)	...........................$1,400-1,500
28-30in (71-76cm)	...........................$2,300-2,500
35-38in (88-96cm)	...........................$4,000-4,500

#969, 14-15in (36-38cm) $6,250-6,750

#979, 25in (64cm) $2,500-3,000

#1009

15-16in (38-41cm)	...........................$600-650
19-21in (48-53cm)	...........................$750-800
24-25in (61-64cm)	...........................$900-1,000

#1039

10in (25cm) flirty eyes	...........................$1,250
16-18in (41-46cm)	...........................$600-650**
23-25in (58-64cm)	...........................$800-900**

#1039, key-wind walking body, (R. & D.),

16-22in (41-56cm)	...........................$1,700-1,800

#1039, walking, kissing, 20-22in (51-56cm) $800-900

#1078, 1079

7-9in (18-23cm) five-piece body	...................$375-425
8in (20cm) fully jointed	...........................$650-750

°Few price samples available.
*Allow extra for strap bootines and square cut teeth.
**Allow $100 extra for flirty eyes.

10-12in (25-31cm)	$700-800
14-15in (36 38cm)	$500-550
17-19in (43-48cm)	$450-550
22-24in (56-61cm)	$500-550
28-30in (71-76cm)	$650-750
36in (91cm)	$1,800-2,200
42in (107cm)	$3,800
45in (115cm) more adult face, at auction	$8,800

#1109

14in (36cm)	$850°
18in (46cm)	$1,100°

#1139, 13in (33cm) ....$1,200°

#1248, 1249, Santa

12in (31cm)	$850
15in (38cm)	$750-800
20in (51cm)	$750-850
26-28m (66-71cm)	$1,200-1,500
31-32in (79-81cm)	$1,500-1,800
38in (96cm)	$2,800-3,200

#540, 550, 570, 22-24in (56-61cm) $450-550

#176, (A. Hülss), Flapper, 18in (46cm) $550-600

Baby Blanche, 23in (58cm) $500-550

22in (56cm) SH/GB child.
Howard & Jan Foulke.

12in (30cm) 1079 child.
Howard & Jan Foulke.

21in (53cm) 540 child.
Howard & Jan Foulke.

°Few price samples available.

Child doll with open mouth and kid body

Ca. 1889 to 1930s. Perfect bisque swivel head on shoulder plate or shoulder head with stationary neck, sleep eyes.

#1010, #1040, 1080, 1260
17-18in (43-46cm) $350-400
21-23in (53-58cm) $450-500
#1009, 1039, 17-19in (43-48cm) $500-550
#1250, 1260, with pink kid body and composition arms
14-16in (36-41cm) $400-450
22-24in (56-61cm) $550-650
29in (74cm) $750-800
#949, 19-21in (48-53cm) $1,200-1,400

So-called "Little Women" type

Ca. 1900. Mold number **1160.** Shoulder head with fancy mohair wig, glass set eyes, closed mouth; cloth body with bisque limbs, molded boots.
5½-7in (14-18cm) $300-325
10-11in (25-28cm) $375-425
14in (36cm) $550-600

5½in (13cm) 1160 so-called Little Women doll.
Howard & Jan Foulke.

Character Child

Ca. 1909. Wig or molded hair, painted or glass eyes, open or closed mouth, character face; jointed composition body.
#120, 21in (53cm) $3,100
#150
15in (38cm) $8,000-10,000
20in (51cm) $30,000-32,000
#151
14-15in (36-38cm) $4,700-5,200
24in (61cm) $13,000

22in (56cm) 120 character child.
Rosalie Whyle.

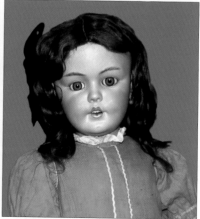

31in (79cm) 1279 character child.
Richard Saxman Antiques.

#153
    12in (31cm) $15,000-18,000
    17in (43cm) $28,000-32,000
#174, 21in (53cm) . . . .$1,750-1,950°
#600
    12in (31cm) $900
    18-19in (46-48cm) toddler $1,400-1,500
#607, 18in (46cm) at auction $1,925
#616, 28in (71cm) flirty eyes $1,320
#1279
    14-15in (36-38cm) $1,200
    19-21in (48-53cm) $1,600-2,000
    26-27in (66-69cm) $2,200-2,700
    34in (86cm) $3,500-4,000
#1299, 18in (46cm) $800-900
#1339
    18in (46cm) . . . .$1,000-1,100°
    28-32 (71-81cm) . . . .$1,900-2,100°
#1388
    19in (48cm) $17,000-20,000
    25-28in (64-71cm) $32,000-40,000
#1398, 23in (58cm) . . . .$20,000°
IV, #1448
    13-14in (33-36cm) $18,000
    17-18in (43-46cm) . . . .$24,000°

Character Baby

Ca. 1909 to 1930s. Molded hair or wig, sleep or painted eyes, open or open/closed mouth; composition bent-limb baby or toddler body.

    #156 (A. Hülss)
      Baby
        15-17in (38-43cm) $375-425
        23in (58cm) $550-600
      Toddler, five-piece body
        9in (23cm) $750
        15in (38cm) $500-600
        29in (73cm) $1,800-2,000

15in (38cm) 1489 *Erica* character baby. *Howard & Jan Foulke.*

25in (63cm) 1488 character toddler. *Richard Saxman Antiques.*

°Few price samples available.

#1294
Baby
17-19in (43-48cm) $400-500
23-25 in (58-64cm) $600-700
28in (71cm) with clockwork eyes ....$2,500°
Toddler, 20in (51 cm) $800-900

#1428
Baby
10-11in (25-28cm) . .$1,000-1,200
13-14in (33-36cm) . .$1,200-1,500
21in (53cm) $2,200-2,400
Toddler
11in (28cm) $1,400-1,600
15-18in (38-46cm) .$1,800-2,200

#1488
Baby
20-23in (51-58cm) .$3,400-3,600
15in (38cm) $3,500-4,000
Toddler
16in (41cm) $3,850
22in (56cm) $5,500

#1489 Erika, baby,
21-22in (53-56cm) ...$3,700-4,200°

#1498
Baby, 16in (41cm) ...$2,000-2,500°
Toddler, 22in (56cm) .....$4,000°

#172, baby,
14-15in (36-38cm) ...$2,500-3,000°

152 lady.
James D. Julia, Inc.

Lady Doll

Ca. 1910. Lady body, molded bust, slim arms and legs.

#1159 **(may have an H. Handwerck body)**
12in (31cm) $1,100-1,200
17-18in (43-46cm) $1,800
21-23in (53-58cm) $2,200-2,400
27in (69cm) $2,800-3,000

#1468, 1469
13-15in (33-38cm) naked ...$2,500
Original clothes $3,500

#1303 lady,
20in (51cm) ......$18,000-20,000°

#152, lady
20in (51cm) $23,000-30,000
24in (61cm) at auction $99,000

#1308 man,
13in (33cm) ....$8,000-10,000°

#1307, 21in (53cm) $12,500

#1303 Indian,
15in (38cm) $3,200-3,500

#1305, 18in (46cm) $12,500

1469 flapper.
James D. Julia, Inc.

°Few price samples available.

Snow Babies and Santas, German

Snow Babies

All-bisque immobile figures with snowsuits and caps of pebbly-textured bisque; painted features; various positions. Incised or stamped "Germany."

Standing
- 1½in (4cm) $35-40
- 2½in (6cm) $100-125
- 4¾in (12cm) $250-300

Sitting
- 1½in (4cm) $35-40
- 3-3½in (8-9cm) $150-200

Jointed arms and legs
- 3½in (9cm) $250-300
- 5¼in (13cm) $350-400

Shoulder head on cloth body
- 4½in (11cm) $185-210
- 10in (25cm) $300-350

Fine early quality with high hood, 2in (5cm) $185-210
With musical instrument, 2in (5cm) $50-60
Twins, 2in (5cm) $85-110
Snowman, 2½in (6cm) $40-50
Snow bear, 1½in (4cm) $35-40

Action Figures

Huskies pulling sled with snow baby, 3in (9cm) $200
Reindeer pulling sled with snow baby, 2in (5cm) $175-200
Snow baby riding reindeer, 2½in (6cm) $225
Snow baby riding snow bear, 3in (9cm) $250
Tumbling snow baby, 2½in (6cm) $100-125

Snow baby on sled
- 1½in (4cm) $50-65
- 3in (8cm) $150-175

Three snow babies on sled $150-175

3in (8cm) snow baby.
Howard & Jan Foulke.

Snow babies sliding on cellar door, 2½in (6cm) $175-225
Snow dog and snowman on sled, 2in (5cm) $200-225
Snow Children
   Seated girl, 1½in (4cm) $75-95
   Boy or girl on sled $125-150
   Sliding on cellar door, 2½in (6cm) $225
   Carollers, 2¼ in (5cm) $110

"No Snows"
Boy and girl on sled, 2in (5cm) $90-125
Elf with teddy, 2in (5cm) $110-135
Skiing boy, 2½in (6cm) $65-75

Santas (with or without snow)
3in (9cm) standing $75-95
2in (5cm) with toy sack $100-125
Riding snow bear, 2½in (6cm) $250
In sleigh with reindeer, 3½in (9cm) $200-225
On igloo with snow baby, 2½in (6cm) $150-175
With bell tower, 2½in (6cm) $225-250
On camel, 2½in (6cm) $300-325

Steiff

History Fräulein Margarete Steiff, Wurtemberg, Germany. 1894-on.
Comment Though better known for their wonderful stuffed animals, Steiff produced quite a few cloth dolls in their early years, always in the superb quality the company is known for. In modern years, Steiff has again made dolls, some copies of early models, but they are not collected as avidly as the original early dolls. To bring the prices listed, dolls must be clean with good color and no moth holes. Faded and dirty dolls in poor condition will bring only one-third of these values.
Description Felt, plush or velvet fabric, jointed; molded head with seam down middle of face, button eyes, inset mohair wigs. Original clothing, many with large feet or shoes to enable them to stand. Adult dolls represented characters from everyday life and the comics.
Mark Steiff metal button in ear.

Steiff Doll
Children (Character Dolls)
   11-12in (28-31cm) $1,000-1,250
   16-17in (41-43cm) $1,500-1,650
   Black child, 19in (48cm) $2,200
Adults (fewer women than men) ....$1,800 up
Gnome, 12in (31cm) $700-900

Schlopsnies
1922-1925. Celluloid head, cloth body, all original with label.
16in (41cm) $500-750

U.S. Zone Germany
12in (31cm) child with glass eyes $600-650

11½in (29cm) Steiff character boy, all original.
Howard & Jan Foulke.

1987/1988 Vinyl Children
20in (51cm) boxed $150-200

1986/1987 Limited Edition felt dolls
Tennis Lady $125
Gentleman $125
Peasant Lady $125
Gusto Clown $140-150

Jules Steiner

History Jules Nicolas Steiner and successors, Paris, France. 1855-1908.
Comment Steiner dolls are high quality products and very popular with collectors. The company was very innovative, always introducing improved designs. Heads must be on Steiner bodies, most of which are marked except for some of the very early models.
Description Perfect bisque socket head, sleeping eyes with wire lever or bulgy paperweight eyes, pierced ears, closed mouth, mohair or skin wig, cardboard pate. Stamped Steiner jointed composition body with straight wrists on early models. Vintage clothing.

Round Face
Ca. 1870s. Very pale bisque, round face, jointed composition body.
Mark None, but sometimes body has a label.
Two rows of pointed teeth, 16-19in (41-48cm) $6,000-7,000
Closed mouth, 18-22in (46-56cm) $10,000-12,000
Täufling-type body, bisque shoulders, hips and lower arms and legs
18-21in (46-53cm) $6,500
Swivel neck $7,500

Gigoteur
Kicking, crying bébé, mechanical key-wind body with composition arms and lower legs.
18-20in (46-51cm) $2,200-2,500

Waltzing Couple
All original $9,350

Series *Bébé Steiner*
1880s. Sleep eyes with wire mechanism or bulgy paperweight eyes with tinting on upper eyelids, round face, pierced ears with tinted tips; jointed composition body with straight wrists and stubby fingers (sometimes with bisque hands). Sizes 4/0 (8in) to 8 (38in). Series "C" more easily found than "A."

Marks	(incised) **Sie A 0**
	(red script) **J. Steiner Bte SgDg J.Bourgoin, Sr.**
	(incised) **Sie C 4**
	(red stamp) **J. STEINER B.S.G.D.G.**

8-10in (20-25cm) $11,000-13,000
15-16in (38-41cm) $5,500-6,500
21-24in (53-61cm) $8,000-10,000
28in (71cm) $11,000-12,000
32in (81cm) $12,500-14,500
36in (91cm) $16,000-18,000
Open mouth, 16-18in (41-46cm) $6,200-6,800
Series E, 16in (41cm) repaired head $3,520
Series F, 9in (23cm) at auction $14,850
Series G, closed mouth
  12in (31cm) $17,600
  18in (46cm) $19,800

Figure *Bébé Steiner*
Ca. 1887-on. Figure "A" more easily found than "C."
Figure A, closed mouth, 1887-1891
  12in (31cm) $4,500-5,000
  18in (46cm) $5,500
  22-24in (56-61cm) $6,000-6,500
  33in (83cm) $11,000
Figure A, closed mouth, 1892-on
  8-10in (20-25cm) five-piece body $3,300-4,000
  8-10in (20-25cm) fully-jointed $5,000-5,500
  15-16in (38-41cm) $4,250-4,500
  22-24in (56-61cm) $5,000-5,500
  28-30in (71-76cm) $6,000-6,500
  35in (89cm) $7,500-8,500
Figure A, open mouth
  17in (43cm) $2,500
  22in (56cm) $2,900
  23-25in (58-64cm) *Le Petit Pas* with
    key wind body $4,500-5,000
Figure B, open mouth with two rows of teeth
  16in (41cm) $5,000-5,500
  23-25in (58-64cm) $6,000-6,500
Figure C, closed mouth, 22in (56cm) $6,500-7,500
Figure F, 30in (76cm) at auction $23,000

23in (58cm) early *Bébé Steiner*
with two rows of teeth.
Richard Saxman Antiques.

29in (73cm) Series C
Bébé Steiner.
Gloria & Mike Duddlesten.

23in (58cm) Figure C
Bébé Steiner.
Kay Jensen Antique Dolls.

24in (61cm) Figure A
Bébé Steiner.
Gloria & Mike Duddlesten.

Swaine & Co.

History Swaine & Co., porcelain factory, Huttensteinach, Sonneberg, Thuringia, Germany. Ca. 1910-on for doll heads.

Comment Swain produced an interesting group of character doll heads with appealing faces.

Description Perfect bisque socket character head, mohair wig if needed. Composition baby body, a few toddler and child models. Appropriate vintage clothing.

Mark Round green stamp
GESCHUTZT
S & Co.
GERMANY

Swaine Character Babies

Ca. 1910-on.

Incised **Lori**, molded hair, glass eyes, open/closed mouth,
    21-24in (53-61cm) $1,600-1,800
#232 (open-mouth Lori)
    8½in (21cm) $350-400
    12-14in (31-36cm) $700-800
    20-22in (51-56cm) $1,000-1,200
DIP (wig, glass eyes, closed mouth)
    8½-9½in (21-24cm) $450-500
    11in (28cm) $650-700
    14-16in (36-41cm) $900-1,000
    14in (36cm) toddler $1,250
DV (molded hair, glass eyes, open/ closed mouth)
    13in (33cm) $900-950
    16in (41cm) $1,000-1,100
DI (molded hair, intaglio eyes, open/ closed mouth),
    12-13in (31-33cm) $550-600
B.P., B.O. (smiling character, child body),
    16-18in (41-46cm) $4,000-5,000
F.P., 8-9in (20-23cm) $500-600
A.P. (wig, painted eyes, closed mouth, child body),
    15in (38cm) $4,000-5,000

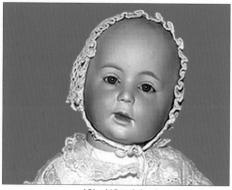

19in (48cm) *Lori.*
Gloria & Mike Duddlesten.

Thuillier

History A. Thuillier, Paris, France. Some heads by F. Gaultier. 1875-1893.
Comment Truly the most coveted of French dolls, the A.T. has a dreamy quality to the face. Very few of these dolls exist, so prices remain firm for the desirable early models.
Description Perfect bisque head, paperweight eyes, eye shadow, pierced ears, closed mouth, mohair wig. Body of wood, kid or composition. Appropriate vintage clothing.

Mark A. 10. T.

Approximate Size Chart
1 = 9in (23cm)
3 = 12in (31cm)
7 = 15½in (39cm)
9 = 18in (46cm)
12 = 22-23in (56-58cm)
15 = 36-37in (91-93cm)

A.T. Child

Early face, soft features and decoration
12-13in (31-33cm) $35,000-40,000
16-18in (41-46cm) $45,000-50,000
24in (61cm) $60,000-63,000
Later face, heavier features and decoration
16-18in (41-46cm) $30,000-33,000
26in (66cm) $40,000-45,000
Open mouth, two rows of teeth
20-22in (51-56cm) $15,000-19,000
36in (91cm) $25,000
A.T. Shoes, size 10 .... $1,000

18in (46cm) A 9 T *bébé*.
Kay Jensen Antique Dolls.

Unis

History Société Française de Fabrication de Bébés et Jouets. (S.F.B.J.) of Paris and Montreuil-sous-Bois, France. 1922 on.

Comment These very late French dolls do not have the quality of the early ones, but charming models can be found if you choose carefully.

Description Perfect bisque head, human hair wig, sleeping eyes, open mouth. Composition and wood jointed body. Appropriate clothing.

Mark

Unis Child Doll

#301 or 60 (fully-jointed body)
- 8-10in (20-25cm) $500-600
- 15-17in (38-43cm) $450-500
- 23-25in (58-64cm) $550-600
- 28in (71cm) $650-750

Five-piece body
- 5in (13cm) painted eyes $160-185
- 6½in (17cm) glass eyes . $250-275
- 11-13in (28-33cm) $275-325

Black or brown bisque,
- 11-13in (28-33cm) $325-375

Bleuette, 11in (28cm) . . See page 56.
Princess . . . . See page 107.

#251 character toddler,
- 14-15in (36-38cm) . . $1,100-1,300

Composition head #301 or 60
- 11-13in (28-33cm) $150-175
- 16-18in (41-46cm) $250-300

Composition head #251 or 247
- toddler, 22in (56cm) . . . $500-600

7½in (19cm) Unis *bébé* with fully jointed body, all original.
Howard & Jan Foulke.

Izannah Walker

History Izannah Walker, Central Falls, RI, U.S.A.1873, but probably made as early as 1840s.

Comment This very desirable American doll has the look of a primitive painting. Hair styles with painted long side curls or short brush strokes are preferred. The patent marked dolls are later and less desirable. Paint may have some wear and cracking, but must be original with no repaint.

Description Stockinet pressed head with facial features and hair painted with oils, applied ears; muslin body with painted limbs. Vintage clothing.

Mark Later dolls are marked in script **Patented Nov. 4th 1873.**

Izannah Walker Doll

Pre-patent dolls

17-19in (43-48cm) $18,000-22,000
Fair condition $8,500-9,500
Very worn $3,000-4,000
1873 patent dolls, molded ears, 18in (46cm) $4,000-6,000

24in (61cm) English poured wax baby.
Private Collection.

Izannah Walker doll with painted side curls.
Nancy A. Smith.

Wax Dolls

Poured

English Poured Wax Doll

Various firms in London, such as Peck, Montanari, Pierotti, Meech, Marsh, Morrell, Cremer and Edwards. 1850s-early 1900s. Head, lower arms and legs of wax; cloth body; sometimes stamped with maker or store; set-in hair, glass eyes; lovely elaborate original clothes or very well dressed; all in very good condition.

Baby

17-19in (43-48cm) $1,250-1,650
23-24in (58-61cm) $1,900-2,200

Child

6in (15cm) all original $650-750
21-24in (53-61cm) $1,800-2,200

Baby or child, lackluster ordinary face,

20-22in (51-56cm) $750-850

Man or Lady, 19-22in (48-56cm) $1,650-2,250

French Fashion Lady
1917, Lafitte-Desirat, all original, 14in (36cm) $1,000-1,200
Ca. 1930. Wax head, couturier outfit, 12in (33cm) $400-600

Mechanical Baby
In satin-lined wood box, musical, 12in (31cm) $350-450

Reinforced
Reinforced Poured Wax Doll
Various firms in Germany. 1860-1890. Poured wax shoulder head lined on the inside with plaster composition, glass eyes (may sleep), closed mouth, open crown, pate, curly mohair or human hair wig nailed on (may be partially inset into the wax around the face); muslin body with wax-over-composition lower limbs (feet may have molded boots); appropriate clothes; all in good condition, but showing some nicks and scrapes.

Child or baby
    11in (28cm) $250-275
    14-16in (36-41cm) $400-450
    19-21in (48-53cm) $600-650
Lady, 19-22in (48-56cm) $800-1,000
Socket head on ball-jointed composition body (Kestner-type)
    13in (33cm) $700-800
    19in (48cm) $1,200-1,300

Wax-Over-Composition
English Slit-head Wax
Ca. 1830-1860. Round face, human hair wig, glass eyes (may open and close by a wire), faintly smiling; all in fair condition, showing wear.
    18-22in (46-56cm) $900-1,100
    28-30in (71 76cm) $1,500-1,800
    16in (41cm), all original and excellent, at auction $1,650

Molded Hair Doll
Ca. 1860-on. German wax-over-composition shoulder head; nice old clothes; all in good condition, good quality.
    14-16in (36-41cm) $325-375
    22-25in (56-64cm) $550-650
Alice hairdo, 16in (41cm) early model, squeaker torso $750-800

Wax-over Doll with Wig
Ca. 1860s to 1900. German. Original clothing or suitably dressed; entire doll in nice condition.
Standard quality
    11-12in (28-31cm) $250-275
    16-18in (41-46cm) $325-375
    22-24in (56-61cm) $450-500
Superior quality (heavily waxed)
    16-18in (41-46cm) $475-525
    25-26in (64-66cm) $700-800
"Blinking" eye doll, eyes open and close with bellows in torso,
    16in (41cm) all original $1,000

16in (41cm) Bartenstein double-faced wax baby. *Howard & Jan Foulke.*

13in (33cm) reinforced wax lady, all original. *Howard & Jan Foulke.*

Molded Bonnet Wax-over Doll

Ca. 1860-1880. German. Nice old clothes; all in good condition.

16-17in (41 -43cm), common model $450-500
13½in (35cm) baby with bonnet and real curls $750-800
20-24in (51-61cm) lady with real curls and
  unusual hat $2,000-3,000

Double-Faced Doll

1880-on. Fritz Bartenstein. One face crying, one laughing, rotating on a vertical axis by pulling a string, one face hidden by a hood. Body stamped "Bartenstein."

15-16in (38-41cm) $850

Norah Wellings

History Victoria Toy Works, Wellington, Shropshire, England, for Norah Wellings. 1926-ca. 1960. Designed by Norah Wellings.
Comment These charming dolls are very well made. Sailors from various ships, Canadian Mounties, Black Islanders and Scotch dolls are the easiest to find. Prices are for clean dolls with good color and no moth holes. Faded and soiled dolls will bring only one-third of listed prices.
Description All-fabric with molded face (sometimes stockinet-covered papier-mâché) and painted features; stitch-jointed shoulders and hips.

| Mark On tag on foot **Made in England by Norah Wellings** |

Wellings Dolls

Characters (floppy limbs)
8-10in (20-25cm) $75-95
13-14in (33-36cm) $125-135
Glass eyes, 16-19in (41-48cm) black $200-250
Children
12-13in (31-33cm) $300-325
16-18in (41-46cm) $450-500
23in (58cm) $700-800
11½in (29cm) chubby toddler $225-275
Glass eyes, 16-18in (41-46cm) $550-650
Boudoir Doll, 22-24in (56-61cm) $300-400
Old Couple, 26in (66cm), pair $1,500
Harry the Hawk, 10in (25cm) $200
Nightdress Case $250-300
Baby
11in (28cm) $300-350
23in (58cm), glass eyes $2,500-3,000
Rabbit, 9in (23cm) $300-350
R.A.F. Aviator, 29in (73cm) at auction $1,760

14in (36cm) Wellings child, all original.
Diane Costa.

8in (20cm) Tiny Tots character girl, all original.
Howard & Jan Foulke.

Martha Wellington

History Martha L. Wellington, Brookline. MA, U.S.A. 1883-on.
Comment These cloth babies are very rarely found. Paint may have some wear and cracking, but must be original with no repaint.
Description All stockinette with needle-sculpted features, oil painted head and lower limbs; distinctive buttocks with rounded cheeks. Appropriate vintage clothing.

Mark
Cloth label on back

Wellington Baby
22-24in (56-61cm)
Excellent condition ....$12,000-14,000°
Fair to good condition ....$6,500-7,500°

Wislizenus

History Adolf Wislizenus, doll factory, Waltershausen, Thuringia, Germany. Heads made by Bähr & Proschild, Simon & Halbig, and Ernst Heubach. 1851-on.
Trademarks Old Glory, Special, Queen Quality
Description Child or character doll with perfect bisque socket head, jointed composition body, open mouth, sleeping eyes, appropriate clothes and wig.

Child Doll. Ca. 1890 on.
17-19in (43-48cm) $225-250
23-25in (58-64cm) $275-325
Character Doll. Ca. 1910.
#110, 115 toddler body, molded hair,
15-16in (38-41cm) $750-850

Marks
Special
4
Germany

110·6
Germany.

24½in (62cm) child.
Howard & Jan Foulke.

22in (56cm) Wellington baby.
Howard & Jan Foulke.

15in (38cm) 110 toddler.
Howard & Jan Foulke.

°Few price samples available.

Wood
American (Springfield Dolls)

History Co-Operative Manufacturing Co. and D.M. Smith Co., Springfield, VT. 1873-1885.

Comment The Springfield dolls are uniquely American and very interesting to collectors. Most dolls have some paint flaking on the face. Prices given are for fair condition. There is some confusion and conflicting information about the Jointed Doll Co., which may have been simply a distributor of the Mason & Taylor dolls rather than a manufacturer.

Joel Ellis Wooden Doll

Co-operative Manufacturing Co., Springfield. Vermont. 1873-1874. All-wood with mortise and tenon joints; carved hair painted black (a few blondes), painted eyes; metal hands and feet painted black (a few bright blue). Marked only with a black paper band around waist with 1873 patent date.

    12in (31cm) $1,200-1,500
    15in (38cm) $1,800-2,000

Martin, Sanders & Johnson Wooden Doll

1879-1885. Jointed Doll Co., Springfield, Vermont. Composition head over wood core (usually blonde); fully-jointed wood body; metal hands and feet painted blue. Marked only with a black paper band around waist with "Improved Jointed Doll" and patent dates ('79, '80 and '82).

    12in (31cm) $850-950

Mason & Taylor Wooden Doll

1879-1885. D.M. Smith Co., Springfield. Vermont. Composition head over wood core (usually blonde); fully-jointed wood body; early dolls had wooden spoon-type hands; blue metal feet.

    12in (31cm) $850-950
    Very good, at auction $1,575

12in (31cm) Mason & Taylor Improved Jointed Doll. *Connie & Jay Lowe.*

English

History Various English craftsman. Ca. 1690-on.

Comment The English woods mark the beginning of dolls as we know them. Only royalty and the very wealthy could afford these toys, and few survive today. Painted wood is rather unstable, so priced condition is only fair, with some crazing and flaking not only acceptable, but expected.

William & Mary Period

Ca. 1690. Carved wooden face, painted eyes, tiny lines comprising eyebrows and eyelashes, rouged cheeks, flax or hair wig; wood body, cloth arms, carved wood hands (fork shaped), wood-jointed legs; appropriate clothes; all in fair condition.

    12-17in (31-43cm) $46,000

Queen Anne Period

Ca. early 1700s. Carved wooden face, dark glass eyes (sometimes painted), dotted eyebrows and eyelashes; jointed wood body, cloth upper arms; appropriate clothes; all in fair condition.

18in (46cm) $18,500
24in (61cm) $25,000

Georgian Period

Mid to late 1700s. Round wooden head with gesso covering, inset glass eyes (later sometimes blue), dotted eyelashes and eyebrows, flax or hair wig; jointed wood body with pointed torso; appropriate clothes; all in fair condition.

12-13in (31-33cm) $2,500-3,200
16-18in (41-46cm) $4,500-5,000
24in (61cm) $6,000

Early 19th Century

Wooden head, gessoed, painted eyes, flax or hair wig; pointed torso; old clothes (dress usually longer than legs); all in fair condition.

13in (33cm) $1,300-1,600
16-21in (41-53cm) $2,000-3,000

13in (33cm) Queen Anne-type doll, wood body with cloth upper arms and forked wood hands. *Private Collection.*

German (Peg-Woodens)

History Craftsmen of the Grödner Tal, Austria, and Sonneberg, Germany, such as Insam & Prinoth (1820-1830), Gorden Tirol and Nürnberg verlagers of peg-wooden dolls and wood doll heads. Late 18th to 20th century.

Comment Early examples of peg-woods are very desirable and very charming. Early dolls will be in fair condition, with some crazing and flaking acceptable.

Mark None.

Early to Mid 19th Century

Delicately carved head, varnished, carved and painted hair and features, with a yellow tuck comb in hair, painted spit curls, sometimes earrings; mortise and tenon peg joints; old clothes.

4in (10cm) $450-550
6-7in (15-18cm) $650-750
12-13in (31-33cm) $1,350-1,450
17-18in (43-46cm) $2,000-2,500
Fortune tellers, 17-20in (43-51cm) $2,500-3,000
Shell dolls, 8½in (28cm) ....$1,500-1,600 pair
Peddler with lovely old wares, 8in (20cm) $2,400
32in (81cm) "Miss Betsy" swivel waist, ribbon banded-coronet.
Ca. 1800 with provenance $34,100

Late 19th Century

Wooden head with painted hair, carving not so elaborate as previously, sometimes earrings, spit curls; appropriate clothing.

1in (2½cm) $100-125
4in (10cm) $135-165
7-8in (18-20cm) $200-250
12in (31cm) $350-375
16in (41cm) $450-500
21in (53cm) $1,000-1,100
Turned red torso, 10in (25cm) $125-150
Wood shoulder head, carved bun hairdo, cloth body, wood limbs
9in (23cm) all original $350-400
17in (43cm) $500-550
24in (6 1cm) $800-900

Early 20th Century

Turned wood head, carved nose, painted hair; peg-jointed; painted white lower legs, painted black shoes.

11-12in (28-31cm) $40-50

18in (46cm) peg-wood doll with tuck comb, very fine quality.
Richard Saxman Antiques.

German (20th Century)

History Various companies, such as Rudolf Schneider and Schilling, Sonneberg, Thuringia, Germany. 1901-1914.

Comment These interesting dolls were made in Germany for the French trade and given a French name. Body may have some paint flaking, but face should be perfect.

Description All wood with a fully jointed body and socket head; human hair wig, inset glass eyes, open mouth with teeth. Appropriate vintage clothing.

Mark Usually none; sometimes Schilling "winged angel" trademark.

24in (61cm) *Tout en Bois.*
Howard & Jan Foulke.

"*Bébé Tout en Bois*" (Doll All of Wood)
Child
13in (33cm) $425-475
17-19in (43-48cm) $650-750
22-24in (56-61cm) $950
18in (46cm) mint, all original $1,100
Baby, 16½in (42cm) $400-500

Swiss

History Various craftsmen, Brienz, Switzerland. 20th century. Peter Huggler, Brienz, Switzerland. Carved by Adolf Thomann and later his son Paul Thomann. 1930s-on.
Comment These charming hand-carved dolls were produced by this family until very recently. They are favorites with collectors of wood dolls.
Description All-wood with hand-carved features and hair, somtimes carved hats on the males; jointed wood body with carved shoes. A few have carved shoulder heads on cloth bodies with wood lower limbs. Original Swiss clothing, excellent condition.
Mark Usually a paper label on wrist or clothes.

Swiss Linden Wood Doll
9-10in (23-25cm) $275-375
12in (31cm) $450-550
15in (38cm) $750-850
17-18in (43-46cm) $1.000-1,200
12in (31cm) boy
   with carved hat $600-650
13in (33cm) wood
   and cloth babies $450

12in (30cm) Swiss wood pair, all original.
Howard & Jan Foulke.

WPA

History Various artists under the sponsorship of the United States Federal Works Progress Administration (later Works Projects Administration). 1935-1943.
Comment These charming dolls are prized by collectors of cloth dolls as well as collectors of W.P.A. items.
Description All-cloth with molded and painted stockinet head, painted features, yarn hair. Cloth body with uniquely jointed legs and black stamp. Original clothing also sometimes with stamp. Excellent condition.

Mark "#7040, Milwaukee, Wis."

WPA Milwaukee Cloth Doll

22in (56cm) $900-1,200
Black $1,200-1,500

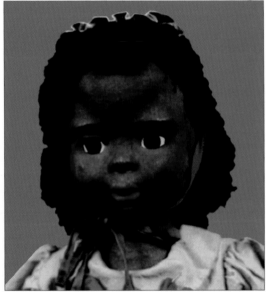

23in (58cm) WPA Milwaukee black cloth child.
Howard & Jan Foulke.

Modern & Collectible Dolls

Dolls in this section are listed alphabetically by manufacturer, material or trade name. Dolls are arranged chronologically by date within a main entry, earliest dolls first.

Unless otherwise stated, values given in this section are retail prices for clean dolls in excellent overall condition with good complexion color and original paint, perfect hair in original set and original unfaded clothing, including underwear, shoes and socks.

Use this chart as a guide for assessing how condition can affect the price of a collectible doll:

For composition dolls:	
Light crazing	none
Cloudy eyes	less 10-15%
Short eye cracks	less 10%
Deep crazing	less 50%
Hair combed	less 20-25%
Replaced clothes	less 35-40%
Dirty, faded, naked, chipped	less 70-90%
Professionally refinished	less 50%
Perfect, unplayed with	add 50-100%
Original box	add 35%
For hard plastic and vinyl dolls:	
Faded cheeks	less 25-30%
Mint in box	add 25-100%

12in (31cm) Alexander *Beau & Belle Brummel,* 1935.
Howard & Jan Foulke.

Madame Alexander Alexander Doll Company

History Alexander Doll Co., Inc., New York, NY, U.S.A. 1923-on, but as early as 1912, the Alexander sisters were designing doll clothes and dressing dolls commercially.

Comment Alexander has been a premiere doll maker for nearly 100 years. Many of today's collectors started with Alexander dolls purchased for special occasions when they were still children. Currently, their hard plastic dolls from the 1950s, particularly *Cissy*, when they are in excellent, unplayed with condition are very hot. Since most Alexanders from 1970-1990 weren't played with, but simply kept in their original boxes, there is a glut of these dolls on the market, and values are often only half or less of the original purchase price.

Mark Dolls themselves marked in various ways, usually "ALEXANDER." Clothing has a white cloth label with blue lettering sewn into a seam which says "MADAME ALEXANDER" and usually the name of the specific doll. Cloth and other early dolls are unmarked and identifiable only by the clothing label.

Cloth Dolls

Original tagged clothing, complete doll clean and in excellent condition with minimal fading.

Characters

Ca. 1933-1940. All-cloth with molded felt or flocked mask face, painted eyes to the side. **Little Women, David Copperfield, Oliver Twist, Edith, Babbie, Alice** and others.

16in (41cm) only
Fair $200-300
Good $350-400
Excellent $700-750
Alice, 19-20in (48-51cm) good $400-500
Kamkins-type, (hard felt face), very good condition,
20in (51cm) . . . .$650-750°
Tiny Twinkle, 15in (38cm) excellent . . . .$800°
Bunny Belle, 12in (31cm) excellent $750
Cloth Baby, Ca. 1936
13in (33cm) very good $300-350
171n (43cm) very good $475-525
24in (61cm) $625
Cloth Dionne Quintuplet, Ca. 1935
17in (43cm) very good . . . . $850-900°
24in (61cm) very good . . . .$1,200-1,300°

19in (48cm) cloth *Alice in Wonderland.*
Howard & Jan Foulke.

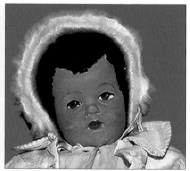

24in (61cm) cloth *Dionne Quintuplet.*
Kathy & Terri's Dolls.

°Few price samples available.

Susie Q. & Bobby Q., Ca. 1938. 12in (31cm) excellent with
   purse or book strap, each $700-750
Little Shaver, 1942. Yarn hair, very good condition
   7in (18cm) $375-425
   10-12in (25-31cm) $400-450
   20in (51cm) $600
Little Shaver, 2000-2001. 10in (25cm) $30-35
Poodles, 16in (41cm) $250-275
Funny, 1963-1977. 18in (46cm) $35-40
Muffin, 1963-1977. 14in (36cm) $50-55

7½in (19cm) composition *Dionne Quintuplet* toddlers, all original.
Howard & Jan Foulke.

Composition Dolls

All in original tagged clothing; excellent condition, with bright color and perfect hair; faint crazing acceptable.

Dionne Quintuplets
1935. (Each Quint has her own color for clothing: Yvonne – pink; Annette –
yellow; Cecile – green; Emelie – lavender; Marie – blue):
   7-8in (18-20cm) $225-275
   Matched set $1,800-2,200
     In bed $2,500
     On Ferris Wheel $3,000
     On Carousel $4,000
     In basket with extra outfits $3,000-3,350
     With five pieces of wooden Dionne furniture $3,750
   10-11in (25-28cm) baby $250-300
   11-12in (28-31cm) toddler ..$375-400
   14in (36cm) toddler $450-500
   16in (41cm) baby with
     cloth body $375-400
   20in (51cm) toddler $600-700
   23-24in (58-61cm) baby with
     cloth body $550-600
   Pins, each $60-90
   Tagged dress and bonnet $100-150

Early Models
   Small Dolls, 7-9in (18-23cm)
     Foreign Countries $150-200
     Storybook Characters ...$200-250
     Special Outfits $300-400
     Birthday Dolls $275-325
     Bride and Bridesmaids,
       each $200-225
     Little Women, each $225-275

7in (18cm) *Bo-Peep*, all original.
Rosemary Kanizer.

11in (28cm) one of *Three Little Pigs*, all original. *Howard & Jan Foulke.*

13in (33cm) *Princess Elizabeth* with closed mouth, all original. *Howard & Jan Foulke.*

Carmen \$300
Scarlett \$300
Black Topsy, at auction \$920
Little Colonel, 1935
8½in (22cm) \$450-550
13in (33cm) \$600-650
Nurse (for *Dionne Quintuplets*), Ca. 1935.
13in (33cm) \$900-1,100
Betty, Ca. 1935. Painted or sleep eyes, wigged or molded hair
13in (33cm) \$375-425
19in (48cm) \$550-600
Baby Jane, 1935.
16in (41cm) \$750-850
Topsy Turvy, Ca. 1936.
7½in (19cm) \$150-200
Dr. DaFoe, 1936.
14in (36cm) \$1,600-1,700
Three Little Pigs, 1938-1939.
12-13in (31-33cm) each ...\$650-750

Marionettes
1935. Character faces.
10-12in (25-30cm)
Tony Sarg \$250-275
Disney \$350-400

Babies
1936-on. Little Genius, Baby McGuffey, Pinky, Precious, Butch, Bitsey; composition head, hands and legs, cloth bodies.
11-12in (28-31cm) \$200-225
16-18in (41-46cm) \$250-300
24in (61cm) \$375-425

Princess Elizabeth Face
Original tagged clothes; all in excellent condition.
Princess Elizabeth, 1937
13in (33cm) closed mouth .\$400-450
16-18in (41-46cm) \$450-500
22-24in (56-61cm) \$650-700
27in (69cm) \$800-900
8in (20cm) *Dionne* head \$500
McGuffey Ana, 1937. Braids.
9in (23cm) painted eyes ...\$350-400
11in (28cm) closed mouth .\$400-450
15-16in (38-41cm) \$450-500
20-22in (51-56cm) \$650-700
Snow White, 1937. Closed mouth, black hair
13in (33cm) \$400-450
16-18in (41-46cm) \$550-600
Flora McFlimsey, 1938
13in (33cm) \$450-500
15in (38cm) \$550-600
22in (56cm) \$750-850
Kate Greenaway, 1938
13in (33cm) \$500-550
16-18in (41-46cm) \$650-700

15in (38cm) *Flora McFlimsey*, all original. *Howard & Jan Foulke.*

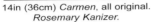
14in (36cm) *Carmen*, all original. Rosemary Kanizer.

11in (28cm) *Scarlett O'Hara*, all original. Howard & Jan Foulke.

Wendy Ann Face

Original tagged clothes; all in excellent condition.

Wendy Ann, 1936
- 9in (23cm) painted eyes $300-350
- 14in (36cm) swivel waist $400-450
- 21in (53cm) $600-700
- 14in (36cm) molded hair $400-450

Scarlett O'Hara, 1937. Black hair, blue or green eyes
- 11in (28cm) $750-800
- 14in (36cm) $800-850
- 18in (46cm) $1,000-1,250
- 21in (53cm) $1,500

Madelaine du Bain, 1938. 14in (36cm) $600-650
Miss America, 1939. 14in (36cm) $800

Bride & Bridesmaids, 1940
- 14in (36cm) $350-400
- 18in (46cm) $450-500
- 21in (53cm) $600-650

Portraits, 1940s. 21in (53cm) $2,500-4,500
Sleeping Beauty, Cinderella, Ca. 1941. 14in (36cm) $450-500

Carmen (Miranda), 1942. Black hair
- 9in (23cm) painted eyes $300-350
- 14-15in (36-38cm) $450-500
- 21in (53cm) $1,000-1,100

Fairy Princess or Fairy Queen, 1942
- 14in (36cm) $450-500
- 18in (46cm) $600-650

18in (46cm) *Bride*, all original. Rosemary Kanizer.

21in (53cm) *Bridesmaid*, all original. Kathy & Terri's Dolls.

Armed Forces Dolls, 1942. WAAC, WAVE, WAAF, AVWS, Soldier, Marine,
    14in (36cm) **$800-900**
Mommy & Me, late 1940s. 14in (36cm)
    and 7in (18cm) Set . .**$1,200-1,400**
Astrological Series, 11in (28cm)
    Aries, at auction **$3,740**

Special Faces

Original tagged clothes; all in excellent condition.
Jane Withers, 1937
    13in (33cm)
        closed mouth **$900-1,000**
    15-16in (38-41cm) . .**$1,000-1,150**
    21in (53cm) **$1,500-1,650**
Sonja Henie, 1939
    14in (36cm) swivel waist $650-750
    18in (46cm) **$800-850**
    21in (53cm) **$1,000-1,200**
Jeannie Walker, 1941
    13-14in (33-36cm) **$700-750**
    18in (46cm) **$1,000**
    13in (33cm) boxed **$1,500-2,000**
    14in (36cm) non-walker **$475-525**
Special Girl, 1942. Cloth body, 22in (56cm) **$400-450**

14in (36cm) *AVWS*, all original.
Howard & Jan Foulke.

16in (41cm) *Jane Withers*, all original. *Howard & Jan Foulke.*

18in (46cm) *Sonja Henie Bride*,
all original.
Howard & Jan Foulke.

14in (36cm) *Jeannie Walker*,
all original.
Howard & Jan Foulke.

Margaret Face

Original tagged clothes; all in excellent condition with perfect hair and pretty coloring.

Margaret O'Brien, 1946. With dark braided wig.
- 14in (36cm) $750-850
- 18in (46cm) $1,150-1,350

Karen Ballerina, 1946. With blonde wig in coiled braids
- 14in (36cm) $700-800
- 18in (46cm) $1,000
- 21in (53cm) $1,250-1,500

Alice-in-Wonderland, 1947
- 14in (36cm) $375-425
- 18in (46cm) $500-550
- 21in (53cm) $700-800

Hard Plastic Dolls

1948-on. Original tagged clothes; excellent condition with bright color and perfect hair. Dolls in crisp and mint "like new" condition will bring higher prices.

18in (46cm) *Margaret O'Brien*, all original. *Howard & Jan Foulke.*

Margaret Face

1948-1956.

Alice-in-Wonderland, 1949-1952. 14in (36cm) $500-600

Babs, 1948-1949
- 14in (36cm) $1,200-1,400
- 18in (46cm) $1,500-2,000

Bride
- **1948**
  - 14in (36cm) $600
  - 20in (51cm) $1,000
- **1950. Pink gown.**
  - 14in (36cm) $700-800
  - 18in (46cm) $800-1,000

Cinderella, 1950.
- Ball gown: 14in (36cm) $650-750
- 18in (46cm) $900-1,000
- "Poor" dress, 14in (36cm) $650

Cynthia (black), 1952-1953.
- 14in (36cm) $800-900
- 18in (46cm) $1,000

Fairy Queen, 1947-1948.
- 14in (36cm) $600-650
- 18in (46cm) $800

Fashions of the Century, 1954.
- 18in (46cm) $2,000-3,000

Glamour Girls, 1953. 18in (46cm) $1,200-1,500

Godey Ladies, 1950. 14in (36cm) $2,000-2,500

Groom, 18in (46cm) $700-750

Margaret O'Brien, 1948
- 14in (36cm) $1,500-2,000
- 18in (46cm) $2,500-3,000

Margaret Rose, 1948-1953
- 14in (36cm) $650-750
- 18in (46cm) $800-850
- 18in (46cm) Beaux Arts Series, 1953 ....$1,650-1,850

18in (46cm) *Nina Ballerina*, all original.
Kathy & Terri's Dolls.

18in (46cm) *Wendy Bride*, all original.
Connie Blain.

Mary Martin, 1950. Sailor suit
 14in (36cm) $850-1,000
 18in (46cm) $1,200-1,500
McGuffey Ana, 1949
 14in (36cm) $1,100-1,200
 18in (46cm) $1,600-2,000
Nina Ballerina, 1949-1951. Blonde
 14in (36cm) $650-750
 18in (46cm) $1,000-1,100
 21in (53cm) $1,600
Peggy Bride, Ca. 1950. 20in (51cm) $1,200-1,500
Prince Charming, 1950
 14in (36cm) $650-750
 18in (46cm) $750-850
Prince Philip, Ca. 1950. 18in (46cm) $700-750
Queen Elizabeth II, 1953
 18in (46cm) with long velvet cape $1,600-1,800
 No cape $1,000-1,200
Snow White, 1952
 14in (36cm) $600-700
 18in (46cm) $800-900
Story Princess, 1954-1956
 14in (36cm) $650-700
 18in (46cm) $750-850
Wendy-Ann, 1947-1948
 14in (36cm) $750-800
 18in (46cm) $900-1,000
Wendy Bride, 1950
 14in (3 6cm) $700-750
 18in (46cm) $900-1,000
Wendy (from Peter Pan set), 1953.
 14in (36cm) mint, at auction $1,485
Winston Churchill, Ca. 1950. 18in (46cm) $700-750

Maggie Face
1948-1956.
Alice-in-Wonderland, 1949-1952
 14in (36cm) $500-600
 18in (46cm) $700-800

Annabelle, 1952
15in (38cm) $550-650
18in (46cm) $750-850
Arlene Dahl, 1950-1951. 20in (57cm) $3,500
Glamour Girls, 1953. 18in (46cm) $1,200-1,500
Godey Man, 1950. 14in (36cm) at auction $3,600
John Powers Models, 14in (3 6cm) $1,500-2,000
Kathy, 1951
14in (36cm) $800-850
18in (46cm) $900-1,000
Margot Ballerina, 1953
14in (36cm) $650-750
18in (46cm) $800-900
Maggie, 1948-1953
14in (36cm) $650-750
17in (43cm) $800-900
20in (5 1cm) $1,000-1,100
Me and My Shadow, 1954. 18in (46cm) $1,600-2,000
Peter Pan, 1953. 15in (38cm) $650-750
Polly Pigtails, 1949
14in (36cm) $600-700
17in (43cm) $800-900
Rosamund Bridesmaid, 1953
15in (38cm) $600-650
18in (46cm) $750-850

Little Women
1948-1956
Floss hair, 1948-1950
14-15in (36-38cm) each $475-525
Amy, loop curls $525-550
Dynel hair, each $375-425

Little Men (Nat, Stuffy, Tommy Bangs)
1952.
Each $950-1,250

Babies (Baby Genius, Bitsey, Butch)
1948-1951. Cloth body, hard plastic or vinyl limbs.
12in (31cm) $250-300
16-18in (41-46cm) $400-450

Winnie and Binnie
1953-1955
15in (38cm) $400-450
18in (46cm) $500-600
25in (64cm) $450
Skating outfit,
15in (38cm) $550-650
Sweet Violet, 18in (46cm)
fully-jointed body $1,000-1,250
Victoria (black, green-and-white
dress), 15in (38cm) $500-550
Flower Girl
15in (38cm) $550
18in (46cm) $850
Mary Ellen,
31 in (79cm) $500-600

14in (36cm) *Binner Walker*, all original.
Howard & Jan Foulke.

21in (53cm) *Cissy Queen*, all original.
Kathy & Terri's Dolls.

Cissy

1955-1959.

21in (53cm)

Street clothes $550-650
Basic underwear, shoes, stockings $450-550
Cocktail dresses $750-850
Ball gowns $1,200-1,500
Queen $1,000-1,200
Bride ....$1,200 up
#2245 Lissy, special hairdo and gown, at auction $2,585
#2250 Renoir, yellow gown, at auction $2,310
Tagged dresses $200-400
Tagged gowns $700-800

Alexander-Kins

1953-to present. All-hard plastic: original tagged clothes; all in excellent condition with perfect hair and rosy cheeks. A played-with doll having partial or faded costume will bring 25 percent of quoted prices.

Wendy, Wendy Ann or Wendy-Kin, 7½-8in (19-20cm)

1953. Straight-leg non-walker $450-650
1954-1955 Straight-leg walker $400-600
1956-1964 Bent-knee walker $350-550
1965-1972 Bent-knee non-walker $275-475
Wendy, basic (panties, shoes and socks), boxed $350-450
Quizkin, 1953. ....$450-550

Wendy in Special Outfits

Agatha, 1953. ....$1,000-1,200
American Girl, 1962-1963. ....$250
Amish Boy or Amish Girl, 1966-1969. ....$250
Aunt Pitty Pat, 1957...........................$1,600
Baby Clown, 1955. ....$700-800
Ballerinas, 1956-1964. ....$450-650
Billy or Bobby, 1955-1963 ....$300-400
Bride, 1955-1960. ....$350-450
Bride, pink, at auction $1,540
Bridesmaid (pink),1955 ....$900
Cherry Twin, 1957, each $1,000-1,200
Cousin Grace, 1957. ....$1,300
Cousin Marie, 1963. ....$900
Cowboy or Cowgirl, 1967-1970 ....$250-300

Davy Crockett Boy or Girl, 1955 ....$350-450
Easter Wendy, 1953. ....$500-600
Edith, 1958 ....$650-700
Groom, 1956-1963 ....$500-600
Guardian Angel, 1954 ....$700-800
Hiawatha, 1967-1969 ....$250
Little Madeline, 1953 ....$700-750
Little Southern Girl, 1953 ....$850-950
Little Victoria, 1954 ....$1,200-1,300
Maypole Dance, 1954. ....$550
McGuffey Ana, 1964-1965 ....$300-350
Miss USA, 1966-1968. ....$350-400
My Shadow, 1954 ....$1,500
Nurse, 1956-1965 ....$550-650
Parlour Maid, 1956 ....$800

8in (20cm) *Wendy*, all original. Rosemary Kanizer.

8in (20cm) *Wendy*, all original. Rosemary Kanizer.

Pocahontas, 1967-1969 ....$250
Prince Charles, 1957 ....$600-700
Princess Anne, 1957 ....$600-700
Priscilla or Colonial Girl, 1962-1970 ....$250-300
Scarlett, 1965-1972 ....$250-350
Southern Belle, 1963 ....$350-450
Wendy Sewing Basket, 1965-1966 ....$2,500
Wendy Dude Ranch, 1955 ....$550-600
Wendy in Easter Egg, 1965 ....$1,700
Wendy Ice Skater, 1956 ....$450
Wendy Loves to Waltz, 1955. ....$350-450
Wendy in Riding Habit, 1965. ....$450-550
Wendy Loves Being Loved, 1992. Boxed set $100-150
Wendy Being Just Like Mommy, 1993.
    With baby carriage $75-85
International Costumes
    Bent-knee walker $50-65
    1965-1972. Bent-knee non-walker $40-45
    Korea, Africa, Hawaii, Vietnam, Eskimo, Morocco,
        Ecuador, Bolivia $150-200

1973-1976. Straight-leg, rosy cheeks $30
1982-1987. Straight-leg, pinched lips $25
1988-on. Current face $25
Storybook, Ballerinas & Brides
Bent-knee non-walker $40-50
1973-1976. Straight-leg, rosy cheeks $35
1982-1987. Straight-leg, pinched lips $30
1988-on. Current face $30
Little Women, set of five
1955. Straight-leg walker $1,200-1,500
1956-1964. Bent-knee walker $700-800
Bent-knee non-walker $300-350
Straight legs $150-175
1994 FAO Schwarz movie outfits $225
1995 Jo Goes to N.Y. Trunk Set $135-165
Exclusive and Special Editions
A Bit of Country, 1997. MADC $75
Springtime, 1991. MADC $75
Round Up Day, 1992 Disney $95
Bobbie Sox, 1990. Disney $75-85
David & Diana, 1989. FAO Schwarz set $75-100
Mouseketeer, 1991. Disney $55-65
Easter Bunny, 1991. Child at Heart $100
Cowboy, 1987. MADC Convention $55-65
Orphan Annie, 1999. . . . .$60
Anne of Green Gables, 1994. Trunk set,
Neiman-Marcus $175-195
Wendy Shops FAO, 1993. FAO Schwarz $50

Little Genius
1956-1962.
Baby with short curly wig, 8in (20cm).
Basic or simple outfit $150-200
Fancy outfit $275
Christening outfit $350

Lissy Face
1956-1958.
Lissy, 12in (31cm) $400-500
Boxed with trousseau, 1957 . . . .$1,500
FAO Schwarz exclusive $950
Bridesmaid, 1956-1957. . . . .$600
Kelly, 1959. . . . .$400-500
Little Women
1957-1958. Jointed elbows and knees $275-300
1959-1967. One-piece limbs $200-250
Southern Belle, 1963 . . . .$1,000-$1,200
McGuffey Ana, 1963 . . . .$1,200-$1,400
Katie, 1962 . . . .$700-800
Scarlett, 1963 . . . .$1,000-$1,200
Tommy, 1962 . . . .$700-800
Cinderella, 1966 . . . .$650
Boxed set $900-1,000
Laurie, 1967 . . . .$350
Pamela, 1962-1963
Boxed with wigs $800-900
Suitcase gift set $1,200-1,400
Columbian Sailor, 1993. UFDC $60-70

16½in (42cm) *Elise*, all original. *Rosemary Kanizer.*

12in (31cm) *Katie & Tommy. Diane Costa.*

12in (31cm) *Lissy Meg from Little Women. Howard & Jan Foulke.*

Elise
1957-1964.

16½in (42cm)
Basic undergarment, shoes, stockings $250-275
Street clothes $300-400
Ball gowns $550-650
Bride $300-350
Sleeping Beauty, Disney $500-600
Bridesmaid $300-350
Ballerina $250-300
Renoir $800

Cissette Face
1957-1973.

Cissette, 1957-1963. 10in (25cm)
Basic doll, mint-in-box . . $350-400
Day dresses $300-400
Cocktail dresses $500-600
Evening gowns $650-800
Bride $450-500
Queen, 1957-1963 . . . . $350
Gold Ballerina, 1959 . . . . . . $500-550
Denmark, 1962 . . . . $300-400
Gibson Girl $700-800
Jacqueline, 1962 . . . . $550-650
Margot, 1961 . . . . $400-500
Klondike Kate, 1962 . . . . $700-800
Sleeping Beauty,
1959-1960 . . . . $250-350
Mrs. Molloy's Millinery Shop,
1994 . . . . $175
Lady Hamilton #975, 1957 . . . . $1,200
Miss Unity, 1991. UFDC $50-100
Portrettes, 1968-1973.
All Models $200-300

10in (25cm) *Cissette*, all original. *Kathy & Terri's Dolls.*

207

10in (25cm) *Cissette Enchanted Doll,*
all original.
Diane Costa.

16½in (42cm) *Maggie Mixup,*
all original.
Kathy & Terri's Dolls.

Shari Lewis
1959.
14in (36cm) $550-650
      Boxed trousseau set $2,200
21in (53cm) $750-850

Maggie Mixup
1960-1961.
16½in (42cm) $300-400
8in (20cm) $350-450
8in (20cm) angel $450-550
Little Lady $350
Little Lady Gift Set $800-900

Vinyl Dolls
Original tagged clothing, excellent never-played-with condition, bright color.
Miss Flora McFlimsey, 1953. 15in (38cm) $350-450
Kathy, Kathy Cry Dolly, Kathy Tears, 1954-1962.
    15in (38cm) $50-60
    18-19in (46-48cm) $75-85
Kelly Face, 1958-1965. 15in (38cm)
    Kelly $275-325
    Pollyana $275-325
    Marybel, complete case $200-250
    Edith $275-325
    Elise, 1964 ....$200-250
        Riding outfit $300
Betty, 1960. Smiling face, walker, 30in (76cm) $300-350
Timmy Toddler, 1960-1961.
    23in (58cm) $125-150
    30in (76cm) $350-400
Chatterbox, 1961. Battery-operated talker,
    24in (61cm) $200-225
Mimi, 1961. 30in (76cm) fully-jointed $300-400
Jacqueline, 1961-1962.
    21in (53cm) suit $450-550
    Riding habit $550-650
    Gown $550-650
Caroline, 1961-1962.
    15in (38cm) $250-350
    Riding habit $375-425

Smarty Face, 1962-1965. 12in (31cm)
- Smarty, 1962-1963 ....$100-125
- With baby $165-185
- Brother $100-125
- Katie (black), 1965 ....$125-175

Portraits, 1962-current. 21in (53cm), all models $100-200

Melinda, 1963. 14in (36cm) $175-225

Janie Face, 1964-1990. 12in (31cm)
- Janie, 1964-1966 ....$100-125
- Lucinda, 1969-1970 ....$100-125
- Rozy, 1969 ....$100-125
- Suzy, 1970 ....$100-125
- Muffin, 1989-1990 ....$25-30

12in (31cm) *Janie*, all original.
Kathy & Terri's Dolls.

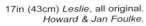

17in (43cm) *Leslie*, all original.
Howard & Jan Foulke.

Brenda Starr, 1964.
- 12in (31cm) $200-225
- Yolanda, 1965 ....$225-250

Patty, 1965. 18in (46cm) $125-150

Polly Face, 1965-1971. 17in (43cm)
- Polly, 1965 ....$200-225
- Mary Ellen Playmate, 1965 ....$225
- Leslie (black), 1965-1971 ....$200-225
- Marlo, 1967 ....$250-300

Mary Ann Face, 1965-current. 14in (36cm)
- Mary Ann, 1965 ....$75
- Orphant Annie, 1965-1966 ....$75-100
- Gidget, 1966 ....$75-100
- Little Granny, 1966 ....$50-60
- Riley's Little Annie, 1967 ....$75-100
- Renoir Girl, 1967-1971 ....$50-75
- Disney Snow White, 1967-1977 ....$165-185
- Easter Girl, 1968 ....$200-300
- Scarlett, 1968. Flowered gown $150-200
- Madame, 1967-1975 ....$50-75
- Jenny Lind & Cat, 1969-1971 ....$100-125
- Gone with the Wind, 1969-1986 ....$40-50
- Jenny Lind, 1970 ....$100-125
- Grandma Jane, 1970 ....$75
- Goldilocks, 1978-1982 ....$40-50

Bonnie Blue, 1989 ....$40-50
Discontinued dolls, 1982-1995 ....$40-50
Anne of Green Gables Trunk Set, 1992-1994 ....$200-250
Babies, 1963-present. Cloth and vinyl
    Littlest Kitten, 1963. 8in (20cm)
        Basic or simple outfit $150-175
    Fancy outfit $200-225
    Sugar Tears, 1964. 14in (36cm) $50-75
    Fischer Quints, 1964. 7in (18cm) set $250-300
    Baby Ellen (black), 1965-1972. 14in (36cm) $50-60
    Sweet Tears, 1965-1982. 14in (36cm) $40-45
        Layette sets $75-100
    Little Bitsey, 1967-1968. 9in (23cm) $110-130
    Victoria, 1967-1989. 20in (51cm) $80-90
    So Big, 1968-1975. 22in (56cm) $85-95
    Mary Cassatt Baby, 1969-1970. 20in (51cm) $175-200
    Pussy Cat (black), 1970-1984
        14in (36cm) $40
        20in (51cm) $55-65
    Happy, 1970. 20in (51cm) $150-175
    Smiley, 1971. 20in (51cm) $150-175
    Baby McGuffey, 1971-1976. 20in (51cm) $100-125
    Baby Lynn, 1973-1976. 20in (51cm) $50-60
    Baby Brother, 1977-1979. 20in (51cm) $40-50
    Mommy's Pet, 1977-1986. 20in (51cm) $50-60
    Mary Mine, 1977-1989 ....$125-150
Sound of Music, 1965-1970. Small set.
    Friedrich, 8in (20cm) $50-75
    Gretl, 8in (20cm) $50-75
    Marta, 8in (20cm) $50-75
    Brigitta, 10in (25cm) $100-125
    Louisa, 10in (25cm) $100-125
    Liesl, 10in (25cm) $100-125
    Maria, 12in (31cm) $100-125

17in (43cm) *Elise*, all original.
Kay Jensen Antique Dolls.

Sound of Music, 1971-1973. Large set (allow 100 percent more for sailor outfits)

Friedrich, 11in (28cm) $75-100
Gretl, 11in (28cm) $75-100
Marta, 11in (28cm) $75-100
Brigitta, 14in (36cm) $75-100
Louisa, 14in (36cm) $75-100
Liesl, 14in (36cm) $75-100
Maria, 17in (43cm) $100-125
Kurt, 11in (28cm) sailor suit $200-250

Coco, 1966. Right leg bent slightly at knee

21in (53cm) $1,800-2,000
Portrait Dolls, 1966 ....$1,800-2,200
Scarlett #2061, white gown $2,500

Elise Face, 1966-1991. Redesigned vinyl face, 17in (43cm)

Elise Portrait, 1972-1973 ....$100-125
Ballerinas $40-50
Brides $40-50
Formals $40-50
Maggie, 1972-1973. ....$100-125

Peter Pan Set, 1969:

Peter Pan, 14in (36cm) $75-100
Wendy, 14in (36cm) $75-100
Michael, 11in (28 cm) $100-125
Tinker Bell, 10in (25cm) $150-200

Nancy Drew Face, 1967-1994. 12in (31cm)

Nancy Drew, 1967 ....$200-225
Renoir Child, 1967 ....$50-75
Pamela, 1969. Boxed set, with wigs $450-500
Poor Cinderella, 1967 ....$50-75
Little Women, 1969-1989 ....$40-50
1989, Sears Exclusive, 5 dolls $250
Romantic Couples, pair $50-55
Discontinued dolls $20-25

First Ladies, 1976-1989. 14in (36cm) each $25-50

American Character

History American Character Doll Co., New York, NY, U.S.A. 1919-on.
Comment Although in business a long time producing better-than-average dolls, A.C. was always in the shadows of other companies until the 1950s when it hit big with *Tiny Tears, Sweet Sue* and *Betsy McCall*. Betsy is listed in her own section.
Trademark Petite.

Marked Petite or American Character Mama Dolls

1923-on. Composition/cloth; original clothes; all in good condition.

16-18in (41-46cm) $175-200
24in (61cm) $225-250

Baby Petite

12in (31cm) $100-125

Puggy

1928. All-composition, frowning face; original clothes; all in good condition.

12in (31cm) $400-500

Marked Petite Girl Dolls

1930s. All-composition; original clothes; all in good condition with nice coloring and perfect hair.

16-18in (41-46cm) $175-200
24in (61cm) $250-275
Petite Toddler, 13in (33cm) $100-125

Sally

1930. All-composition; painted eyes, molded hair or wigged with sleep eyes; original clothes; all in good condition with nice coloring.

12in (31cm) $100-125
16in (41cm) $175-200
Sally-Joy, 1930. Composition, cloth.
    18in (46cm) $225-250
    21in (53cm) $250-275

Carol Ann Beery

1935. All-composition "Two-Some Doll" with special crown braid, matching playsuit and dress.

13in (33cm) $500-600
16½in (42cm) $700-800

Toodles

1956. Hard rubber, drink-and-wet baby; original clothes; excellent condition.

18-20in (46-56cm) $175-200
Tiny Toodles, 10in (25cm) $200-225

Toodles Toddler

1960. Vinyl and hard plastic, "Peek-a-Boo" eyes; original clothes.

24in (61cm) $225-250
30in (76cm) $275-300

11in (28cm) *Tiny Tears* with hard plastic head, in original layette.
Kathy & Terri's Dolls.

Tiny Tears

1950s. Hard plastic head with tear ducts; drink-and-wet baby; original clothes; excellent condition.

Rubber body
    13in (33cm) $200-250
    18in (46cm) $300-350

Original box and accessories
    13in (33cm) **$300-400**
    15in (46cm) **$500-600**
All-vinyl, 1963
    12in (31cm) **$75-95**
    15in (38cm) **$100-125**
    Boxed with accessories **$250**
Clothing and Accessories
    Pink piqué dress
        and bonnet **$40-45**
    Romper suit **$25-30**
    Plastic cradle **$40-50**
    Bottle **$25-30**
    Shoes **$18-22**
    Bubble pipe **$35-40**
    Bracelet **$30**

20in (51cm)
Sweet Sue Sophisticate.
Kathy & Terri's Dolls.

Sweet Sue

1953. All-hard plastic or hard plastic and vinyl, some with walking mechanism, some fully-jointed including elbows, knees and ankles; original clothes; all in excellent condition, with perfect hair and pretty coloring.
    14in (36cm) **$200-225**
    18-21in (46-53cm) **$250-275**
    24in (61cm) **$275**
    30in (76cm) **$300**
    Annie Oakley, 1955. 14in (36cm) **$350**
    Alice-in-Wonderland, 18in (46cm) **$275-300**
    Sweet Sue Sophisticate, vinyl head. 20in (51cm) **$200-250**
    Toni, 1958. Vinyl head, all original.
        10½in (26cm) **$190-210**
        20in (51cm) **$225-275**
    Ricky, Jr., 1955. All-vinyl, all original.
        14in (36cm) **$110-125**
        21in (53cm) **$200-225**

Eloise

Ca. 1955. All-cloth; yellow yarn hair; original clothing; in excellent condition. Designed by Bette Gould from the fictional little girl "Eloise" who lived at the Plaza Hotel in New York City.
21in (53cm) **$450-500**

Whimsies

1960. Characters; original clothing; excellent condition.
Hedda Get Bedda (three faces), Wheeler the Dealer, Lena the Cleaner, Polly the Lolly, Bessie the Bashful Bride, Dixie the Pixie and others.
    19-21in (48-53cm) **$125-150**
    Mint-in-box with tag **$225**
Little Miss Echo, 1962. Recorded voice; original clothing, excellent condition.
    30in (76cm) boxed . . .**$250-300**
    Out of box **$100-150**

15in (38cm) *Sweet Sue,*
early face, all original.
Howard & Jan Foulke

Tressy, 1963-1965. Growing hair.
    12½in (32cm) boxed $50-60
    Doll only $40-45
Pre-teen Tressy, 1963. Growing hair,
    14in (36cm) boxed $75-85
Cricket, 1965. Boxed $75-85
Mary Make-up, 1965. Boxed $75-85

Arranbee

History Arranbee Doll Co., New York, NY, U.S.A. 1922-1960.
Comment R & B produced high quality dolls, but never achieved the popularity and success of Alexander or Effanbee. Vogue purchased the company in the late 1950s, and the *Littlest Angel* line was continued through Vogue.
Mark "ARRANBEE" or "R & B.".

My Dream Baby
1924. Bisque head, cloth body.
    15-16in (38-41cm) $225-250

Storybook Dolls
1930s. All-composition; original storybook costumes; all in excellent condition, with perfect hair and pretty coloring.
    9-10in (23-25cm) $150-175
    Boxed $225-250

Bottletot
1926. All-composition; molded celluloid bottle in hand; appropriate clothes; all in good condition.
    13in (33cm) $125-150

Nancy
1930. All-composition; original clothes; all in good condition, with pretty coloring.
    12in (31cm) molded hair, painted eyes $90-100
    12in (31cm) with trousseau in wardrobe trunk $150-200
    16in (41cm) sleep eyes, wig, open mouth $225-250

Debu'Teen and Nancy Lee
1938-on. All-composition; original clothes; all in good condition with perfect hair and pretty coloring.
    11in (28cm) $275-325
    14in (36cm) $225-250
    18in (46) $250-300
    21in (53cm) $350-400
    Skating Doll, 18in (46cm) ..$350-400
    Brother, 14in (36cm) $225-250
    WAC, 18in (46cm) $400-500

Little Angel Baby
1940s. Composition, cloth; original clothes; all in good condition.
    16-18in (41-46cm) $200-250
    Hard plastic, 18in (46cm) $250

11in (28cm) *Surprise Doll*,
boxed and original.
Mary Jane's Dolls.

14in (36cm) *Nancy Lee*, all original. Mary Jane's Dolls.

17in (43cm) *Nancy Lee*, all original. Rosemary Kanizer.

Nanette and Nancy Lee

1950s. All-hard plastic, original clothes; all in excellent condition, with rosy cheeks.

14in (36cm)	**$300-350**
17in (43cm)	**$375-425**
20in (51cm) Skater	**$450-500**
Cinderella, 14in (36cm)	**$400-450**
Alice-in-Wonderland	**$400-450**

Littlest Angel

1956. All-hard plastic, jointed knees, walker; original clothes; all in excellent condition.

10-11in (25-28cm)	**$150-175**
Boxed	**$250-300**
Boxed outfits	**$65-95**

Coty Girl

1958. All-vinyl, fashion body, high-heeled feet.

10½in (27cm) boxed	**$175-200**

Artist Dolls
Traditional

Comment Today's doll artists owe much to the early doll artists of the 1960s and 1970s, who espoused the concept of the doll as art and promoted their art dolls through organizations, such as NIADA and ODACA. These artist names are familiar to older doll collectors, but hardly known to newer and younger collectors, who are usually unaware of this whole area of collecting.

Traditional Artists

All dolls original and excellent.

Barrie, Mirren; cloth historical characters,
11½in (30cm)	**$75-85**
Beckett, Bob & June; carved wooden children	**$125-150**
Blakeley, Halle; high-fired clay lady dolls	**$350-400**

Bringloe, Frances; carved wooden American Pioneer Children,
6¼in (16cm) pair	**$500-600**

Bruyere, Muriel; biscuit-fired clay, Little Vie,
    8in (31cm) $75-85
Bullard, Helen; carved wood
    Holly, Barbry Allen $165-195
    Hitty $350
    American Family Series (16 dolls) each $300
Clear, Emma
    Porcelain, china and bisque shoulder head dolls $250-300
    Danny $300-350
    George & Martha Washington pair $300-400
    Gibson Girl $275-325

12in (31cm) *Adam* by June
Beckett, one of a kind.
Howard & Jan Foulke.

Group of carved wood dolls by
Sherman Smith.
Howard & Jan Foulke.

DeNunez, Marianne; Bru Jne,
    10in (25cm) $200-300
Flather, Gwen; Katharine Hepburn, 13½in (34cm) $295
Florian, Gertrude
    Ceramic dressed ladies $250-300
    Mother and Baby $300-400
Heizer, Dorothy; cloth sculpture
    Fashion Ladies of the 1940s,
        16in (41cm) each $1,500-2,000
    Queens, 10-13in (25-33cm) $1,500
    Mary, Mary, 16in (41cm) $3,100
Hale, Patti
    Carved wood heads $300-400
    Hitty, all-wood $300
Kane, Maggie Head; porcelain, Gypsy Mother $200-250
Ling, Tita; Philippines, carved wood, 12in (30cm) $650
Nordell, Carol; porcelain ballerinas $125
Oldenburg, Maryanne; porcelain children $125-175
Park, Irma; wax-over-porcelain, miniature vignettes $100-200
Parker, Ann; historical characters $200
Redmond, Kathy; embellished porcelain shoulder heads
    Historical Characters $250-350

Henry VIII $400
Henry's Wives $300
Elizabeth I & Edward, each $250
Medieval Ladies $250-275
Children $200-225
Saucier, Madeline; cloth, 15in (38cm) $200-250
Shreve Island Plantation; flat wood, painted underwear.
   Julie Ann, 3¾in (9cm) $45-50
Smith, Sherman; carved wood
   5-6in (13-15cm) $300
   Pinocchio, 7½in (19cm) $350-400
   Hitty $350
   Miss Unity, 12½in (31cm) $550
Sorensen, Lewis; wax
   Father Christmas $1,000-1,200
   Toymaker $400-500
   Gibson Girls $200-300
Thompson, Martha; porcelain
   Princess Caroline, Prince Charles,
      Princess Anne, each $600-800
   Little Women, each $300-400
   Betsy $500-600
   McKim Child (not bisque) $600
   Royal Ladies $600
   The Eisenhowers, pair $1,500
Tuttle, Eunice
   Miniature porcelain children $350-400
   Angel Baby, boxed $350
   Alice-in-Wonderland Set $1,000
Vargas; black wax characters $300-400
Walters, Beverly; porcelain, miniature fashions ....$500 up
Wilson, Lita; porcelain, Carolyn & John Kennedy, pair ...$125-165
Zeller, Fawn; porcelain
   Angela, Jeanie $300-350
   Jackie Kennedy $400
   Polly Piedmont, 1965 ....$300-400
   Polly II, 1989, U.S. Historical Society $150-200

14in (36cm) *Betsy* by Martha Thompson.
Howard & Jan Foulke.

UFDC

Comment Created by doll artists in limited editions and distributed to convention attendees as souvenirs. Before 1982, most dolls were given as kits; after 1982, most dolls were fully made up and dressed. Except as noted, dolls have porcelain heads, arms and legs; cloth bodies. A few are all-porcelain.

U.F.D.C. National & Regional Souvenir Dolls

Alice in Wonderland; Yolanda Bello, 1990 Region 10,
complete doll $100-125
Alice Roosevelt; Kathy Redmond, 1990 National,
complete doll $85-95
Eleanor, companion doll $225-250
Baby Stuart; Pat Robinson, 1996 National,
complete doll $60-65
Bo-Peep; Fred Laughon, 1989 Region 15,
carved wood with staff and sheep $50-60
Charity; Fred Laughon, 1995 National, peg-wooden $65-75
Cookie; Linda Steele, 1987 Regional, complete doll $175-200
Crystal Faerie; Kazue Moroi and Lita Wilson, 1983
Midwest Regional, complete doll $25-35
Emma; Rappahannock Rags, 1993 National, cloth $25
Father Christmas; Beverly Walters, 1980 National,
(kit) fully made up $250-300
Gibson Girl Bathing Beauty; Phyllis Wright, 1993 Regional,
with bathing costume and beach chair $40-50
Janette; Fawn Zeller, 1991 National, complete doll,
undressed $125-150
Kate; Anili, 1986 National, all-cloth,
with original box $125-135
Katrena & Dimitri; Wendy Lawton 2000 National, pair $400
Ken-Tuck; Janet Masteller, 1972 Regional,
(kit) fully made up $25-35

Li'l Apple, 1979 Convention Doll.
Howard & Jan Foulke.

Eleanor Roosevelt, companion
to 1990 National Convention
Doll *Alice Roosevelt.*
Howard & Jan Foulke.

Laurel; Lita Wilson and Muriel Kramer, 1985 Regional,
fully made up $25-35
Li'l Apple; Faith Wick, 1979 National, fully made up
with romper suit $25
Apple Lil, Companion doll $40
Lindbergh; Faith Wick, 1981 National, complete doll $75-85
Lissette; Cathy Hansen, 1998 National, all-bisque doll
with trunk $200-300
Little Miss Sunshine; Diana Lence Crosby, 1974 National,
(kit) fully made up $25-35
Louise; Marilyn Stauber, 1997 National, complete doll $35-40
Mary; Linda Steele, 1987 National, complete doll $50-60
Lewis, Companion doll $125-150
Miami Miss; Fawn Zeller, 1961 National:
(kit) fully made up $100-125
Dressed $175-200
Nellie Bly; Muriel Kramer, 1985 Pittsburgh Regional,
complete doll $25-35
Osceola; X. Kontis, 1954 National, composition,
all original $100-110
PaPitt; X. Kontis, 1953 National, composition,
all original $100-110
Portrait of a Young Girl; Jeanne Singer, 1986 Rochester
Regional, complete doll $50-60
Precious Lady; Maori Kazue, 1992 National,
fully made up $25
Princess Kimimi; Lita Wilson, 1977 Ohio Regional,
(kit) fully made up $25
Queen Victoria; Virginia Orenyo, 1994 National,
complete doll $75-100
Princess Louise, 5in (12cm) companion baby $200
Rose O'Neill; Lita Wilson, 1982 National,
complete doll $35
Scarlett; Beverly Walters, 1976 Regional, half-doll,
fully made up $90-100
Scarlett; Lita Wilson and Muriel Kramer, 1989 Florida
Regional, half-doll, fully made up $90-100
Sunshine; Lucille Gerrard, 1983 National,
complete doll $35
Wain, Companion doll $45
Tammy; Jeanne Singer, 1989 Western New York Doll Club,
complete doll $35-40
Trick or Treat; Dana Martindale, 1991 Regional,
complete doll with "Nose" $35-40

Commercial

Comment Prices are for a factory perfect doll, never-played-with,
including all accessories, wrist tag, certificate and box, if any.

Commercial Doll Artists
Deval, Brigitte; Wax-over-porcelain children $1000-1500
Good-Kruger, Julie
Vinyl children, 21in (53cm) $75-125
A Trip to Grandma's, 1994. Doll, suitcase, clothes and
accessories. 16in (41cm) $125-150
Gunzel, Hildegard
Wax-over-porcelain children,
28-31in (71-79cm) $800-1200
Vinyl, large children $400-600

Alexander Doll Co., 1990-1993. Vinyl.
    17in (43cm) $25-30
    27in (69cm) $50-60
Gunzel Kids, 1992. 13in (33cm) $35-40
Porcelain babies, My Little Miracle, 2006.
    19in (48cm) $25-35
Hartmann, Sonja; Vinyl children $75-100
Heath, Philip
    Vinyl, large children
        Jezebel, only 22 made $500
        Titi $450
        Mindiyana $455
        Marisol $280
        Seraphina $230
Heller, Karin; Cloth children. 20in (51cm) $80-100
Iacono, Maggie; Cloth children, fully jointed $450-650
Kish, Helen
    UFDC Riley $360
    Ballerinas, 12in (31cm) $95-105
    Kristina,1994, fully-jointed $200
    Veronica's Bridal Day, 2001. ....$850
    Christmas Morning Bethany, 2003. ....$560
    Bitty Bethany, 2003. ....$325
    Pippa, 1998. ....$290
    Kitten, 1998. ....$255
    Alice, 1996. ....$160
    African Madonna, 1989. ....$1800
Lawton, Wendy
    Little Colonel, 1990. ....$150
    Bessy & Her Bye-Lo, 1995. ....$185
    Katie & Her Kewpie, 1994. ....$150
    Bon Voyage, 2003. 9in (23cm) $350
    Laura Emeline, 2001. 9in (23cm) $260
    Marie, 1987. ....$180
    Secret Garden Trousseau Set, 2000, 9in (23cm) $250
    Henrietta & Hilda, 1996. 17in (43cm) $325

19in (48cm) *Sylvie*, by Heidi Ott.
Kay Jensen Antique Dolls.

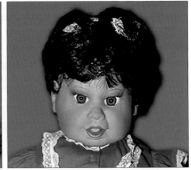

1989 *My Lee*, by Lee Middleton.
Kay Jensen Antique Dolls.

Middleton, Lee
    Honey Love and other vinyl babies $50-70
    Bubba Chubbs, 22in (56cm) vinyl $100-125
Ott, Heidi
    Lucie & Baby, Sylvie, Imelda, 1984.
        19in (48cm) vinyl $100-150
    Vinyl children, 12in (31cm) $40-50
Pongratz, Elisabeth
    All-wood children, 14in (36cm) $1200

Roche, Lynne & Michael
Porcelain and wood children
    20-22in (51-56cm) $750-1000
All-bisque children, 15in (38cm) $350-450
Sandreuter, Regina
    All-wood children, 17in (43cm) $2200-2500
Schrott, Rotraut, for Gadco
    Martina, 1988.
        Porcelain, 28in (71cm) $125-150
        Vinyl $75-100
    Marlene, 1990.
        Porcelain, 28in (71cm) $300-400
        Vinyl $125-150
    Puyi, 1989. 26in (66cm) $65-75
    Suzi, 1989. 28in (71cm) $65-75
    Ricardo, 1992. 30in (81cm) $125
    Jasmine, 1991. 28in (71cm) $125
Spanos, FayZah
    Sheer Elegance, 30in (81cm) $230
    40in (102cm) sitting girl dressed in Battenberg
        lace holding 15in (38cm) baby $225
    Vinyl babies and children $75-125
Thompson, Pat
    Porcelain girls in fancy outfits, 1987.
        22in (56cm) $275-375
    Beauty & the Beast $550
Treffeisen, Ruth
    Porcelain children, 25-30in (64-76cm) $400-600
    Vinyl children $125-150
Turner, Virginia
    Large children, 25-30in (64-76cm) $75-100
    Small children, 21in (53cm) $35-55
Woods, Robin
    Vinyl children and characters
        8in (21cm) $10-15
        12-14in (31-36cm) $15-25
    Easter doll in egg with wardrobe, 8in (21cm) $155
    Alice trunk set $115

Ashton-Drake Galleries

> Comment Prices are for dolls in mint condition with certificates and boxes.

Designer — Yolanda Bello
Picture Perfect Babies
    Jason (1st) $150-200
    Heather (2nd, Jennifer (3rd), Matthew, 1987 (4th),
        Amanda (1988), Sarah (1989), Jessica (1989),
        Lisa (1990), Michael (1990), Emily (1991),
        Danielle (1991), each $30-35
Playtime Babies
    Lindsey (1994), Shawna (1994), Todd (1994), each ...$15-25
Lullaby Babies $15-25
Moments to Remember
    Jill (1993), Justin (1991), each $15-20
Magical Moments of Summer
    Whitney (1995), Dana (1996), each $15
Heaven Scent Babies
    Megan Rose (1994), Sweet Carnation, each $15

Designer — Wendy Lawton
Little Women, set of five,
    16in (41cm) $125-150
Mary Had a Little Lamb, 1994 . . . .$15
Little Bo-Peep, 1994. 15in (38cm) $15
Little Miss Muffet, 1995.
    14in (36cm) $15

Designer — Joan Ibarolle
Little House on the Prairie, 1992-1995
    Ma & Pa each $75-85
    Baby Grace $200

Designer — Dianna Effner
Heroines from the Fairy Tale Forest,
16in (41cm)
    Goldilocks, Cinderella, Snow White,
      Red Riding Hood, Rapunzel,
      each $15-20
What Little Girls Are Made Of, 15in (38cm)
    Sunshine & Lollipops (1997),
      Peaches & Cream, Christmas &
      Candy Canes (1999),
      each $15-20
Mother Goose Series, 14in (36cm)
    Mary, Mary (1991), Girl with curl
    (1992), Curly Locks (1993), Snips &
    Snails (1993), each $15-20
Classic Collection, Hillary (1995), 15in (38cm) $20-25
Babies, Sugar Plum (1994), 8in (20cm) $25

Gene in *Teatime at the Plaza*,
FAO Schwartz Exclusive.
Sidney Jeffrey Collection.

Designer — Julie Good-Krüger
Amish Blessings
    Rebeccah, Rachael, Adam, each $20-25

Designer — Jenny Lundy
Simple Pleasures, Special Days, Amish Children
    Molly (1999), Gretchen (1998), each $20-25

Designer — Mary Tretter
Wizard of Oz
    Dorothy, Scarecrow, Cowardly Lion,
      Tinman, each $25-35

Designer — Brigitte Deval
Fairy Tale Princesses, 18in (46cm), each $40-50

Designer — Titus Tomescu
From This Day Forward (Brides) 1994. . . . .$25-35
Barely Yours (Babies)
    Snug as a Bug $30
    Cute as a Button, 1993 . . . .$30
    Pretty as a Picture, 1996. . . . .$30
    Good as Gold, 1997. . . . .$30
    Snow Babies $10
    Jesus, Water into Wine $30-40

For Walt Disney
Mickey Mouse Club Annette $200
Disney Babies $35-45
Disney World Girl or Boy, 2001. 16in (41cm) $25-35

Designer — Mel Odom
Gene
Premiere, 1996 ....$100-125
Holiday Magic, 1996. First Christmas, outfit only $90-110
Broadway Medley, 1998 Convention doll $200-225
King's Daughter, 1997 ....$75
Ransom in Green, 1988, at auction $810
Night at Versailles, 1997 ....$225
An American Countess, 1999 ....$100

BAPS

History Frau Edith von Arps, Burgkunstadt, Germany. 1946 on. Many sold on military bases and in Pxes.
Description Felt face with hand-painted features (latered stenciled), yarn hair, wire-framed body with felt covered limbs, metal feet; original clothing, often felt; excellent condition.
Mark BAPS, on stand or box, dolls unmarked.

Baps Storybook Characters and German Costume Dolls (Trachtenpuppen)
5in (12cm) adults $30-40
3½in (9cm) children $30-40
Animals $25-35
Family of 4 ....$225
Storybook Characters $65-85
Man and lady pair $135-165
Puss in Boots $145
Hansel, Gretel and Witch Set $145

Alice in Wonderland with
the White Rabbit.
Kathy & Terri's Dolls.

Peter Pan and Tinkerbell.
Kathy & Terri's Dolls.

#1 *Barbie*® #850, 1959 wearing
Enchanted Evening #983 1960-1963.
Kiefer Collection.

#2 *Barbie*® wearing
Sweater Girl #976.
Kiefer Collection.

BARBIE®

BARBIE® is a registered trademark of Mattel, Inc.

History Mattel, Inc., Hawthorne, CA, U.S.A. 1959 to present. Hard plastic and vinyl. 11½-12in (29-31cm).
Comment Condition is extremely important in pricing BARBIE® dolls. Mint condition means the doll has never been played with, coloring is beautiful, hair is perfect, all accessories are present. Rule of thumb dictates that to price out-of-original-box dolls and accessories, deduct 50 percent; for lightly played-with items, deduct an additional 25 percent.
Mark 1959-1962: "Barbie TM/Pats. Pend./© MCMLVIII/by/Mattel, Inc."
1963-1968: "Midge TM/© 1962/Barbie®/© 1958/by/Mattel, Inc."
1964-1966: "© 1958/Mattel, Inc/U.S. Patented/U.S. Pat. Pend."
1966-1969: "© 1966/Mattel, Inc/U.S. Patented/U.S. Pat. Pend./Made in Japan."

#1 BARBIE®

1959. Vinyl, solid body; very light complexion, white irises, pointed eyebrows, gold hoop earrings, ponytail; black and white striped bathing suit; holes in feet to fit stand; mint condition.

11½in (29cm)
    boxed $4,500-5,500*
Doll only, no box or accessories
    Mint $2,000-2,500
    Very good $1,200-1,600
    Stand $1,200-1,500
    Shoes, spikes $75-95
    Shoes, closed toe $35-45
    Hoop earrings $75

1961 Ponytail *Barbie*® Bride.
Kiefer Collection.

*Brunette harder to find than blonde.

#2 BARBIE®

1959-1960. Vinyl, solid body; very light complexion; same as above, but no holes in feet; some wore pearl earrings; mint condition. Made three months only.

11½in (29cm) boxed **$4,500-5,500***
Doll only, no box or accessories, very good **$1,200-1,600**

#3 BARBIE®

1960. Vinyl, solid body; very light complexion; same as #2, but with blue irises and curved eyebrows; no holes in feet; mint condition.

11½in (29cm) boxed **$1,200-1,400**
Doll only, mint **$600-800**

#4 BARBIE®

1960. Vinyl; same as #3, but with solid body of flesh-toned vinyl; mint condition.

11½in (29cm) boxed **$500-600**
Doll only, mint **$250-300**
Dressed doll box #865 Negligee, at auction **$1,525**

#5 BARBIE®

1961. Vinyl; same as #4; ponytail hairdo of firm Saran; mint condition.

11½in (29cm) boxed **$325-425**
Doll only, mint **$225-275**

Other BARBIE®s

All prices are for mint-in-box dolls unless otherwise noted.

Bubble Cut BARBIE®, 1961 on **$250-350**
Doll only, mint **$125-175**
Bubble side part, doll only, mint **$300-350**
White Ginger, 1962, boxed **$625**
Fashion Queen BARBIE®, 1963 . . . .**$550-750**
Doll only with three wigs **$80-110**
Miss BARBIE®, 1964 . . . .**$900-1,100**
Swirl Ponytail BARBIE®, 1964 . . . .**$550-650**
Doll only, mint **$250-350**

#3 *Barbie*® wearing
Solo in the Spotlight.
Kiefer Collection.

#4 *Barbie*® wearing
Sweater Girl #976.
Kiefer Collection.

1961 Ponytail *Barbie*®
wearing *After Five*
from1962-1964.
Kiefer Collection.

Bendable Leg BARBIE®, 1965 and 1966
   American Girl
      Center part, mint-in-box $1,200-1,800
           Side part $2,500-3,500
Color Magic BARBIE®, 1966
      Brunette $1,600-2,200
      Blonde $1,200-1,800
      Midnight to ruby red $1,600
   Doll only, mint
         Brunette $1,000-1,200
         Blonde $500-650
Twist 'N Turn BARBIE®, 1967 ....$375-425
   Trade-In box, mint $700-750
   Doll only $225-275
Talking BARBIE®, 1970 ....$225-250
Living BARBIE®, 1970 ....$100-125
Live Action BARBIE®, 1970 ....$200-250
Hair Happenin's BARBIE®, 1971 ....$1,200
Montgomery Ward BARBIE®, 1972 ....$200-225
Growin' Pretty Hair, 1971-1972 ....$325-375
Quick Curl, 1972 ....$125-150
Gift Sets, mint-in-box
      Fashion Queen BARBIE® & Ken, 1964 ....$2,800-3,200
      Wedding Party, 1964 ....$3,000
      On Parade (BARBIE®, Ken and Midge), 1964. ...$2,500-3,200
      Silver Blue, 1967. ....$2,500-3,200
      Tennis BARBIE® & Ken $2,600-3,200

1963 *Barbie®, Ken & Midge On Parade Gift Set.*

1962 Swirl Ponytail *Barbie®*, boxed.

Outfits

All never-removed-from-package. Deduct 50 percent for complete but out-of-package outfits.
   Roman Holiday ....$3,000 up
   Gay Parisienne ....$2,000 up
   Easter Parade ....$2,500 up
   Shimmering Magic ....$1,400 up
   Here Comes the Bride ....$950 up
   Pan Am Stewardess ....$4,000 up
   BARBIE® Baby Sits $200-300
   Dogs & Duds $150-175
   Enchanted Evening $250-300

1600 Series and Jacqueline
   Kennedy-style outfits . . .$450 up
Dinner at 8 . . . .$200-250
Commuter Set $1,250-1,500
Picnic Set $300-350
Midnight Blue $700-800
Silken Flame $125-150
Senior Prom $250-300
Plantation Belle $300-350
Open Road $275-350
Registered Nurse $285

Accessories
Mint-in-package.
BARBIE® doll's First Car . .$250-300
BARBIE® doll's First
   Dreamhouse $125-150
Fashion Shop, at auction $500
Little Theatre $400-500
Cases . . . .$25 up
BARBIE® doll's bed $90-100
Ken's Hot Rod Roadster $200

Fashion Queen Barbie® wearing Senior Prom gown. Kiefer Collection.

Other Dolls
All prices are for mint-in-box dolls unless otherwise noted.
Ken #1
   1961 . . . .$150-175
   Bendable legs $175-200
   Dressed boxed doll $250-350
Midge
   1963 . . . .$175-195
   1966, bendable legs $300-350
Allan, 1964-1966
   Bendable legs $200-250
   Straight legs $100-125
Skipper, 1964.
   Straight legs $150-175
   Dramatic New Living Skipper $125-150
   Bendable Legs $175-200
   Skipper Dream Room, 1968 . . . .$200
   Party Time Gift Set $200
Ricky, 1965 . . . .$150-175
Scooter, 1965. Straight legs $150-175
Francie, 1966-1967
   Doll only, bendable legs, mint $175-210
   Straight legs $175-210
   Twist 'N Turn $260-285
   Black
      1967, mint-in-package $1,500-1,900
      Doll only, mint $750-850
   "No Bangs"
      1970 . . . .$1,500
      Doll only, mint $700-900
   Growin' Pretty Hair $250-275
   Hair Happenin's, 1970 . . . .$225-275
Casey, 1967 . . . .$250-300
Twiggy, 1967 . . . .$275-325
   Boxed outfits $150-200
Christie, 1968-1972. (Black) Twist 'N Turn $300-350
Stacey, 1968-1971
   Twist 'N Turn $300-350
   Talking $300-350

P.J., 1969-1971
    Twist 'N Turn $225-275
    Live Action on Stage $215
Truly Scrumptious
    1969 ....$425-475
    Doll only, mint $275-300
Julia, 1969 ....$225-275
    Talking $150-200
Tutti, 1967-1970 ....$125-150
Chris, 1967-1970 ....$95-110
Todd, 1967-1970 ....$95-110
Pretty Pairs
    Angie 'N Tangle $200-250
    Nan 'N Fran $175-225
    Lori 'N Ron $200-250

Bob Mackie BARBIE® Dolls
1990 Gold $125-175
1991 Platinum $100-125
1991 Starlight Splendor (black) $150-175
1992 Empress Bride $250-350
1992 Neptune Fantasy $300
1993 Masquerade Ball $75-125
1994 Queen of Hearts $75-125
1995 Goddess of the Sun $75-125
1996 Moon Goddess $75-125
1997 Madame du BARBIE® $250
1997 Jewel Essence Collection, five dolls $175-225

Holiday BARBIE® Dolls
1988, English language box $225-275
1989 ....$75-125
1990 ....$50-75
1991 ....$50-75
1992 ....$40-50
1993 ....$35-45
1994 ....$35-45
1995 ....$25-30
1996 ....$25
1997 ....$25
1998 ....$25
1999 ....$25-30
2000 ....$25-30
2001 ....$20-25

Exclusive Store Specials
1990 Winter Fantasy
    (FAO Schwarz) $25-35
1993 Little Debbie, First $10
1993 Rockettes
    (FAO Schwarz) $35-40
1994 Nicole Miller
    (Bloomingdales) $25
1994 Victorian Elegance
    (Hallmark) $15-20
1994 Silver Screen
    (FAO Schwarz) $25-30
1994 Tooth Fairy (WalMart) $5
1995 Shopping Chic (Speigel) ...$15-20

1972 Montgomery Ward Reissue *Barbie*®.
Kay Jensen Antique Dolls.

1995 Jeweled Splendor **(FAO Schwarz)** $25-35
1995 Circus Star **(FAO Schwarz)** $20-25
1995 Donna Karan **(Bloomingdales)** $30-35
1995 Royal Enchantment **(J.C. Penney)** $5
1995 Statue of Liberty **(FAO Schwarz)** $35-40
1996 Pink Ice **(Toys R Us)** $25-30

Timeless Creations (now BARBIE® Collectibles)

Stars and Stripes Collection
   1990 Air Force BARBIE® $15
   1991 Navy BARBIE® $15
   1992 Marine BARBIE® $15-20
   1992 Marine Gift Set $30-35
   1993 Army Gift Set $25-30
   1994 Air Force Gift Set $25-30
Classique Collection
   1992 Benefit Ball $25-30
   1993 Opening Night $25-30
   1993 City Style $20-25
   1994 Uptown Chic $20-25
   1994 Evening Extravaganza $20-25
   1994 Evening Extravaganza **(black)** $20-25
   1995 Midnight Gala $25-30
Nostalgia Series
   1994 35th Anniversary $30
   1994 Gift Set $55-65
   1994 Solo in the Spotlight $20-25
   1995 Busy Gal $25
   1996 Enchanted Evening $20-25
   1996 Poodle Parade $20-25
   1997 Fashion Luncheon $40-50
Scarlett Series, 1994 & 1995
   Green Velvet $50-60
   Red Velvet $50-60
   Barbecue $50-60
   Honeymoon $50-60
   Ken as Rhett Butler $40-50
Great Eras
   1993 Gibson Girl $20-25
   1993 1920s Flapper $30-40
   1994 Egyptian Queen $30-40
   1994 Southern Belle $25-30
   1995 Medieval Lady $20-25
   1996 Grecian Goddess $20-25
   1997 Chinese Empress $20-25
Other BARBIE® Dolls
   1986 Blue Rhapsody **(porcelain)** $75-125
   1988 Mardi Gras $15
   1989 Pink Jubilee $1,000
   1990 Wedding Fantasy $15
   1992 My Size $80-90
   1994 Snow Princess $30-40
      (brunette) $125
   1994 Gold Jubilee $100
   1994 Evergreen Princess $20-25
   1994 Evergreen Princess **(Disney with red hair)** $75
   1995 Peppermint Princess $20-25
   1995 Starlight Waltz $15-20
   1995 Dior, First $50-60
   1995 50th Anniversary **(porcelain)** $60-125
   1995 Rapunzel $15-20

1996 Pink Splendor $225-275
1996 Jewel Princess $15
1996 Jewel Princess (Disney, brunette) $40-50
1996 Escada $35-40
1996 Dior, Second $50-60
1996 Wedding Fantasy Gift Set $40
1996 Erté Stardust $200-225
1997 Bill Blass $25-30
1997 Midnight Princess $15-20
1997 Midnight Princess (Disney, brunette) $40-45
1997 Illusion $50-60
1997 1st Harley-Davidson $200-250
1998 Harley-Davidson, Second $40-45
1998 Crystal Jubilee $90-110
1998 Rendezvous $35-40
1998 Fabregé Imperial Elegance (porcelain) $200-225
Silkstone Lingerie BARBIE®
   #1 . . . .$125-150
   #2 . . . .$150-175
   #3 . . . .$65-85
   #4 . . . .$55-60
   #5 . . . .$35-40
   #6 . . . .$35-40
2003 Chataine (FAO Schwarz exclusive) $475-525

Betsy McCall

Comment *Betsy McCall* started in 1951 as a paper doll in the now defunct *McCall's* magazine. She was so popular with little girls that a 14-inch real doll version was licensed to Ideal in 1952. But she didn't become a smash-hit doll until 1957 when the 8-inch version with a large wardrobe available separately was licensed by American Character. Today, Betsy is still very popular with collectors, and a modern version is made by Robert Tonner.

American Character Doll Co.

1957. All-hard plastic, jointed knees; molded eyelashes, rooted Saran hair on wig cap; original clothes; excellent with rosy cheeks.
   8in (20cm) basic, (undergarment, shoes and socks) $250-275
      Mint-in-box, basic $375-425
      In dresses $250-300
      In gowns $300-400
      Mint-in-box, pink dress
         and hat $600-650
      Mint-in-blister pack $575
   Clothes, clean and in very good
   condition
      Dresses $40-65
      Shoes and socks $35-40
      Boxed outfits $100-150

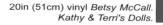

20in (51cm) vinyl *Betsy McCall*.
Kathy & Terri's Dolls.

American Character
1960. All-vinyl, slender limbs; lashed sleep eyes, original clothes; excellent condition.

    14in (36cm) $350-375
    20in (51cm) $450-500
    30in (76cm) $350-400
    36in (91cm) $400-500
    Boxed, all original
        14in (36cm) $700-775
        20in (51cm) $900-1,000
    Jointed at wrists, waist, knees and ankles
        22in (56cm) $350-400
        30in (76cm) $525-575

Ideal Novelty & Toy Co.
1952. Vinyl head, hard plastic body; original clothes; excellent condition.

    14in (36cm) $225-250
    Mint-in-box $550-650

Ideal Novelty & Toy Co.
1959. All-vinyl; original clothes; excellent condition.

    Betsy McCall, 36in (91cm) $400-500
    Sandy McCall, 38in (96cm) $350-450

8in (20cm) hard plastic *Betsy McCall. Kathy & Terri's Dolls.*

Uneeda
1959-1961.

    All-vinyl, 11½in (29cm) $95-115
    Boxed $275-300

Horsman
1974.

    All-vinyl, 29in (73cm) boxed $225-275
    Beauty Box, 13in (33cm) boxed $50-60

Tomy
1984. Porcelain/cloth, all original and boxed.

    Four Seasons, 16in (41cm) $40-50

Rothschild
1986.

    Hard vinyl, 8in (20cm), all original $25-30

Tonner, Robert
1997. All original, boxed and mint.

    8in (20cm)
        Tiny Betsy Loves Disney, 2002 ....$220
        Gift Set, Pink Perfection, 2002 ....$200
        Tiny Betsy, 50th Anniversary $350
        Just Peachy Gift Set $250
        UFDC Ready to Travel $255
    14in (36cm)
        San Antonio Betsy $76
        Betsy Baking Bread Trunk Set $125

Boudoir Dolls

History Various French, U.S., English and Italian firms. Early 1920s into the 1940s.

Comment These dolls with a very distinctive look were made primarily as bedroom decorations, appealing to teen-agers and ladies. Many have exquisite costumes in the Art Deco style, and these bring the highest prices.

23in (58cm) boudoir
doll purse.
Private Collection.

Boudoir Doll

Head of composition, cloth or other material, painted features, mohair wig; composition or cloth stuffed body, unusually long extremities; usually high-heeled shoes; original clothes elaborately designed and trimmed; all in excellent condition.

Cloth Face, 1920s
    Exceptional quality art doll, silk
    face and hair,
        28-30in (71-76cm) $350-450
    Standard quality, 28-30in (71-76cm)
        Dressed $200-225
        Naked $80-90
Composition Head
    1920s, dressed $150-175
    Smoker
        (Apache Dancer) . . .$350-450
    1940s, dressed $100-125
Lenci . . . . .See page 134.
Poured Wax, 22in (56cm) $600
Blossom Doll Co. Wedding Party.
    All original, set of 10 dolls,
    at auction $4,400
Printed Cloth, 34in (86cm) $110
Vintage high-heeled shoes $40-50

Buddy Lee

History H.D. Lee Co., Inc., garment manufacturers of Kansas City, MO, U.S.A. 1920-1962.

Comment *Buddy Lee* was an advertising doll for the manufacturer of the Lee denims. Dolls must be dressed in Lee-made clothes and uniforms of delivery truck drivers or gas station attendants to have full value. They have cross-over value with collectors of denim, soft drinks, and gasoline and trucking companies.

Mark "Buddy Lee" embossed on back.

13in (33cm) hard plastic
Buddy Lee, replaced hat.
Kay Jensen Antique Dolls.

Marked Buddy Lee

Molded hair, painted eyes to side; jointed at shoulders, stiff hips, legs apart, painted shoes; dressed in original Lee clothes; all in very good condition.

Composition, 1920-1948. 13in (33cm) $300-400
Hard Plastic, 1949-1962. 13in (33cm) $350-450

22in (56cm) Burgarella child, boxed.
Bart Boeckmans.

Burgarella

History Gaspare Burgarella, Rome, Italy. Ca. 1925 until World War II. Designed by Ferdinando Stracuzzi.
Comment These high-quality Italian dolls are very desirable and rarely found. Though they are not marked, their distinctive facial look and construction is unmistakeable. Allow extra for an outstanding costume.
Mark Cloth label sewn on clothes "BURGARELLA Made in Italy."

Burgarella Child

Excellent quality; all-composition; jointed at neck, shoulders, elbows, hips and knees; human hair or mohair wig, short face with chubby cheeks, dramatic painted eyes, small mouth; all in excellent condition.

All original clothing
    16-18in (41-46cm) $600-750
    22in (56cm) $750-850
Sexed boy, all original $1,000

Cameo Doll Company

History Cameo Doll Company, New York, NY, later Port Allegany, PA, U.S.A. Original owner: Joseph L. Kallus. 1922-on.
Comment J.L. Kallus, a very talented doll designer, took the line drawings of Rose O'Neill's Kewpie and Scootles and transformed them into three-dimensional form. The wood-segmented dolls were his own designs.

Kewpie, 1913 ....See page 121.
Bundie, 1918-1925. All-composition, 11in (28cm) ....$300°

°Few price samples available.

Scootles, 1925. Designed by Rose O'Neill. All-composition; appropriate clothes; all in very good condition.

7-8in (18-20cm)	$450-500
12-13in (31-33cm)	$300-350
15-16in (38-41cm)	$450-550
20in (51cm)	$650-750
Boxed with tag, 8in (20cm) at auction	$1,100
Sleep eyes	
12in (31cm)	$500-550
20in (51cm)	$900-1,000
Black, 13-14in (33-36cm)	$500-600
All-bisque (Japan)	
4½in (11cm)	$325-375
6-7in (15-18cm)	$500-550
Baby Bo Kaye, 1925	See page 40.

14in (36cm) composition
Scootles, all original.
Howard & Jan Foulke.

Wood Segmented Characters

Designed by Joseph L. Kallus. Composition head, segmented wood body; undressed; all in very good condition.

Margie, 1929	
10in (25cm)	$150-165
15in (38cm)	$275-325
17in (43cm)	$350-400
Pinkie, 1930. 10in (25cm)	$175-200
Joy, 1932	
10in (25 cm)	$175-200
15in (38cm)	$300-325
Betty Boop, 1932	
12in (31cm)	$650-750
With molded bathing suit and composition legs;	
wearing a cotton print dress	$750-850°
Pop-Eye, 1935. 14in (36cm)	$500
Hotpoint Man, 16in (41cm)	$1,300
RCA Radiotron, 16in (41cm)	$1,000
Bandy, General Electric, 18in (46cm)	$800
Pete the Pup, 9in (23cm)	$450-500
Howdy Doody, 12½in (32cm) boxed, at auction	$720

°Few price samples available.

13in (33cm) *Giggles*.
Howard & Jan Foulke.

15in (38cm) *Baby Blossom*.
Howard & Jan Foulke.

Giggles
1946. Designed by Rose O'Neill. All composition; original romper; all in very good condition.
14in (36cm) $350-400
Boxed $550-600

Pretty Bettsie
All composition.
18in (46cm) at auction $1,050

Little Annie Rooney
1925. Designed by Jack Collins. Composition; painted eyes, yarn wig; all original.
16in (41cm) $700-800

Baby Blossom
1927. Composition and cloth.
19-20in (48-51cm) ....$550-$650°

Champ
1942. Composition, molded hair, freckles, all original.
16in (41cm) ....$500-600°

Vinyl Dolls
Miss Peep, 1957. Black or white. All original.
16-18in (41-46cm) $45-55
Boxed $95
Newborn Miss Peep, 1962. 14in (36cm) boxed $45
Baby Mine, 1961. All original. 20in (51cm) boxed $150-175
Margie, 1958. All original. 17in (43cm) boxed $150-175
Scootles, all original
1964, 14in (36cm) $75-85
19-20in (48-51cm) sleeping eyes $225
1973 Ltd. Ed. (Maxines), 16in (41cm) $125-150
1980s, (Jesco), all original
12in (31cm) $35
16in (31cm) $50
1997 Lee Middleton Stamp Doll, 12in (31cm) $25-35

°Few price samples available.

Campbell Kids

Comment These very appealing dolls originally designed by Grace G. Drayton as advertising for the Campbell Soup Co. have been in production for nearly 100 years. In all of their myriad versions, they continue to be extremely popular collectibles.

Mark on head:
E. I. H. © 1910

Cloth label on sleeve:
**The Campbell Kids
Trademark by
Joseph Campbell.
Mfg. by E.I. Horsman Co**

E.I. Horsman Co.

1910-1914. Designed by Grace G. Drayton. Composition head, molded and painted bobbed hair; original cloth body; appropriate or original clothes; all in good condition.

10-13in (25-33cm) $175-225
16in (41cm) $300-325

American Character & E.I. Horsman Co.

1923. Designed by Grace G. Drayton. sometimes called *Dolly Dingle*. All-composition; molded bobbed hair, painted eyes to side; original clothes; all in good condition.

12in (31cm) ....$400-500°

12in (31cm) 1948 *Campbell Kid.*
Kiefer Collection.

E.I. Horsman Co.,

1948. All-composition; molded bobbed hair, painted eyes to side, watermelon mouth; original clothes; all in good condition.

12-13in (31-33cm) $350-375
With Campbell Soup outfit and label $500-550

All-Vinyl

1950-on. Original clothes, bright color, unplayed-with condition.

8in (20cm) $30-40
Boxed $45-50
16in (28cm) $50-55

°Few price samples available.

All-Cloth, Knickerbocker
1973.
12in (31cm) boxed $20-25

Porcelain
1997. Soup Can box.
11½in (29cm) $20-25

1997 Horsman Reproductions
1948. 12½in (32cm) pair $25-35
1910. 10in (25cm) $20

Cloth Caricature Dolls

History Made by various companies, such as Klumpe and Roldan, both in Barcelona, Spain. Ca. 1952 - 1975.
Comment Prices are for excellent, clean condition with good color and accessories, if any. Values are higher for occupational and hobby dolls.
Description Molded cloth face with painted features and amusing expressions; posable wire armature cloth-covered bodies; large balancing feet; original clothing with accessories, if any; many are occupational or hobby related.
Mark Cardboard tag only, unmarked doll.

Cloth Caricature Doll
      9in-11in (23-28cm) $45-65
      Butterfly catcher $175
      1920s Paris Dancing Pair $285
      Doctor, nurse, professor, musician $100-125

10½in (27cm) Klumpe character, all original with tag.
Howard & Jan Foulke.

Cloth, Russian

History Unknown craftsman, Ca. 1930-1940s.

Comment Sometimes the cloth label gives information about the area represented by the doll, such as *Ukrainian Woman* or *Smolensk District Woman*. All dolls must be clean with bright and original clothes.

Description All cloth with molded and handpainted stockinet head and arms. Authentic original regional clothes.

Mark Cloth tag Made in Soviet Union.

6½in (16cm) child	.......$25-30
11in (28cm) child	........$60-70
15in (38cm)	..........$150-175
Tea Cosy, 20in (51cm)	...$150-175

15in (38cm) Russian cloth
Ukrainian Woman, all original.
Howard & Jan Foulke.

Dewees Cochran

History Dewees Cochran, Fenton, CA, U.S.A. 1940-on.

Comment Dewees Cochran had a gift for sculpting dolls which looked like real children. She adapted some of her models for the Effanbee Doll Co. *American Children* recognized by collectors as the ultimate composition dolls. She developed a latex material for her own production dolls, but it can deteriorate and even break with the passage of years, so examine dolls carefully.

Mark Signed under arm or behind right ear.

Dewees Cochran Doll

Latex with jointed neck, shoulders and hips; human hair wig, painted eyes, character face; dressed; all in good condition.

Cindy, 1947-1948. 15-16in (38-41cm) $800-900
Grow-up Dolls, 1952-1958.
  Stormy, Angel, Bunnie, J.J. and Peter Ponsett
    each at ages 5, 7, 11, 16 and 20 ....$1,400-1,800

Dewees Cochran *Angel* (smiling) and *Cindy*, all original.
Connie Lowe Collection.

Look-Alike Dolls (six different faces) $1,400-1,800
Individual Portrait
    Children $1,500-1,800
    Baby, 9in (23cm) $1,000-1,200
Asian $2,400
American Children (Composition) ....See page 251.

Composition
American

> Comment Unless otherwise noted, all dolls should be all original with perfect hair, good coloring, original clothes; light crazing acceptable.

All-Composition Child Doll
1912-1920. Various firms, such as Bester Doll Co., New Era Novelty Co.. New Toy Mfg. Co., Superior Doll Mfg. Co.. Artcraft Toy Product Co., Colonial Toy Mfg. Co. Ball-jointed composition body; appropriate clothes; all in good condition. These are patterned after German bisque-headed dolls.
    22-24in (56-61cm) $225-250
    Character baby, all-composition, 19in (48cm) $175-225

Early Composition Character Doll
Ca. 1912. Composition head with molded hair or wig and painted features; cloth body; appropriate clothes.
    12-15in (31-38cm) $110-125
    18-20in (46-51cm) $150-175
    24-26in (61-66cm) $225-250

Molded Loop Dolls
Ca. 1930s. Composition head with molded bobbed hair and loop for tying on a ribbon; quality is generally mediocre.
    12-15in (31-38cm) $100-125

17in (43cm) unmarked *Patsy*-type child, all original.
Howard & Jan Foulke.

Patsy-type Girl
Ca. 1930s. All-composition with molded bobbed hair; of good quality.
    9-10in (23-25cm) $100-125
    14-16in (36-41cm) $175-200
    20in (51cm) $225-250
    Kewty, 13in (33cm) $350
    Mitzi, 12in (31cm) $275

Mama Dolls

Ca. 1920-on. Composition head with hair wig; composition lower limbs, cloth body.

16-18in (41-46cm) $175-200
20-22in (51-56cm) $225-275
24-26in (61-66cm) $300-350

Babies and Infants

Ca. 1920 on. Composition head with molded hair; composition lower arms, cloth body (may have composition lower legs).

14-16in (36-41cm) $150-200
18-20in (46-51cm) $225-250

Dionne-type Doll

Ca. 1935. All-composition with molded hair or wig; of good quality.

7-8in (18-20cm) baby $125-135
13in (33cm) toddler $200-225
18-20in (46-51cm) toddler $275-300

Alexander-type Girl

Ca. 1935. All composition; of good quality.

13in (33cm) $200-225
16-18in (41-46cm) $250-300
22in (56cm) $325-350

11in (28cm) Junel doll,
all original.
Kay Jensen Antique Dolls.

16in (41cm) unmarked
Alexander-type child, all original.
Howard & Jan Foulke.

11in (28cm) unmarked
costume doll, all original.
Diane Costa.

Shirley Temple-type Girl
Ca. 1935-on. All-composition; of good quality.
16-18in (41-46cm) **$300-400**

Storybook or International Costume Doll
Ca. 1940. All-composition.
11in (28cm)
    Excellent quality **$125-150**
    Standard quality **$65-75**

Miscellaneous Specific Dolls
Carmen (Miranda), Eegee
    14in (36cm) **$200-225**
    20in (51cm) **$300-350**
Cat, Rabbit or Pig head, naked.
    10-11 in (25-28cm) **$300-400**
David, Bible Doll Co. of America.
    11in (28cm) boxed **$285**
Famlee, 1921. Boxed with six heads and
    six costumes **$750-850**
Grace C. Drayton,
    14in (36cm) **$325-375**
Hedwig/DiAngeli
    Elin, Hannah, Lydia, Suzanne, 14in (36cm) **$625-675**
Indian child, 1940s. 8in (21cm) boxed **$50-60**
Jackie Robinson, 13½in (34cm) **$700-800**
Jerry Mahoney, Juro Novelty, 24in (61cm) **$200-250**
Kewpie-type characters, 12in (31cm) **$50-60**
Little Miss Movie, Eegee, 27in (69cm) **$600-650**
Lone Ranger, with hat, holster and gun,
    16in (41cm) **$650-750**
Miss Curity, 18in (46cm) **$450-500**
Monica, 1941-195. Inset human hair,
    17-18in (43-46cm) **$450-500**
P.D. Smith, 22in (56cm) . . . .**$2,600°**
Paris Doll Co. Peggy, 28in (71cm) walker **$250-300**
Puzzy, 1948. H. of P., 15in (38cm) **$350-400**
Royal "Spirit of America," 15in (38cm) with
    original box and outfits **$300-350**
Santa Claus, 19in (48cm) **$225-275**

12in (31cm) unmarked costume doll, all original. *Kay Jensen Antique Dolls.*

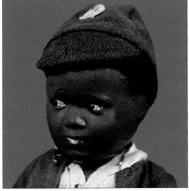

13½in (34cm) *Jackie Robinson*, all original. *Howard & Jan Foulke.*

11in (28cm) unmarked baby. *Kay Jensen Antique Dolls.*

Sizzy, 1948. H. of P.,14in (36cm) $250-300
Sterling Doll Co. Sports Dolls, 29in (74cm)
  all original $300-350
Trudy, 1946. Three faces, 14in (36cm), all original $175-225
Tonto, 16in (41cm) $650-750

Black Composition Dolls

Ca. 1930. Original or appropriate clothes; some have three yarn tufts of hair on either side and on top of the head; all in good condition.

"Topsy" Baby
  10-12in (25-31cm) $165-195
  16in (41cm) $250-275
Toddler, 15-16in (38-41cm) $250-275
Girl, 17in (43cm) $300-325
1910 character, 13½in (34cm) $200-250
Patsy-type, 13-14in (33-36cm) $225-250
Tony Sarg Mammy with Baby, 17in (43cm) $900
Alexander's Ragtime Kids, 13in (33cm), pair $950

Ming Ming Baby

1930. Quan-Quan Co., Los Angeles and San Francisco, California. Ca. 1930. All-composition baby; original Oriental costume of colorful taffeta with braid trim; feet painted black or white for shoes.
  10-12in (25-31cm) $200-300

13in (33cm) Eugenia Doll Co.
Juliette, all original.
Howard & Jan Foulke.

9½in (24cm) black composition child.
Kay Jensen Antique Dolls.

°Few price samples available.

14in (36cm) Kammer & Reinhardt
917 flapper girl with flirty eyes.
Howard & Jan Foulke.

Dora Petzoldt child, all original.
James D. Julia, Inc.

German

> **History** Various German firms as König & Wernicke, Kämmer & Reinhardt and others. Ca. 1920s on.

All-Composition Child Doll
Socket head with good wig, sleep (sometimes flirty) eyes, open mouth with teeth; jointed composition body; appropriate clothes; all in good condition; of excellent quality.
12-14in (31-36cm)	**$175-200**
18-20in (46-51cm)	**$250-300**
22in (56cm)	**$325-350**
Character face, 18-20in (46-51cm)	**$325-425**
Double-Face Googly, 14in (36cm)	**$425-475**
K & R 917, 13in (33cm)	**$750**

Black Composition Doll
All-composition; molded hair or wig, glass eyes (sometimes flirty); appropriate clothes; all in good condition.
11in (28cm)	**$275-300**
16-18in (41-46cm)	**$400-500**

Dora Petzoldt Child
1919-on. Molded composition (sometimes cloth) head, closed mouth, pensive character face, painted eyes, mohair wig; cloth body, sometimes with long arms and legs; original clothing; all in very good condition.
19-22in (48-56cm)	**$850-950**
Moderate wear, re-dressed	**$400-450**

Character Baby
Composition head with good wig, sleep eyes, open mouth with teeth; bent-limb composition baby body or hard-stuffed cloth body; appropriate clothes; all in good condition; of excellent quality.
All-composition baby	
16-18in (41-46cm)	**$200-225**
23in (58cm)	**$250-275**
Cloth body, 18-20in (46-51cm)	**$200-225**
All-composition toddler, 16-18in (41-46cm)	**$300-350**
K & R "Puz", 16-17in (41-43cm)	**$350-400**

Japanese

> **History** Unidentified Japanese Companies, 1920-1940.
> **Mark** "Japan" incised or stamped on back torso.

Japanese Composition Doll

All-composition with molded hair, painted features; original rayon panties with "Japan" stamp or naked; all in excellent condition.

Dionne Quintuplets
    Baby, 7in (18cm) $125-150
    Baby, 9in (23cm) $175-225
    Toddler, 7½in (19cm) $125-150
    9in (23cm) $175-225
Choir Boy, with book molded in hands,
    10in (25cm) $100-125
Toddler, 8in (20cm), all original $125-135
Shirley Temple, 7½in (19cm) $125-175

9in (23cm) *Dionne Quintuplet* baby.
Howard & Jan Foulke.

8in (20cm) *Ginger*, all original.
Mary Jane's Dolls.

Cosmopolitan

> **History** Cosmopolitan Doll & Toy Corp., Jackson Heights, NY, U.S.A.
> **Comment** Cosmopolitan dolls have come into their own after taking a back seat to *Ginny*. Quality is good, but not up to Vogue standards. The Disney costumes are the most sought-after.

Ginger

1954 on. All-hard plastic walker; sleep eyes; original clothes; excellent condition with good color and perfect hair.

    Unmarked, 8in (20cm) $150-175
        Mint-in-box $225-250
        Roundup, Mouseketeer or Davy Crockett $225-250
        Disneyland Costumes $300-350
        Girl Scout or Brownie $175-225
        Boxed outfits $40-60
        Vinyl head doll, all original $50-60
        Zippy $150

Ginger Baby
1955-on.
All vinyl, original clothes $65-75

Miss Ginger
1957 on. Vinyl head; hard plastic body with adult figure, high-heeled feet; original clothes; excellent condition. Mark "GINGER" on head.
10½in (27cm) $165-195
Dresses $20-30
Boxed Outfits $75-80
Gift Set with Trousseau, at auction $412

Little Miss Ginger
1958-on. Vinyl head; rigid vinyl body, adult figure with high-heeled feet: original clothes; excellent condition; eyes not askew. Mark "GINGER" on head.
8in (20cm) $75-85
Shoes $20
Dresses $20-30
Boxed Outfits $65-75

Deluxe Reading

> **Comment** This company, also known as DeLuxe Premium and Topper Toys, made an inexpensive line of dolls which were sold in supermarkets, hardware stores and drug stores. They were often large and eye-catching. Their most famous doll was *Dawn*, still vastly popular with collectors today.

Bride Dolls
1958. All-vinyl, fashion doll; complete original bride clothes.
24-29 in (61 -74cm) $100
Boxed with Accessories $200-300

Candy
1962. All-vinyl fashion doll. three extra costumes, hats and accessories; boxed.
20in (51cm) $150-200

Penny Brite
1963. All-vinyl child doll, with accessories and wardrobe sold separately.
8in (20cm) original dress $25-30
Boxed doll $50-60
Boxed outfit $30-45
Beauty Salon $45
Kitchen Set $45

Dawn
1969-on. Topper. All-vinyl play doll with accessories, wardrobe and friends.
6in (15cm) $30-40
Boxed doll $65-75
Boxed or packaged outfit $40-60
Angie, boxed $75-95
Kip Majorette $65-75
Gary $55-65

6in (15cm) *Dancing Dawn*, boxed.
Sidney Jeffrey Collection.

Suzy Homemaker
1964. Vinyl and hard plastic, jointed knees.
21in (53cm) $55-65

Suzy Smart
1962-on. Vinyl and hard plastic, bendable knees, talks.
24in (61cm)
    Doll only $95
    With desk, chair and all accessories $250

Snow White & Seven Dwarfs
1958-on. All vinyl.
22in (56cm) & 8in (20cm) $200

EFFanBEE

History EFFanBEE Doll Co., New York, NY, U.S.A. 1912-on.
Comment Comment Effanbee was a premiere producer of dolls through the 1940s, and still continues today as part of the Robert Tonner Doll Co. Effanbee produced high-quality dolls with lovely costumes. *Patsy* and her family was their first big success, followed by *Dy-Dee Baby*.

Mark Various, but nearly always marked "EFFanBEE" on torso or head, sometimes with doll's name. Wore a metal heart-shaped bracelet; later a gold paper heart label.

EFFanBEE
DURABLE
DOLLS

Original Metal Heart Necklace or Bracelet with chain $30-35
Metal Pinback Button $65-75

Composition Dolls
Early Characters
Composition character face, molded painted hair; cloth stuffed body; appropriate clothes; in good condition. Some marked "Deco."
12-16in (30-41cm)
    Baby Grumpy, 1912. Molds 172, 174 or 176 ....$275-325
    Miss Coquette, Naughty Marietta, 1912 ....$300-325
    Pouting Bess, 1915. 162 or 166 ....$275-325
    Billy Boy, 1915 ....$275-325
    Whistling Jim, 1916 ....$275-325
    Harmonica Joe, 1924 ....$325-375
    Katie Kroose, 1918 ....$300-350
    Buds, 1915-1918
        7in (18cm) $125-135
        Black $150-165
    Aunt Dinah, 1915. 16in (41cm) $500-600
    Johnny Tu-Face, 1912 ....$400-450
    Betty Bounce, 1913 ....$300-325
    Baby Huggins, 1915 ....$200
    Oriental Baby, 1914 ....$300-325

18in (46cm) *Katie Kroose*, all original.
Howard & Jan Foulke.

12in (31cm) *Pennsylvania Dutch Dolls*, Amish Man and Brethern Lady, all original. *Howard & Jan Foulke.*

Shoulder Head Dolls

Composition shoulder head; cloth torso, composition arms and legs; original clothes; all in good condition.

Baby Grumpy, 1925-1939:
  12in (31cm) white $225-250
  Black $275-325
Pennsylvania Dutch Dolls, 1936-1940. All original
  and excellent $175-225
Baby Dainty, 1912-1922. 15in (38cm) $200-225
Patsy, 1925. 15in (38cm) $250-275
Rosemary, 1925; Marilee, 1924; and other name dolls
  14in (36cm) $200-225
  17in (43cm) $275-300
  25in (64cm) $350-400
  30in (76cm) $500-600
Mary Ann, 1928
  19-20in (48-51cm) $275-325
  All-composition $350-400
Mary Lee, 1928
  16-17in (41-43cm) $250-275
  All-composition $300-325
Mae Starr, Phonograph doll, 1928. 30in (76cm) $650-750

Babies

Composition head, light crazing acceptable; perfect hair and good coloring; cloth body; original clothes; all in good condition.

Bubbles, 1924.
- 16-18in (41-46cm) $300-350
- 20-22in (51-56cm) $400-450
- 25-26in (63-66cm) $550-600
- 29in (51cm) re-dressed $325-350

Lovums, 1928.
- 16-18in (41-46cm) $275-325
- 22-24in (56-61cm) $400-450
- 28in (71cm) $500-550

Mickey, Baby Bright Eyes, Tommy Tucker, Katie, 1939-1949.
- 16-18in (41-46cm) $300-350
- 22-24in (56-61cm) $400-500

Sweetie Pie, 1942.
- 16-18in (41-46cm) $300-350
- 22-24in (56-61cm) $425-475

Baby Effanbee, 1925.
- 12in (31cm) $125-135

Lambkin, 1930s.
- 16in (41cm) $350-375
- Boxed, with pillow $650-700

Sugar Baby, 1936. Caracul wig,
- 16-18in (41-46cm) $300-350

Babyette, 1943. Eyes closed, boxed with
- pillow, 13in (33cm) $400-450

Pat-O-Pat, 1925. Clap hands.
- 13in (33cm) $150-165
- 15in (38cm) all cloth, boxed,
  - at auction $740

Mark EFFanBEE
BUBBLES
COPYR 1924
Made in U.S.A.

Mark EFFanBEE
LOVUMS
©
Pat No. 1,283,558

18in (46cm) *Baby Bright Eyes*, all original. *Howard & Jan Foulke.*

Patsy Family

Mark EFFanBEE
PATSY
DOLL

1928-on. All-composition; original or appropriate old clothes, may have some light crazing.

Wee Patsy
- 6in (15cm) $350-400
- Boxed $500
- Boxed with extra outfits $650
- Sewing set, boxed $650
- Storybook Doll, all original $600
- Black maid $1,000

Baby Tinyette, 7in (18cm) $275-300

Quintuplets, set of five, boxed,
- all original $1,500-2,000

Tinyette Toddler
- 8in (20cm) $275-300

Patsy Babyette
- 9in (23cm) $300-325
- Twins in layette set $750

Patsyette
- 9in (23cm) $275-300
- Brown $650
- Hawaiian $650

George and Martha Washington,
- pair $650
- Little Red Riding Hood $350

Patsy Baby
- 11in (28cm) $350-400
- Brown $650-750
- In three-tiered trunk
  - with accessories $1,300

9in (23cm) *Patsyette.*
Howard & Jan Foulke.

9in (23cm) *Patsy Babyette*
pair with layette.
Gloria & Mike Duddlesten.

16in (41cm) *Patsy Joan,*
all original.
Howard & Jan Foulke.

Patsy Jr., Patsy Kins, Patricia Kin
    11in (28cm) **\$350-400**
    Brown **\$800-900**
    Movie Anne Shirley, red wig **\$500-600**
Patsy
    14in (36cm) **\$400-450**
    1946, unmarked **\$300-350**
        Boxed **\$450-550**
    Black, at auction **\$2,860**
Patricia
    15in (38cm) **\$400-450**
    Movie Anne Shirley, red wig **\$500-600**
Patsy Joan
    16in (41cm) **\$400-450**
    1946 (different mold) **\$325-375**
        Brown **\$550**

11in (28cm) *Patsy Baby*, all original.
Howard & Jan Foulke.

14in (36cm) *Patsy.*
Howard & Jan Foulke.

Patsy Ann
    19in (48cm) \$400-450
    Brown \$1,250
    With trunk and vintage wardrobe \$650
Patsy Lou, 22in (56cm) \$400-450
Patsy Ruth, 26in (66cm) \$1,200-1,500
Patsy Mae, 30in (76cm) \$1,500-1,600
Skippy, 1929. 14in (36cm)
    Soldier, Sailor \$325-375
    Boy's Suit \$650
    Policeman \$800
    Cowboy \$1,000
    Re-dressed \$250-275
    Brown \$850

W.C. Fields

1930. Composition head, hands and feet; cloth body; original clothes.
    19in (48cm) at auction \$1,425

15in (38cm) *Dy-Dee Baby* with hard plastic head, caracul wig, rubber body. *Mary Jane's Dolls.*

26in (66cm) *Patsy Ruth*, all original. *Howard & Jan Foulke.*

Dy-Dee Baby

1933-on. Hard rubber head with applied rubber ears, soft rubber body; appropriate old clothes; good condition.

	Mark
	EFF-AN-BEE
	DY-DEE BABY
	US PAT.-1-857-485
	ENGLAND-880-060
	FRANCE-723-980
	GERMANY-585-647
	OTHER PAT PENDING

    9in (23cm) \$275-300
    11in (28cm) \$275-300
    13in (33cm) \$200-225
    15in (38cm) \$275-300
    20in (51cm) \$375-400
    24in (61cm) \$450-500
With box and layette
    13in (33cm) \$525
    15in (38cm) \$575
Carded five-piece nursery set with Dy-Dee booklet \$150
Dy-Dee pajamas \$32
Bottle, bubble pipe \$25
Book, Dy-Dee Dolls Days \$95
Hard plastic head with applied ears. soft rubber body; appropriate old clothes; good condition.
    11in (28cm) \$150-175
    15in (38cm) \$225-250
    20-21in (51-53cm) \$325-350

21in (53cm) *Little Lady*, all original.
Howard & Jan Foulke.

All-Composition Children

1933-on. Original clothes; all in very good condition; nice coloring and perfect hair.

Anne Shirley, 1935-1940; Little Lady, 1940-1949.
    14-15in (36-38cm) $125-150
    17-18in (43-46cm) $175-200
    21 in (53cm) $225-250
    27in (69cm) $300-350
    WAAC outfit, 14in (36cm) $450
    Little Eva, 15in (38cm) $1,400
    Honey, 1949. 21in (53cm) $350-400
American Children, 1936-1939. Dewees Cochran.
    Closed mouth, 19-21in (48-53cm) marked "American Children" head on "Anne Shirley" body.
        Peggy Lou and others, painted eyes $2,200
        Gloria Ann and others, sleep eyes $2,000
        17in (43cm) girl, sleep eyes $1,800
        17in (43cm) boy, unmarked, painted eyes $1,800

17in (43cm) *American Child* with sleep eyes.
Howard & Jan Foulke.

21in (53cm) *American Child* with painted eyes.
Howard & Jan Foulke.

Open mouth, unmarked.
Barbara Joan
15in (38cm) $700-750
Ice Queen (skater) $750
Barbara Ann,
17in (43cm) $750-800
Barbara Lou,
21in (53cm) $900-950
Suzette, 1939. Painted eyes,
11½in (29cm) $250-275
Suzanne, 1940. 14in (36cm) ...$250-275
Portrait Dolls, 1940. Ballerina, BoPeep,
Gibson Girl, bride, groom, dancing
couple, colonial.
11in (28cm) each $200-225
Candy Kid, 1946. Toddler, molded hair.
12in (31cm) $300-325
Boxed $500
Betty Brite, 1933. Caracul wig.
6½in (42cm) $250-275
Betty Bounce, 1933.
"Lovums" head, caracul wig,
19in (48cm) $300-325
Butin-Nose, 1939.
9in (23cm) $225-250
Oriental $500
Brother and Sister, 1943. Yarn hair,
16in (41cm) and 12in (31cm),
each $200-225

14in (36cm) *Suzanne*,
all original with magnet hands.
Howard & Jan Foulke.

Charlie McCarthy

1937. Strings at back of head to operate mouth; original clothes, all in very
good condition.
17-20in (43-51cm) $450-550
Mint-in-box with button $750

14in (36cm) *Charlie McCarthy*,
all original.
Mary Jane's Dolls.

14in (36cm) Historical Doll Replica
1816 Monroe Doctrine.
Rosemary Dent Collection.

Historical Dolls

1939. All-composition. Three each of 30 dolls portraying the history of American fashion, 1492-1939. "American Children" heads with elaborate

human hair wigs and painted eyes; elaborate original costumes using velvets, satins, silks and brocades; all in excellent condition.

21in (53cm)	**$1,500-1,800**
Historical Doll Replicas, 1939.	
14in (36cm)	**$400-500**
Boxed	**$650**

14in (36cm) Historical Doll Replica *1682 Quaker Colony.*
Rosemary Dent Collection.

Hard Plastic Dolls

Howdy Doody

1949-1950. Hard plastic or composition head and hands; molded hair, sleep eyes; cloth body; original clothes; all in excellent condition.

19-23in (48-58cm)	**$300-400**
Mint-in-box	**$525-575**

Noma, the Electronic Doll

1950. Battery operated talking mechanism.

28in (71cm)	**$325-375**
Boxed	**$500**

Honey

1949-1955. All-hard plastic; original clothes; all in excellent condition. Later dolls have walking mechanism. Mark **EFFanBEE**

14in (36cm)	**$250-275**
18in (46cm)	**$325-350**
24in (61cm)	**$400**
In Schiaparelli outfits, 18in (46cm)	**$500**
Prince Charming	**$500-600**
Cinderella	**$500-600**
Alice	**$400-450**
Tintair Honey	
14in (36cm)	**$400**
In original box with accessories	**$600-650**
18in (46cm)	**$550**

18in (46cm) *Honey.*
Kathy & Terri's Dolls.

Vinyl Dolls

All original and excellent condition.

Mickey, 1956.
    10-11in (25-28cm) $40-50
Champagne Lady, 1959.
    19in (48cm) $200-225
Fluffy*, 1957 on.
    8in (20cm) $15-20
    11in (28cm) $25-30
    Boxed Outfits $20-25
Patsy Ann, 1960 on.
    15in (38cm) $75-100
Suzette*, 1962. 15in (38cm) ... $65-75
Melodie, 1953-1956. Battery operated singing talking doll, all original.
    27in (69cm) $325-375
Mary Jane, 1959 on.
    32in (81cm) $225-275
    Nurse $275-325
Little Lady, 1958.
    19in (48cm) $125-150
Fashion Lady, Ca. 1958.
    19in (48cm) $200-225
Most Happy Family, 1958. (Mother, Sister, Brother, Baby), boxed.
    8-21in (20-53cm) $250-300
Alyssa, Ca. 1960.
    23in (58cm) $125-150

15in (38cm) *Patsy Ann Girl Scout*, all original. *Howard & Jan Foulke.*

Bud, Ca. 1960. 24in (61cm) $175-200
Happy Boy, 1961. 10½in (27cm) $40
Half Pint, 1966 on. 11 in (28cm) toddler $15-20
Boudoir Lady, 1961. 30in (76cm) boxed $200-225
Dy-Dee Darlin', 1971. 18in (46cm) $50-60
Baby Lisa, 1980, designed by Astry Campbell, in basket with accessories, 11in (28cm) $35-40
Disney Dolls
    1977. Alice in Wonderland, Cinderella, Snow White, Sleeping Beauty, 14in (36cm), each $30-35
    1985. Cinderella & Prince Charming Set, 12in (31cm) ... $50
Hagara, Jan; 1984. 15in (38cm).
    Christina with teddy $25-30
    Laurel $35-40
Hibel, Edna; 1984.
    Flower Girl of Brittany $25
    Contessa Isabella $25
Suzie Sunshine, 1961-1979. Designed by Eugenia Dukas,
    8in (46cm) boxed $25-30
Sugar Pie, 1962-1964. 18in (46cm) boxed $30-35
Effanbee Club Limited Edition Dolls
    1975 Precious Baby $75
    1976 Patsy $65-75
    1977 Dewees Cochran $20
    1978 Crowning Glory $15-25
    1979 Skippy $65-75
    1980 Susan B. Anthony $15-20
    1981 Girl with Watering Can (Renoir) $15-20
    1982 Princess Diana $25-30
    1983 Sherlock Holmes $15-25
    1984 Bubbles $15-25
    1985 Red Boy $15-25

*For Girl Scouts, see page 260.

```
1986 China Head ............................$10-15
```
Legend Series, mint-in-box.
```
   W.C. Fields, 1980 ................................$40
   John Wayne, (cowboy), 1981 ......................$50
   John Wayne, (cavalry), 1982 ......................$50
   Mae West, 1982 ..................................$25
   Groucho Marx, 1983 .............................$25
   Judy Garland, 1984 ..........................$90-100
   Lucille Ball, 1985 ................................$35
   Liberace, 1986 ..................................$50
   James Cagney, 1987 ...........................$40-45
   Humphrey Bogart, 1988 ...........................$50
   George Burns, 1996 ..............................$25
   Gracie Allen, 1996 ..............................$25
   Carol Channing, 1998 ........................$40-50
```
Presidents, mint-in-box.
```
   Abraham Lincoln, 1983 .......................$25-35
   George Washington, 1983 .....................$25-35
   Teddy Roosevelt, 1984 .......................$25-35
   Franklin D. Roosevelt, 1985 .................$25-35
   Andrew Jackson, 1989 ........................$25-35
```
Personalities, mint-in-box.
```
   Mark Twain, 1984 ...............................$20
   Louis Armstrong, 1984-1985 .....................$27
   Sir Winston Churchill, 1984 .....................$25
   Eleanor Roosevelt, 1985 ........................$20
   Babe Ruth, 1985 ................................$40
Pride of the South, 1981-1983. 13in (33cm) mint-in-box ..$15-20
Grande Dames, 1976-1983. 15in (38cm) mint-in-box .....$20-25
Gigi, 1979-1980. 11in (28cm) mint-in-box ..............$15-20
International & Storybook, 1976 on.
   11in (28cm) mint-in-box ......................$10-$15
Wizard of Oz, 1994. Six-doll set .......................$65
Mary Poppins, 1985 ..................................$20
Heidi, 1984 .........................................$20
Peter Pan, 1994. Three-doll set .....................$30-35
```

16½in (42cm) 1983 *Groucho Marx*, all original.
Kay Jensen Antique Dolls.

Freundlich

History Freundlich Novelty Corp., New York, NY, U.S.A. 1923-on.
Comment Freundlich made some very interesting dolls, but they were
inexpensive items of mediocre quality.

General Douglas MacArthur

Ca. 1942. All-composition portrait doll; molded hat, original
khaki uniform; all in good condition.

Mark Cardboard tag,
"General MacArthur"

18in (46cm) $400-450

Military Dolls

Ca. 1942. All-composition with molded hats,
original clothes; Soldier, Sailor, WAAC and
WAVE; all in good condition.
15in (38cm) $225-275

Baby Sandy

1939-1942. All-composition; appropriate
clothes; all in good condition.
8in (20cm) $200-225
12in (3 1cm) $250-300
14-15in (36-38cm) $350-400
20in (51cm) boxed $650-750
Baby Sandy Doll Button,
at auction $90

15in (38cm) *Sailor*, all original.
Howard & Jan Foulke.

20in (51cm) *Baby Sandy*,
all original.
Howard & Jan Foulke.

Other Composition Dolls

Orphan Annie & Sandy, 1936.
12in (30cm) pair
with tags $600-650
Three Little Pigs and Wolf,
boxed set $800-1,000
Red Ridinghood, Wolf & Grandmother
Set, 1934. All original.
9in (23cm) $800-900
Dionne Quints and Nurse Set,
all original $650-750
Dummy Dolls, 1938. Clown, Dan, Davy
Crockett and others,
14-18in (36-46cm) $65-75
Goo Goo Eva and others, 1937.
20in (51cm) $65-75
Goo Goo Topsy, 1937. Black,
20in (51cm) $85-95
Pig Baby, 9in (23cm) $400
Animal Head Dolls; Cat, Rabbit,
Pig or Wolf.
10-11in (25-28cm),
naked $300-400

G.I. Joe®

History Hasbro (Hassenfeld Brothers, Inc.), Pawtucket, RI. 1964-1979
Description 12in(31cm) hard plastic and vinyl figure, fully jointed.
Molded and painted hair and features with scar on right cheek. All G.I.
Joes have a scar on the right cheek except foreign Action Soldiers of the
World and the Nurse.
Comment All prices are for mint-in-box dolls with complete outfit and
accessories unless indicated otherwise. Flocked hair and beard must
be excellent. Figures less than perfect sell for 25 to 30 percent of
these prices.
Mark **G.I. Joe //Copyright 1964//By Hasbro//Patent Pending//
Made in U.S.A.**

12in (31cm) *Action Soldier,* boxed.   12in (31cm) *Black Action Soldier.*
Howard & Jan Foulke.   Doodlebug Dolls.

G.I. Joe Action Figures
1964.

Action Soldier, painted hair	**$300-350**
Naked doll	**$75**
Action Sailor, painted hair	**$550-650**
Action Marine	**$300-350**
Action Pilot	**$350-450**
Action Soldier, black, painted hair	**$1,500**
Naked doll	**$450**

Action Soldiers of the World
1966, painted hair, no scar.

German Storm Trooper	**$1,250**
Dressed doll only, no accessories	**$225-250**
Russian Infantryman	**$1,200**
Dressed doll only, no accessories	**$200-225**
British Commando	**$1,200**
Dressed doll only, no accessories	**$200-225**

12in (31cm) *Action Soldier of the World, French Resistance Fighter. Doodlebug Dolls.*

French Resistance Fighter $1,250
Dressed doll only,
 no accessories $200-225
Australian Jungle Fighter $1,000
Dressed doll only,
 no accessories $200-225
Japanese Imperial Soldier $1,600
Dressed doll only,
 no accessories $250-275

Nurse Action Girl
1967.
Boxed $3,000-4,000
Dressed doll only $1,625
Naked doll $400-500

Talking G.I. Joe
1967.
Action Soldier $300-400
Action Sailor $600-700
Action Marine $600-700
Action Pilot $800-1,000

Man of Action
1970-1975.
Lifelike hair $200-250
With Kung-Fu Grip $225
Talking, lifelike hair $200-250

Adventurers
1975, lifelike hair and beard.
Land $175-190
Air $240-265
Sea $225-250
Astronaut, talking $400-450
 Dressed doll only, no accessories $225-250
Black $300
Naked doll $60

Accessories
Footlocker with accessories $400
Footlocker, green, empty $40
Space Capsule, boxed $400-450
Desert Patrol Jeep, boxed $1,500
Motorcycle, boxed $225-250

Outfits in Unopened Packages
#5300 State Trooper, at auction $1,500
#7532 Green Beret Special Forces $450-500
#7521 Military Police, brown $350-400
#7531 Ski Patrol $250-300
#7620 Deep Sea Diver $250-300
#7612 Shore Patrol, at auction $1,000
#7710 Marine Dress Parade, at auction $1,700
#7807 Scramble Set, at auction $1,800
Smoke Jumper $225
Frogman $140

Ginny–Type Dolls*

Comment The great success of Vogue's *Ginny* spurred the creation of lots of knock-offs. Of these inexpensive copies, the Virga dolls seem to be the nicest. The *Lolly-Pop* dolls with the colored hair are the most popular. Prices are for dolls in excellent overall condition with perfect hair, pretty coloring and original outfits. All dolls are hard plastic and about 7-8in (18-20cm) tall. Ca. 1950-1960.

A & H Doll Mfg. Corp.
Gigi $45-50
    Boxed $100-125
    Outfits $10-15
    Boxed outfits $25-30
Julie $35-40

8in (20cm) Fortune Doll Co. *Pam* dolls.
Kiefer Collection.

Doll Bodies, Inc., Mary Lu $40-50
Fortune Doll Co.
    Pam $65-75
        Outfits $10-15
        Boxed Outfits $25-30
    Pam Ballerina, pointed toes $85-90
    Ninette $40-50
Hollywood Doll Mfg. Co.
    Girl $40-45
Miss Rosebud, England $45-55
Stashin Doll Co., Andrea, molded white strap shoes $50-60
Unidentified, black $100-125
Virga (Beehler Arts), molded white strap shoes.
    Lolly-Pop
        Colored hair $100-110
        Boxed $175-200
    Lucy $90-110
    Play-Mates $90-110
        Boxed $150-175
    Schiaparelli (GoGo) $150-175
    Twinkle Ballerina, boxed $175-200

*See separate entries for Cosmopolitan Ginger, Vogue Ginny, Nancy Ann Storybook Muffie and Alexander Wendy.

Girl Scout

Comment With millions and millions of members over the years, nearly every little girl in America, it's no wonder that Girl Scout dolls are popular collectibles. Prices are for dolls in excellent overall condition with perfect hair and original clothes, including hat, scarf, belt, shoes and socks.

Georgene Novelties, Inc.
1930s and 1940s. All cloth.
Girl Scouts and Brownies
Flat face, 15in (38cm) $350-400
Molded cloth face, 13in (33cm) $225-250
Molded plastic face, 13in (33cm) $100-125

Terri Lee Sales Corp.
Ca. 1950. Hard plastic.
Girl Scouts and Brownies
Terri Lee
16in (41cm) $400
Dress and hat only $125-135
Tiny Terri Lee,
10in (25cm) $175-200
Ginger
8in (20cm) $175-200
Outfit only $75-85

Vogue Dolls, Inc.
Ca. 1956. Hard plastic.
Girl Scouts and Brownies
Ginny, painted eyelash walker
8in (20cm) $275-325
Complete outfit only $100-125
80th Anniversary, 8in (20cm)
Boxed $75-100
Black, boxed $125

Uneeda Doll Co.
Ca. 1960. Vinyl head/hard plastic body, "U" on head.
Janie, 8in (20cm) $125-150
Carry Case $100

Effanbee Doll Co.
Ca. 1960 through 1970s. Vinyl.
Patsy Ann, 15in (38cm): Girl Scout $250-350
Brownie $250-350
Blue Bird, Camp Fire ....$550°
Suzette, 15in (38cm): Girl Scout $300-400
Brownie $300-400
Blue Bird, Camp Fire ....$550°
Fluffy, 8in (20cm): Girl Scout, Brownie $50-60
Boxed $100-125
Camp Fire, Blue Bird $200-225
Camp outfit or bathing suit sold separately $50-75
Fluffy, 11in (28cm): Girl Scout, Brownie $60-65
Camp Fire, Blue Bird $55-65
2002, 11in (28cm), boxed $55-65

°Few price samples available.

Hallmark
1979. All cloth.
Juliette Low, founder of the Girl Scouts,
7in (18cm) $30

Jesco, Inc.
Ca. 1985. Vinyl.
Katie, 9in (23cm) $75-85

Madame Alexander
1992. Hard plastic.
8in (20cm) (blonde harder to find) $75-95

Pleasant Co.
1999.
American Girl of Today
Outfit only $50-60
Brownie outfit only $50-60

Avon, Tender Memories
Bisque.
14in (36cm) boxed $20-25

15in (38cm) Georgene Novelties *Girl Scout*, all original.
Howard & Jan Foulke.

Godey's Little Lady Dolls

History Ruth Gibbs, Flemington, NJ, U.S.A. 1946. Designed by Herbert Johnson.

Comment Ruth Gibbs was inspired by the old *Godey's Lady's Book* magazine from the mid-19th Century for the costuming of her old-fashioned dolls.

Mark Paper label inside skirt "Godey's Little Lady Dolls;" "R.G." incised on back plate.

Ruth Gibbs Doll

Pink or white china head; cloth body with china limbs and painted slippers; original clothes; excellent condition.

7in (18cm)	$70-80
Boxed	$125-135
Little Women, set of five	$850
Trousseau, boxed set (four outfits)	$575
Fairy Tale, boxed set	$575
Williamsburg, boxed set (two outfits)	$500
Black, boxed	$300-350°
10in (25cm) skin wig	$250-295
Boxed	$350-395
12in (31cm)	$125-135
Boxed	$185-195

12in (31cm) Lady Doll exclusive for Fox Department Store. *Howard & Jan Foulke.*

7in (18cm) *Patty*, all original. *Howard & Jan Foulke.*

°Few price samples available.

Hard Plastic Dolls

> **Comment** Hard plastic dolls came on the scene after World War II in the late 1940s. By 1950, they had replaced composition dolls. Plastic was perfect for dolls. It didn't break, and it had a lovely luminescent, natural looking finish.

14in (36cm) unmarked child, all original.
Kathy & Terri's Dolls.

Marked "Made in U.S.A." or with various letters.

Ca. 1950s. All-hard plastic; sleep eyes, perfect wig; original clothes; all in excellent condition with very good coloring.

14in (36cm) $165-195
18in (46cm) $225-250
24in (61cm) $275-300

Miscellaneous Specific Dolls

All original clothes including underwear, shoes and socks; excellent condition with lovely complexion and perfect hair; unmarked except as indicated.

Answer Doll, 1951. Block Doll Corp., toddler with yes/no button, 10in (25cm) $75-85

Baby Walker, 1950s. Block Doll Corp., toddler, 10in (25cm) $65

Artisan Doll Co., 1951-1955.

Raving Beauty, 1951. Open mouth, tag on some clothing. "Original Michelle//California;" separate clothing was available.
19-20in (48-51cm) . . .$250-300

Miss Gadabout, 1953. Open mouth walker, marked with "Heady-Turny" label.
20in (51cm) $175-200

Duchess Doll Corp., 1950s. Slender storybook and fashion dolls in various costumes, marked on back.
7-8in (18-20cm) $10-12
Boxed $15-20

Walt Disney's Peter Pan and Tinker Bell
Each $20-25
Boxed Set $95-100

10in (25cm) baby boy.
Kathy & Terri's Dolls.

Eugenia Doll Co.
Juliette, 1953. 21in (53cm) $450
Personality Pla-Mate, 1949.
16-18in (41-46cm) $350-400

Gigi Perreau, 1952. Goldberger Doll Mfg. Co. Portrait doll of the movie star with smiling mouth and teeth, Dynel hair, vinyl head, excellent face color. Hard plastic body,
20in (51cm) . . . .$600 up°

Haleoke, 1950s. Roberta Doll Co., 18in (46cm), with accessories and additional clothing $350-450

Heddi Stroller, 1952. Belle Doll & Toy Corp., walker, Saran braids,
20in (51cm) $140-150

°Few price samples available.

263

Hollywood Doll Mfg. Co., 1947 on. Storybook and fashion dolls in various costumes; marked on back.

4½-5½in (12-14cm) $15-20

     Boxed $30-40

Ballerina, 5in (12cm) boxed $65-75

Rock-a-Bye Baby, boxed $90-100

LuAnn Simms, 1953. Roberta, Horsman & Valentine. Mark: ."Made in U.S.A." or "180." walker. 16in (41cm) $350-400

Marion, 1949. Monica Studios, rooted hair, sleep eyes,

18in (46cm) ....$400°

Mary Jane, 1955. G.H.&E. Freydherg, Inc. Terri Lee-type doll,

17in (43cm) $200-225

Rita, 1952. Paris Doll Co., walker. 27-29in (69-74cm) ...$200-250

Roxanne, Beat the Clock, 16in (41cm) boxed $400-450

Susan Stroller, 1953. Goldberger Doll Mfg. Co.. walker. Saran hair; Mark: "Eegee." 23in (58cm) $150-165

Wanda the Walking Wonder, 1950s. Advance Doll Co.,

17-19in (43-48cm) $125-175

17in (43cm) Ottolini girl with flirty eyes, all original. *Howard & Jan Foulke.*

16in (41cm) *LuAnn Simms,* Roberta Doll Co., all original. *Rosemary Kanizer.*

Italian Hard Plastic

Ca. 1950-on. Bonomi, Ottolini, Ratti, Furga, Magda and others. Heavy fine quality hard plastic; human hair wig, sleep eyes, sometimes flirty; original clothes; all in excellent condition. Mark Usually on head.

12in (31cm) $100-110

15-17in (38-43cm) $125-150

19-21in (48-53cm) $175-225

25in (64cm) fashion $275

English Black Hard Plastic Characters

1950s. Pedigree and others. Curly black wig, sometimes over molded hair.

14-16in (36-41cm) $150-175

21in (53cm) $225-275

°Few price samples available.

Hasbro

Jr. Miss Sewing Kit
1957.
7½in (19cm) doll $65-75

Little Miss No Name
1965. Large round eyes, molded tear, forlorn expression; original ragged clothes; all in excellent condition, with tear.
15in (38cm) $150-175
Boxed $300-350

Dolly Darlings
1965. All-vinyl characters.
4in (10cm) complete, no box $10-20
Shary, boxed with accessories $50
John, boxed with accessories $50

Peteena Poodle
1966. Poodle dog head, rooted poodle-like hair, real eyelashes; fashion doll body, retractable tail.
9in (23cm) in original bikini $75-100
Boxed, perfect condition $165
Boxed outfits $75-125

Aimee
1972.
All-vinyl; original clothing; all in excellent condition $15-20

Charlie's Angels
1977.
8½in (21cm)
Boxed $25-30
Gift set, boxed $125

Jem Series
1986-1987. 12½in (32cm) all-vinyl fashion dolls; original clothing; all in excellent condition; in original box. Deduct one-third for an out-of-box doll.
Jem, Jerrica $45-50
Kimber $45-50
Aja $50-55
Synergy $50-55
Roxy $60-65
Pizazz $65-75
Stormer $65-75
Rio $30-35
Boxed outfits $35-55
Rock Backstager Play Set $55-65
Rolls Royce Play Set $70

G.I. Joe
See page 257.

Raggedy Ann
See page 158.

Himstedt, Annette

History 1986 on. Hard vinyl and cloth. Designed by Annette Himstedt.
Comment Since 1986 when her Barefoot Children were introduced, Annette Himstedt has been a leader in the artist doll field. Her dolls are portraits of real children, appropriately sized so that they can wear actual child clothes, an aspect that collectors love. Her collections of the last three or four years have really energized her line, as she continues her concept of presenting children of the world.
Mark Wrist tag with doll's name; cloth signature label on clothes; signature on lower back plate and on back of doll's head under wig.

Marked Himstedt Doll

Hard vinyl head swivels on long shoulder plate, cloth lower torso, vinyl arms and curved legs; inset eyes with real eyelashes, painted feathered eyebrows, molded upper eyelids, open nose, human hair wig; original cotton clothing, bare feet; all in excellent condition with original box and certificate.

1986 Barefoot Children, 26in (66cm).
    Ellen, Kathe, Paula, Fatou, Lisa, Bastian, each **$175-225**
1987 American Heartland Dolls, 19-20in (48-51cm).
    Timi **and** Toni, each **$125-150**
1988 The World Children Collection, 31in (79cm).
    Kasimir **$325**
    Malin **$350**
    Michiko **$200-250**
    Friederike **$450-550**
    Makimura **$280-380**
1989 Reflections of Youth, 26in (66cm).
    Adrienne, Janka, Ayoka, Kai, each **$175-200**
1990
    Fiene, Taki **(baby)**, Annchen **(baby)**, each **$300-350**
1991 Faces of Friendship
    Liliane **$300-350**
    Neblina **$200-250**
    Tinka **$225-275**
    Shireem **$125-175**
1993 Images of Childhood
    Kima, Lona, Tara, Jule, each **$200-250**

36in (91cm) Mithi, Asian girl, limited edition of 277, from *The 2005 1st World's Children Summit*, all original. *Connie Lowe Collection.*

36in (91cm) Marthy, English girl, limited edition of 277, from *The 2005 1st World's Children Summit*, all original. *Connie Lowe Collection.*

1994
Panchita, Pancho, Melvin, Elke, each $150-200
1999
Mia Yin $300-350
Mirte & Little Mirte (club doll) $250-300
2002 Puppen Kinder Collection
Annika $700-800
Midori $800-900
Krinchen $700-750
2003 Kinder Collection
Lisi, Kristina, Luis, Kuki, each $300-350
Tammi, Theresa, Elsa , each $400-425
Hanni $475
2004 Kinder Collection
Ginni, Silvi, Elina, Pauline, each $325-375
Inga, Julika, Ineke, Lilli, Ella, each $400-450
2005 1st World's Children's Summit
Mithi $1,500-1,700
Bunda $850
Marthy $850-900

Horsman

History E.I. Horsman Co., New York, NY, U.S.A. Manufacturer; also distributor of French and German dolls. 1878-on.
Comment Horsman is one of the oldest distributors and manufacturers of dolls in the U.S. They spurred the character dolls movement here with the introduction of Baby Bumps and their "Can't Break 'Em" composition dolls.

Mark

Early Composition Dolls
Original or appropriate old clothes; all in good condition.
Billiken, 1909. Composition head, velvet or plush body.
MARK: Cloth label. 12in (31cm) $200-250
"Can't Break 'Em" Characters, Ca. 1911. Character head; hard stuffed cloth body. MARK: "E.I.H. 1911."
11-13in (28-33cm) $100-125
Polly Pru, 13in (33cm) . . . .$350-375°
Little Mary Mix-Up, 15in (31cm) . . . .$350-375°
Cotton Joe, black, 13in (33cm) $325-375
Uncle Sam's Kid, 1917. Composition/cloth; all original.
16in (41cm) $300-350
Baby Bumps $200
Black $250
Puppy & Pussy Pippin, 1911. Grace G. Drayton. Plush body; composition head; cloth label. 8in (20cm) sitting.
Puppy Pippin $300-325
Pussy Pippin $400-450
Peek-a-Boo, 1913-1915. Grace G. Drayton. Composition head, arms, legs and lower torso, cloth upper torso.
MARK: Cloth label on outfit. 7½in (19cm) $100-125
Baby Butterfly, 1911-1913. Oriental doll; composition head; cloth body; original costume. 13in (33cm) . . . .$500°
Peterkin, 1914-1930. All-composition; various boy and girl clothing or simply a large bow. 11in (28cm) $275-300

°Few price samples available.

Gene Carr Characters, 1916. Composition/cloth. Snowball (black boy), Mike and Jane (eyes open), Blink and Skinney (eyes closed). Designed by Bernard Lipfert from Gene Carr's cartoon characters.

    13-14in (33-36cm) $200-250
    Snowball $350-400

Jackie Coogan, 1921. Composition/cloth, appropriate old clothes.

    14in (36cm) $550-650

HEbee-SHEbee, 1925. All-composition; blue shoes indicate a HEbee; pink ones a SHEbee.

    11in (28cm) $425-475
    Fair condition, some peeling $200-225
    Mint, all original $700-800
    All-Bisque ....See page 28.

Ella Cinders, 1925. Composition/cloth. From the comic strip by Bill Conselman and Charlie Plumb for Metropolitan Newspaper Service. MARK: "1925©MNS." 18in (46cm) $650-750

Baby Dimples, 1928. Composition/cloth, appropriate old clothes. MARK: "© E.I.H. CO. INC."

    16-18in (41-46cm) $150-175
    22-24in (56-61cm) $200-225

Mama Doll, Late 1920s-on. Composition/cloth. MARK: "HORSMAN" or "E.I.H. CO. INC."

    Babies, including Brother and Sister
        12-14in (31-36cm) $100-125
        18-20in (46-51cm) $150-175
    Girls, including Rosebud and Peggy Ann
        14-16in (36-41cm) $175-200
        22-24in (56-61cm) $250-300

19in (48cm) mama doll, all original.
Kathy & Terri's Dolls.

6in (9cm) all-bisque *Tynie Baby.*
Howard & Jan Foulke.

Tynie Baby, 1924. Slightly frowning face; cloth/composition; appropriate clothes. Designed by Bernard Lipfert.

    Bisque head, 14-16in (36-41cm) ...$650-750
    Composition head
        15in (38cm) long $175-225
        19-21in (48-53cm) $275-300
    All-bisque, swivel neck, glass eyes, wigged or molded hair.
        6in (15cm) $1,500-1,650
        8-10in (20-25cm) $2,200-2,500
    Vinyl, 1950. 15in (38cm), boxed $70-80

Mark
"© 1924 E.I. Horsman Inc. Made in Germany"

°Few price samples available.

All-Composition Dolls

1930s and 1940s. Original clothes, all in very good condition; may have "Gold Medal Doll" tag. Mark "HORSMAN"

Slender Girl
  13-14in (33-36cm) $125-150
  16-18in (41-46cm) $175-200
Chubby toddler, 16-18in (41-46cm) $200-225
Jo-Jo, 1937. 12in (31cm) $125-150
Jeanie, 1937. 14in (36cm) $125-150
Naughty Sue, 1937. 16in (41cm) $300-325
Roberta, 1937.
  16in (41cm) $300-325
Bright Star, 1937
  13in (33cm) $250-300
  17-20in (43-51cm) $450-550
Sweetheart, 1938. Teenager
  21in (53cm) ....$600°
  24in (61cm) ....$700°
  28in (71cm) ....$850°

20in (51cm) *Nan*, all original.
Howard & Jan Foulke.

15in (38cm) *Cindy* bride with lady body, all original.
Kathy & Terri's Dolls.

All-Hard Plastic Dolls

1950s. Original clothing, perfect hair, good coloring; all in excellent condition. Mark "160 or ["170" or "180"] Made in U.S.A."
  Cindy, 1950-1955. Open mouth with teeth and tongue, synthetic wig; walker body. 16-18in (41-46cm) $175-200
  LuAnn Simms, Ca. 1953. Long brunette wig with front and side hair pulled to back, blue eyes; mold number 180 or 170.
    18in (46cm) $350-400

Vinyl Dolls

Original clothing; all in excellent condition with perfect hair and excellent color.
  Rene Ballerina, 1957. Fully-jointed with high-heeled feet, rooted hair. MARK: "82//HORSMAN." 19in (48cm) $75-100
  Cindy, 1957. Fashion Doll, 19in (21cm) $100-125
  Cindy Strutter, child, 23in (58cm) boxed $90-110
  Tweedie, 1958. Slender limbs, short hair. MARK: "38 Horsman."
    14½in (37cm) $30-50
    Boxed $125

°Few price samples available.

Couturier Doll, 1958. Fashion doll with stuffed vinyl body,
20in (51cm) boxed $125-150
Jackie Kennedy, 1961. Rooted black hair, blue sleep eyes; pearl
jewelry. MARK: "HORSMAN//19 © 61//JK25."
25in (64cm) $165-185
Poor Pitiful Pearl, 1963. Cartoon character. MARK: "1963//Wm
Steig//Horsman"
11-12in (28-31cm) $100-115
Boxed $175-200
16in (41cm) $165
Boxed $250-275
Hansel & Gretel, 1963. Character faces. MARK: "Michael
Meyerberg, Inc."
15in (38cm) $125-150
Walt Disney's Cinderella Set, 1965. Extra head and costume for
"poor' doll. MARK: "H"
11½in (29cm), boxed $100-125
Mary Poppins, 1964. Several different costumes:
12in (31cm) $40
Boxed Wardrobe Set $125-175
Boxed set with 7in (18cm) Jane and Michael $150-165
36in (91cm) $300-350
Flying Nun, 1965.
12in (31cm) $95
Boxed $175-185
Patty Duke, 1965. Gray flannel pants, red sweater.
12in (31cm) $75-85
Boxed $150-175
Elizabeth Taylor, 1976. 11½in (29cm) $45-55
Angie Dickinson, Police Woman, 1970s.
9in (23cm) boxed $55-65
Princess Peggy, 1959. 36in (91cm) $200-225
Ruthie, 1962. 28in (71cm) $150-175

11in (28cm) *Poor Pitiful Pearl*, boxed.
Jean Grout.

7in (18cm) *Jane and Michael*, boxed.
Mary Jane's Dolls.

14in (36cm) Mary Hoyer ballerina,
all original.
Kathy & Terri's Dolls.

18in (46cm) Mary Hoyer *Gigi,*
all original.
Sidney Jeffrey Collection.

Mary Hoyer

History The Mary Hoyer Doll Mfg. Co., Reading, PA, U.S.A. Ca. 1925-on.
Comment Most Mary Hoyer dolls were sold nude with patterns for cro-
cheting or knitting clothing, but labeled factory-made clothing, as well
as accessories like shoes, hats, parasols and skis were also available.
It was primarily a mail-order company, but had a store on the board-
walk in Ocean City, NJ.
Mark Embossed on torso, "The Mary Hoyer Doll" or in a circle, "ORIGINAL
Mary Hoyer Doll"

Marked Mary Hoyer

Original tagged factory clothes or garments made at home from Mary Hoyer
patterns; all in excellent condition.

Composition, 14in (36cm)	**$300-400**
Hard plastic	
14in (36cm)	
In knit outfit	**$325-375**
In tagged Hoyer outfit	**$375-425**
In tagged gown	**$400-500**
14in (36cm) boy with caracul wig	**$400-500**
18in (46cm), Gigi	
In tagged outfits	**$850-1,250**
Boxed	**$1,250-1,650**
Vinyl Play doll, 1990s, 14in (36cm)	**$60-80**
Mary's Dollies **booklets, each**	**$5-10**
McCalls pattern, uncut	**$30-40**

Ideal

History Ideal Novelty & Toy Co., Brooklyn, NY, U.S.A. 1907-on.
Comment Ideal produced a wide variety of dolls of excellent quality over a period of 80 years. Many were sold by catalog companies. Reasonable prices and appealing faces made the dolls extremely popular when they were new. Ideal dolls are equally sought after by collectors today.

Mark

Composition Dolls

Early Composition Dolls

1910-1929. Composition heads; cloth bodies, composition lower arms; some with molded composition shoes; original or appropriate old clothes; all in good condition; some wear acceptable.

Happy Hooligan, 1910. Comic character, 21in (53cm) . . . . . .$500°
Snookums, 1910. Plush body, 14in (36cm) $500-600
Ty Cobb, 1911. Baseball outfit . . . .$500°
**Naughty Marietta (Coquette), 1912. Molded hair with
  ribbon band** $300-325
Captain Jenks, 1912. Khaki uniform $275-325
**Uneeda Kid, 1914-1919. Molded black boots; original bloomer suit,
  yellow slicker and rain hat, carrying a box of Uneeda Biscuits,
  showing some wear. 16in (41cm)** $300-350
**Bronco Bill, 1915. Cowboy outfit with
  gun and holster** $275-325
**ZuZu Kid, 1916-1917. Original clown suit, National Biscuit Co.,
  16in (41cm)** $275-325
**Liberty Boy, 1917. Molded clothes, cloth hat, some wear,
  12in (31cm)** $125-175
Soozie Smiles, 1923. Two faces, crying and smiling $400-425
**Flossie Flirt, 1924-1931. Eyes move side to side.
  14in (36cm)** $175-225
  20in (51cm) $250-300
Buster Brown, 1929. Red suit with hat, 17in (43cm) $325-375
Peter Pan, 1929. Original felt suit and hat, 18in (46cm).
  Excellent with label $550-600
  Good, some wear $300-400
Early Children, 12-15in (31-38cm) $150-175
**Early Babies, Baby Mine, Prize Baby and others,
  15-16in (38-41cm)** $150-175

Composition Babies

1930s and 1940s. Composition heads and lower limbs, cloth bodies, original or appropriate clothes; all in good condition with nice coloring, light crazing acceptable.

**Tickletoes, 1930-1947, soft rubber arms and legs, flirty eyes,
  16in (41cm)** $200-250
**Baby Smiles, 1931. Toddler with rubber arms,
  17in (43cm)** $200-225
**Snoozie, 1933. Designed by Bernard Lipfert. Yawning mouth. may
  have rubber arms. MARK: "© By B. LIPFERT,"
  16-20in (41-51cm)** $400-450
Cuddles, 1933. Rubber limbs. 22in (56cm) $250-300
Bathrobe Baby, 1933. Rubber body, 12in (31cm) $100-125

°Few price samples available.

18in (46cm) *Peter Pan*,
all original.
George & Kathleen Bassett.

16in (41cm) *Betsy Wetsy* with
hard plastic head and vinyl
body, boxed.
Kathy & Terri's Dolls.

Princess Beatrix, 1938. Magic eyes.

    16in (41cm) $225-275

    22in (56cm) $350

Betsy Wetsy, 1937-on. Drink-and-wet baby. HEAD MARK: "IDEAL:"

    Composition or hard rubber head/rubber body,

        14-16in (36-41cm) $275-300

    Hard plastic head/rubber body,

        12-14in (31-36cm) $225-250

    Hard plastic head/vinyl body

        14-16in (36-41cm) $210-235

        15in (38cm) original box and layette, mint $400-450

    All-vinyl

        8in (20cm) boxed $85

        12in (31cm) $75-100

Composition Children

1935-1947. All-composition in excellent condition with perfect hair and good cheek color; original clothes.

    Shirley Temple, 1935 . . . . See page 296.

    Snow White, 1937. Black wig, gown with rayon skirt showing figures of seven dwarfs. TORSO MARK: "SHIRLEY TEMPLE;" DRESS TAG: "An Ideal Doll."

        13in (33cm) $500-550

        18in (46cm) $550-600

        All-cloth, 16in (41cm) . .$525-575

Deanna Durbin, 1938. Smiling mouth with teeth, metal button with picture. HEAD MARK: "Deanna Durbin Ideal Doll, USA."

    14in (36cm) $550-650

    20-21in (51-53cm) . .$900-1,000

    24in (61cm) $1,300-1,400

24in (61cm) *Deanna Durbin.*
Howard & Jan Foulke.

Judy Garland as Dorothy from The Wizard of Oz, 1939. HEAD MARK: "IDEAL DOLL MADE IN USA:"
  16in (41cm) ....$1,500-$1,650
  Replaced clothes ....$1,000-$1,100
Scarecrow from The Wizard of Oz, 1939. All cloth,
  17in (43cm) $1,400
Betty Jane, Little Princess, Pigtail Sally, Ginger, Cinderella, 1935-1947.
  14in (36cm) $200-250
  18in (46cm) $275-325
Soldier, Ca. 1942. Character face; army uniform with jacket and hat, 13in (33cm) $275-325
Miss Curity, Ca. 1945. Nurse uniform, 14in (36cm) $325-375
Flexy Dolls, 1938 on. Wire mesh torso, flexible metal cable arms and legs, 12in (31cm).
  Baby Snooks (Fanny Brice) $200-225
  Mortimer Snerd $200-225
  Soldier $100-125
  Children $100-125
Judy Garland from *Strike up the Band*, 1940. HEAD MARK: "MADE IN U.S.A." BODY MARK: "IDEAL DOLL [backwards 21]"
  21in (53cm) $1,000-1,200

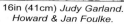

16in (41cm) *Judy Garland.*
Howard & Jan Foulke.

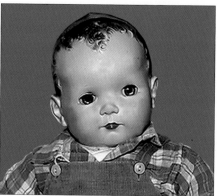

28in (71cm) *Brother Coos.*
Mary Jane's Dolls.

Composition and Wood Segmented Characters

1940. Label on front torso.
  Pinocchio
    10½in (27cm) $475-525
    20in (51cm) $800-900
  King Little, 14in (36cm) $275-325
  Jiminy Cricket, 9in (23cm) $450-500
  Gabby, 11in (28cm) $375-425
  Ferdinand the Bull, 9in (23cm) $175-225
  Superman, 13in (33cm), at auction $880

Magic Skin Dolls

1940-on. Stuffed latex rubber body in very good condition (subject to easy deterioration); original clothes; all in excellent condition.
HEAD MARK: "IDEAL"
  Magic Skin Baby, 1940. 14-15in (36-38cm) $85-95
  Plassie, 1940. 16in (41cm) $85-95
    Toddler, all-hard plastic. 14in (36cm) $125-150

Sparkle Plenty, 1947. 15in (38cm) baby $200-225
Joan Palooka, 1953. 14in (36cm) $125-135
Baby Coos, 1948-1952. Sounds like a baby when squeezed,
   14-16in (36-41cm) $110-135
Brother or Sister Coos, 25-30in (64-76cm),
   dressed like toddlers $200-300

Hard Plastic Dolls

Howdy Doody
1947-1955. Hard plastic head, movable jaw; stuffed body; all original.
   21in (53cm) $300-325
   25in (64cm) $400-450

Toni Family
1948-on. Hard plastic "Toni" home permanent doll and derivatives; nylon wig,
perfect hair, pretty cheek color; original clothes; all in excellent condition.
HEAD MARK: "IDEAL DOLL; **BODY MARK:** "IDEAL DOLL P-90 Made in USA"
   Toni
      14-16in (36-41cm)
         P-90 & P-91 . . . .$225-300
         Naked, untidy hair $40-60
         Mint-in-box $400-500
         19-21in (48-53cm) P-92 & P-93 . . . .$350-450
         Mint-in-box $900-1,100
         22½in (57cm) P-94 . . . .$950
         Playwave Box and contents $75
         Tagged dress $50-100
         Shoes $45-60

16in (41cm) *Toni Walker.*
Howard & Jan Foulke.

19in (48cm) *Toni P-92.*
Kathy & Terri's Dolls.

Mary Hartline
- **14in (36cm)** $275-325
- **22½in (57cm)** $1,100-1,200

Harriet Hubbard Ayer, vinyl head makeup doll.
- **14in (36cm)** $200-225
- **Mint-in box with accessories** $400-450
- **21in (53cm)** $400-450

Miss Curity, Nurse
- **14in (36cm)** $275-325
- **Mint-in-box with accessories** $650

Sara Ann, Saran hair,
- **14in (36cm)** $250-300

Hopalong Cassidy
1949-1950.
- **24in (61cm)** $375

Saucy Walker
1951-1955. All-hard plastic with walking mechanism; original clothes; excellent hair and cheek color. MARK: "IDEAL DOLL"
- **16-17in (41-43cm)** $135-165
- **20-22in (51-56cm)** $185-225
- **Mint-in-box** $250-300

14in (36cm) *Mary Hartline*, all original.
Kathy & Terri's Dolls.

Vinyl Dolls

Posie
1954-1956.
- **Vinyl head, 17in (43cm)** $90-110

13in (33cm) *Bonny Braids.*
Doodlebug Dolls.

Saralee
1950. Black vinyl/cloth body. Designed by Sarah Lee Creech; modeled by Sheila Burlingame. Original clothes; excellent condition.
- **17-18in (43-46cm)** $300-350
- **Undressed** $125

Bonny Braids
1951. Vinyl character head; hard plastic body; original clothes; excellent condition.
- **13in (33cm)** $100-125
- **Mint-in-comic-strip-box** $200-250

Revlon Dolls
1955-1959. Vinyl head with rooted hair, perfect hair, bright cheek color; hard plastic body with jointed waist, high-heeled feet, original clothing, excellent condition.

Miss Revlon
- **18-20in (46-51cm)** $250-300
- **Mint-in-box, dress** ....$400 up
- **Mint-in-box, gown** ....$475 up
- **25in (63cm) at auction** $1,850

10½in (27cm) *Little Miss Revlon*, all original.
Kathy & Terri's Dolls.

18in (46cm) *Miss Revlon*, tagged dress.
Diane Costa.

Little Miss Revlon
 10½in (27cm) $150-175
  Boxed $225-250
Patti Playpal Family, 1959-1962.
 Patti, 35in (89cm) $500-600
  Mint-in-box $1,100
 Peter, 38in (97cm) $750-850
 Daddy's Girl, 42in (107cm) $1,000-1,200
 Miss Ideal
  25in (64cm) $175-225
  30in (76cm) $225-275
 Patti, 18in (46cm) $300-350
 Bonnie & Johnny, 24in (61cm) babies $225-250
 Penny, 32in (81cm) $275-325
 Saucy Walker, 32in (81cm) $275-325
 Patti, 1982.
  Mint-in-box $125-150
  Black, Mint-in-box $225

Tammy Family

1962-1966. Mint-in-box, deduct 50 percent for an out-of-box doll.

 Tammy, 12in (31cm) $100-125
 Pos'n Tammy,
  12in (31cm) $175-225
 Ted (big brother),
  12½in (32cm) $100-125
 Mom, 12½in (32cm) $150-175
 Dad, 13in (33cm) $100-125
 Pepper (sister),
  9in (23cm) $75-85
 Pete (little brother),
  7¾in (20cm) $150-200
 Patti (*Pepper*'s friend),
  9in (23cm) . . . .$250 up
 Dodi (*Pepper*'s friend),
  9in (23cm) $85
 Salty (*Pepper*'s friend),
  7¾in (20cm) $150-200

13in (33cm)
Tammy's Dad, boxed.
Howard & Jan Foulke.

Bud (*Tammy*'s boyfriend), 12½in (32cm) $200
Boxed outfits $30-65
Tammy Car, boxed $225

Miscellaneous Vinyl Dolls

All original, excellent coloring; perfect condition.
Lori Martin (National Velvet), 1961. 38in (97cm) $750-850
Magic Lips, 1955. 24in (61cm) $100-125
Thumbelina, 1961. Vinyl and cloth; wriggles like a real baby.
    19-20in (48-51 cm) $300-375
    Tiny Thumbelina, 14in (36cm) $225-250
    Newborn Thumbelina, 9in (28cm) $125-150
Kissy, 1961-1964. Toddler.
    22in (56cm) $110-135
    Mint-in-box $200-225
Tearie Dearie, 1963-1967. 9in (23cm) $30-40
Bam Bam, 1963.
    12in (31cm) $60-70
    16in (41cm) $90-100
Pebbles, 1963.
    8in (20cm) $40-50
    12in (31cm) $80-90
    16in (41cm) boxed $225-250
Betty Big Girl, 1968. 32in (81cm) $125-150
Little Lost Baby, 1968. Three faces, 22in (56cm), boxed ...$95-110
Flatsy, 1968-1970.
    Each with accessory $20-25
    Boxed $40-50
    Early style, boxed with frame $75-95
Joey Stivic, 1976. Archie Bunker's grandson.
    15in (38cm), boxed $35-45
Dorothy Hamill, 1977. 11½in (29cm) boxed $25
Honey Moon, 1965. From Dick Tracy comic strip,
    mint, boxed $100
Diana Ross, 1969. 17½in (45cm) $300-350
Giggles, 1966
    18in (41cm) $75-85
    Boxed $125-150

Crissy and Family

1968-1974. Growing hair dolls. all original and excellent.
    Crissy, Beautiful Crissy $125-150
    Black Crissy $175-200
    Velvet, boxed $75-100
    Black Velvet $65-75
    Cinnamon $25-35
    Black Cinnamon $75
    Mia $45-55
    Kerry $40-50
    Tressy $70-80
    Brandi $50-60
    Dina $50-60
    Cricket $225-275
    Baby Crissy $100-125
    Black Baby Crissy $100-125
    Packaged clothes $25-50

Tiffany Taylor

1974.
    19in (48cm) $30-40
    Boxed $55-65
    Black $34-45

Kenner

Blythe
1972. Changes eye color.
Excellent and all original $1,000-1,300
Boxed $1,800-2,200
Red hair $1,800-2,000

Dusty
1974. Smiling face, freckles.
12in (31cm), boxed $25-35
Outfits $10-15

Skye
1974. Black skin.
12in (31cm), boxed $25-35
Outfits $10-15

Cover Girls
1978-1980. Fashion dolls with bendable elbows and knees, jointed wrists.
12in (31cm)
    Darci $55-65
    Erica (auburn) $125
    Dana (black skin) $70-75
  Outfits $30-40

Hardy Boys
1978. Mint-in-box dolls.
Shaun Cassidy, Parker Stevenson, each $35

Star Wars
1974-1978. Mint-in-box dolls. For excellent out-of-box dolls, deduct 50 percent.
Darth Vader, 15in (38cm) $200-225
Han Solo, 12in (31cm) $450-475
Luke Skywalker, 12in (31cm) $225-250
Princess Leia, 11½in (29cm) $200-225
Stormtrooper, 12in (31cm) $175-200
Obi Wan Kenobi, 12in (31cm) $75-100
R2D2, 7½in (19cm) $125-150
C3PO, 12in (31cm) $125-150
Boba Fett, 13in (33cm) $150-175
Jawa, 8½in (22cm) $75-85
IG88, 12in(31cm) $400-450
Chewbacca, 15in (38cm) $110-135
Yoda, 9in (23cm) $65-75

Six Million Dollar Man
1975-1978. 13in (33cm) boxed figures.
Bigfoot Bionic, at auction $225
Steve Austin $175-185
Jaime Sommers $175
Bigfoot $75-85
Fembot $100-125
Oscar Goldman $80

Strawberry Shortcake

1980-1986.

Vinyl doll with pet, boxed $30-60
Boxed and complete
    Plum Pudding $120-130
    Peach Blush $125-135
    Raspberry Tart $30-35
    Lemon Meringue $30-35
    Lime Chiffon $25-30
    Blueberry Muffin $30-35
    Huckleberry Pie $45-50
    Orange Blossom $40-45
    Mint Tulip $45-50
    Almond Tea $45-50
Berry Happy Home Dollhouse with furniture $450
Attic Playset, boxed $200-225
Cloth Dolls, 16in (41cm) $20-25

Strawberry Shortcake series:
Huckleberry Pie and *Lemon Meringue*.
Rosemary Kanizer.

16in (41cm) cloth *Strawberry Shortcake*.
Rosemary Kanizer.

Knickerbocker

History Knickerbocker Doll & Toy Co New York, NY, U.S.A. 1937-on.
Head Mark "WALT DISNEY KNICKERBOCKER TOY CO."

Composition Snow White

1937. All-composition; black mohair wig with hair ribbon; original clothing; all in very good condition.

    15in (38cm) $350-400
    20in (51cm) $450-500
    With molded black hair and blue ribbon,
        13-15in (33-38cm) $350-450
    Set, 15in (38cm) Snow White and seven
        9in (23cm) Dwarfs $2,000-2,200

Composition Seven Dwarfs

All-composition; individual character faces; original velvet costumes and caps with identifying names, Sneezy, Dopey, Grumpy, Doc, Happy, Sleepy and Bashful; very good condition.

9in (23cm) each **$200-225**

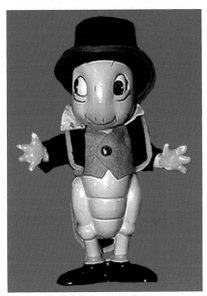

10in (25cm) *Jiminy Cricket.*
George & Kathleen Bassett.

Additional Composition Dolls

Jiminy Cricket, **10in (25cm)** **$450-550**
Pinocchio, 14in (36cm) **$550-650**
Figero the Cat **$500-550**
Blondie, 11in (28cm) all original and
     boxed, at auction **$1,680**
Dagwood, 13in (33cm) at auction **$2,970**
Alexander, 9in (23cm) **$1,500**
Baby Dumpling, at auction **$2,970**

Additional Cloth Dolls

Seven Dwarfs, 14in (36cm) each **$175-200**
Snow White, 16in (41cm) **$375-425**
Donald Duck **$500-600**
Mickey Mouse, 1935 . . . .**$550-650**
Minnie Mouse **$500**
Raggedy Ann & Andy . . . .**See page 156.**
Little Lulu, 18in (46cm) **$400-500**
Child Doll, 1935. Mask face (washable), original clothes,
    12-14in (31-36cm) **$100-125**
Little Orphan Annie and Sandy, 1977. 16in (41cm) **$25**

13in (33cm) baby of the type made by Krueger.
Howard & Jan Foulke.

Krueger

History Richard G. Krueger, Inc., New York, NY, U.S.A. 1917-on.
Head Mark Cloth tag or label.

All-Cloth Doll

Ca. 1930. Mask face; oilcloth body with hinged shoulders and hips; original
clothes, in excellent condition.

7in (18cm) $50-60
12in (31cm) $100-125
16in (41cm) $150-165
20in (51cm) $200-225

Pinocchio

Ca. 1940. Mask character face; cloth torso, wood jointed arms and legs;
original clothes, all in good condition.

15in (38cm) ....$400-450°

Kewpie

See page 121.

Dwarfs

Ca. 1937.

All-cloth, mask face,
12in (30cm) $175-200
Set of seven,
with Snow White $2,200

Scootles

1935. Rose O'Neill. All-cloth, mask face,
yarn hair.

10in (25cm) ....$450°
18in (46cm) ....$850°

13in (33cm) velveteen
monkey with Krueger tag.
Howard & Jan Foulke.

Mattel, Inc.

> **Comment** Unless otherwise indicated. all dolls should be in excellent unplayed-with condition, in original clothes with all accessories. perfect hair, excellent coloring.

Chatty Cathy Family
1960-1965.
Chatty Cathy
    20in (51cm) $225-325
    Boxed $375-475
    Black $800-1,000
    Canadian $400-450
Charmin' Chatty
    25in (64cm) $110-135
    Boxed $175-200
Chatty Baby
    18in (46cm) $95-115
    Boxed $150
Tiny Chatty Baby
    15in (38cm) $75-80
    Black $110-125
Tiny Chatty Brother, 15in (38cm) $60-70
Singing Chatty, 17in (43cm) $75-100

20in (51cm) *Chatty Cathy* in original tagged pajamas. *Norman & June Verro.*

19in (48cm) black *Chatty Cathy.* *Kiefer Collection.*

Buffy & Mrs. Beasley
1967. All-vinyl Buffy, vinyl/cloth Mrs. Beasley.
    6in (15cm) boxed $110-125
    10in (25cm) boxed $200-250
Mrs. Beasley, vinyl and cloth, with glasses.
    16in (40cm) $175-225
    Boxed $350

Skediddles
1966.
    Mint-in-package $65-85

Sunshine Family
1977.
    Boxed set $50-75
    Grandparents, boxed $45

Toddlers and Babies

All original and excellent, unplayed-with, in working condition.

Baby Secret, 1966. 18in (46cm) $50-60
Baby First Step, 1966.
    18in (46cm) $65-75
    Boxed $150
Baby Pattaburp, 1964. 16in (41cm) $40-50
Baby Tenderlove, 1970-1972.
    Newborn, 13in (33cm) $45-55
    Living, 20in (51cm) $50-60
    Brother (sexed), 12in (31cm) boxed $50-65
Cheerful, Tearful, 1966.
    7in (17cm) with play case $45-50
    13in (33cm) $45-50
Dancerina, 1970.
    12in (31cm) $30-35
    16in (41cm) $45-55
    24in (61cm) $125-150
Hi Dottie, 1969. 17in (43cm) boxed $40-50
Sister Belle, 1961. 17in (43cm) $35-40
Matty Mattel, 1961. 17in (43cm) $35-40
Timey Tell, 1964.
    17in (43cm) with watch $30-40
    Boxed $125
Tippy Toes, 1967.
    17in (43cm) with tricycle or horse, good face $70-80
    Boxed $165

Dolls from Television Shows

All prices are for mint-in-box or package dolls.

Charlie's Angels, 1978. 11½in (29cm) $35-40
Debbie Boone, 1978. 11½in (29cm) $35-40
Dick Van Dyke, 1969. 25in (64cm), talks $125
Donny Osmond, 1978. 12in (31cm) $30-35
Marie Osmond, 1978. 12in (31cm) $30-35
Jimmy Osmond, 1979. 10in (25cm) $45-50
Grizzly Adams, 1971. 10in (25cm) $30-35
Herman Munster, 1965.
    Hand Puppet $125
    Full body $200-225
How the West Was Won, 1971. 10in (25cm), each $15-20
Welcome Back Kotter, 1973. 9in (23cm), each $25-35

Liddle Kiddles

1966. Out-of-package doll with all accessories, in excellent condition. Add at least 100% for mint on card doll. **BODY MARK: "1965//Mattel, Inc//Japan"**

    Sleeping Biddle $150
    Liddle Biddle Peep $165
    Peter Pandiddle $225
    Liddle Middle Muffet $185-210
    Liddle Red Riding Hiddle $185-210
    Sizzly Friddle, mint on card $280
    Soapy Sliddle, mint on card $310
    Howard Biff Boodle $135
    Kone Kiddle $45-55
    Kologne Kiddle, mint on card $50-60
    Locket Kiddle, mint on card $45-55
    Heart Pin Kiddle, mint on card $35-40
    Bracelet Kiddle, mint on card $30-40

Zoolery Kiddle, mint on card $200
Kozmik Kiddle, mint on card $300
Pretty Priddle, mint on card $200
Kiddles 'n Kars, mint on card $160-180
Chitty, Chitty, Bang Bang, mint on card $150

15in (38cm) *Little Miss Muffet*, all original.
Kathy & Terri's Dolls.

Mawaphil Dolls

History The Rushton Co., Atlanta, GA, U.S.A. 1923-on.
Mark Cardboard hangtag.

Mawaphil Stockinette Doll
One-piece stockinette dolls, some with attached limbs; hand-painted faces,
rosy checks, painted hair; clothing usually an integral part of the body, but
may have an added item, excellent condition.
   6-10in (15-25cm) ....$75-95°

Mawaphil Cloth Character Doll
Mask face, painted features, rosy cheeks, mohair wig; cloth body, original
clothing.
   15in (38cm) ....$165-195°

Mego Corporation

Television, Movie and Entertainment Dolls
All prices are for mint-in-box or package dolls.
   Batman, **1974. 8in (20cm)** $125-175
   Penguin, **1974. 8in (20cm)** $75-85
   Captain & Tennille, **1977. 12½in (32cm), each** $40-50
   Cher, **1976. 12in (31cm)** $35-45
      Sonny $40
°Few price samples available.

CHiPs, 1977. 8in (20cm), each $20
Diana Ross, 1977. 12½in (32cm) $90-100
Charlie's Angels, 1975. 12½in (32cm), each $50-60
Happy Days, 1976. 8in (20cm), each $65-85
KISS, 1978. 12½in (32cm), each $125-175
Kojack, 1977. 9in (23cm) $65-70
Laverne & Shirley, 1977. 11½in (29cm), each $45-55
Joe Namath, 1971. 12in (31cm) $125
Our Gang, 1975. 5in (13cm) $15-20
Planet of the Apes, 1974. 8in (20cm), each $100-150
Pirates, 1971. 8in (20cm), each $100-125
Robin Hood Set, 1971. 8in (20cm), each $25-35
Starsky & Hutch, 1976. 8in (20cm), each $35-40
Suzanne Somers, 1978. 12½in (32cm) $35-45
The Waltons, 1975. 8in (20cm),
    two dolls in each box, per box $25-35
Wild West, 1974.
    Buffalo Bill, Cochise, Davy Crockett, Sitting Bull,
        Wild Bill Hickok, Wyatt Earp, each $35-40
Wonder Woman, 1976. 12½in (32cm) $150-200
Wizard of Oz, 1974.
    Dorothy, Glinda, Scarecrow,
    Wicked Witch, Tin Man,
    Cowardly Lion, each . . .$30-$35

Star Trek

1975. Fully-jointed plastic; packaged on blister card. For unpackaged dolls, deduct 50 percent.

8in (20cm)
    Captain Kirk $50-60
    Mr. Spock $35-45
    Dr. McCoy $110-125
    Mr. Scott $110-135
    Klingon $50
    Lt. Uhura $50-60
    Andorian, at auction $700
    The Keeper $175-200
    Romulan $800-1,000
    Neptunian $150
Star Trek, 1979. Mint-in-box, 12½in (32cm).
    Captain Kirk $60
    Mr. Spock $50
    Ilia $50

12½in (32cm) *Star Trek* character, boxed.
Rosemary Kanizer.

Molly-'es

History International Doll Co., Philadelphia, PA, U.S.A. Made clothing only. Purchased undressed dolls from various manufacturers. 1920s-on.
Comment Mollye Goldman was an extraordinary designer of doll costumes. Not only did she have her own company, but she worked for some of the large doll manufacturers, and did clothing for Ideal's Shirley Temple doll.
Mark A cardboard tag.

Molly-'es Composition Dolls

Beautiful original outfits; all in good condition.

Babies,
 15-18in (38-46cm) **$175-200**
Girls,
 12-13in (31-33cm) **$175-190**
Toddlers,
 14-16in (36-41cm) **$200-225**
Ladies,
 18-21in (46-53cm) **$500-550**

Internationals

All-cloth with mask faces; all original clothes; in excellent condition with wrist tag.

 13in (33cm) **$65-75**
 Mint-in-box **$100-125**

12in (31cm) Dutch girl, all original.
Howard & Jan Foulke.

Raggedy Ann & Andy

See page 156.

Thief of Baghdad Series

1939. Orange hangtag.

 Sabu, Composition, 15in (38cm) **$550-600**
 Sultan, 19in (48cm) cloth **$650-750**
 Princess, 15in (38cm) composition
  or 18in (46cm) cloth **$500-600**
 Prince, 23in (58cm) cloth **$650-750**

Hard Plastic

All original and excellent.

 Stewardess, 14in (36cm) **$425-475**

18in (46cm) bride, all original.
Mary Jane's Dolls.

Vinyl Dolls

All original and excellent.

Darling Little Women
- 8in (20cm) $25-35
- 12in (31cm) $40-50
Internationals, 8in (20cm) $15-20
Perky, 8in (20cm) $15-20

Nancy Ann Storybook Dolls

History Nancy Ann Storybook Dolls Co., South San Francisco, CA, U.S.A. 1936-on.

Comment Nancy Ann Abbott's forte was the costuming of her dolls, which made them very appealing to little girls. She used only excellent quality fabrics and trimmings, as well as special little details. By 1950, she was making and dressing two million dolls per year.

Painted Bisque Marked Storybook Doll

Mohair wig, painted eyes; one-piece body and head, jointed legs and arms; original clothes; excellent condition with sticker or wrist tag and box. Deduct 25 to 30 percent for out-of-box dolls. 5½-7in (13-19cm).

1936. Babies only. Gold sticker on dress; sunburst box.
MARK: "88 Made in Japan" or "87 Made in Japan."
- 3½-4½in (8-10cm) $450-550

1937-1938. Gold sticker on dress. Sunburst box, gold label.
MARK: "Made in Japan 1146," "Made in Japan 1148." "Japan," "Made in Japan" or "AMERICA" $700-1,000
- Molded hair $1,800

1938-1939. Gold sticker on dress; sunburst transition to silver dot box. MARK: "JUDY ANN USA" (crude mark), "STORYBOOK USA" (crude mark). Molded socks/molded hangs.
- Mark, "StoryBook Doll USA" $550-750
- Masquerade Series, each $800
- Topsy and Eva, pair $1,500
- Judy Ann $600-700
- Oriental $1,700
- Gypsy $1,500
- Pirate $1,300
- Storybook Set $4,300
- Sports Series, each $1,200
- #179 Babes in the Woods, pair, no box $2,235

1940. Gold sticker on dress; colored box with white polka dots; molded socks. MARK: "StoryBook Doll USA" $250-350
- Margie Ann $400-500
- "Pudgies" $250-350
- Hansel & Gretel, pair $1,600

1941-1942. Gold wrist tag; white box with colored polka dots; jointed legs. MARK: "StoryBook Doll USA" $110-125
- White socks $135-165
- "Pudgies" $250-300
- Black Topsy $175-200

1943-1947. Gold wrist tag; white box with colored polka dots; frozen legs. MARK: "StoryBook Doll USA" (some later dolls with plastic arms) $55-65
- Socket head $75-85
- Operetta Series $175-225
- All Time Hit Parade Series $175-200
- Powder and Crinoline Series $150-175
- Holiday inserts $80-100

Hard Plastic Marked Storybook Doll

Swivel head, mohair wig, painted eyes; jointed legs; original clothes; gold wrist tag; white box with colored polka dots, excellent condition.
MARK: "StoryBook Doll USA"

5½-7in (13-19cm) $45-50
Topsy, (black) $100-125
Holiday inserts $75-85
Big or Little Sister $90-100

Storybook Doll Babies

Bisque, Star hand $200-250
Bisque, Closed fist, open mouth $175-200
Bisque, Hard plastic arms $100-125
Hard plastic $100
Boxed furniture ....$300 up

Jesco Storybook Dolls

1986.
Boxed $15

Muffie

All-hard plastic; wig, sleep eyes, 8in (12cm) tall. **MARK:** "StoryBook Dolls USA" some with "Muffie."

1953. Straight-leg non-walker; painted eyelashes, no eyebrows, Dynel wig (side part with flip); 54 complete costumes; original clothes; excellent condition $300-400*
1954. Walker; molded eyelashes, eyebrows after 1955, side part flip or braided wig; 30 additional costumes; original clothes; excellent condition $200-250*
1955-1956. Hard plastic walker or bent-knee walker; rooted Saran wig (ponytail. braids or side part flip); vinyl head and hard plastic body; molded or painted upper eyelashes $165-185

5in (13cm) *East Side, West Side* with jointed legs, missing jacket. *Howard & Jan Foulke.*

8in (20cm) *Muffie*, molded lash walker, boxed. *Mary Jane's Dolls.*

*Allow extra for red hair.

Nancy Ann Style Show
18in (46cm) hard plastic . . .**$750-1,250**
Miss Nancy Ann
    10½in (27cm) teenage body,
         high-heeled feet **$125-150**
    Boxed **$225-250**
    Boxed outfits . . . .**$85 up**
Debbie, hard plastic toddler
    10in (25cm) **$175-200**
    Mint-in-box **$350**
Little Miss Nancy Ann, 9in (23cm)
    boxed **$225**

House of Nisbet

History House of Nisbet, Ltd., England.
1952-1995. Designed by Peggy Nisbet.
Mark Black printed paper wrist tag.

10in (25cm) *Debbie Big Sister*,
all original.
Howard & Jan Foulke.

Nisbet Portrait & Costume Doll
Historical personages and traditional characters of the United Kingdom. All-hard plastic;
portrait face, painted eyes, styled wig; body jointed at arms only; painted
shoes; original costume; excellent condition with box.
    7½-8in (19-20cm) **$25-50**
    Princess Elizabeth, wedding gown **$90**
    Princess Victoria, wedding gown **$90**
    Mary Poppins **$70**
    Judy Garland **$60**
    King James IV **$100**

Old Cottage

History Old Cottage Toys, Allargate,
Rustington, Littlehampton, Sussex, Great
Britain. 1948. Designed by Greta
Fleischmann and her daughter, Susi.
Mark Paper label - "Old Cottage Toys hand-
made in Great Britain."

Old Cottage Doll
Rubber compound or hard plastic head with
hand-painted features, wig; stuffed cloth body;
original clothing; excellent condition.
8-9in (20-23cm)
    Children and
        Storybook outfits **$115-135**
        Scotch, Pearlies **$90-100**
12-13in (31-33cm), mint-in-box . . .**$350°**

Tweedledee & Tweedledum
9in (23cm), pair **$1,000**

9in (23cm) Old Cottage doll, all original.
Howard & Jan Foulke.

°Few price samples available.

Princess Diana Dolls

Dolls must be mint-in-box, complete with all accessories and have their certificates.

Madame Alexander, 1998. Hard plastic, 10in (25cm) $50-65
Ashton-Drake, 1998. Porcelain, designed by Titus Tomescu, in blue, red or green evening gown. Edition of 5,000.
    18in (46cm) $50-60
Danbury Mint, 1982.
    Porcelain, wedding gown, 19in (48cm) $65-75
    Royal Wardrobe Collection, doll with nine outfits $150-200
    Trunk $70
Effanbee, 1982. Vinyl, wedding gown $25-30
Franklin Mint, 1998
    Porcelain, headed gown and others,
        17in (43cm) $100-125
    People's Princess, 1998. 16in (41cm) vinyl, blue suit.
        Doll only $50-55
        Boxed outfits $15-25
    Little Diana, 11in (28cm) $80
    Millennium Princess, Limited Edition of 2000 . . . .$185
    Princess of Radiance, 2003. Limited Edition of 75 . . . .$700-800
    Princess of Loveliness $250
    Princess of Sophistication $275-300
Gadco, 1998.
    Young Diana, red coat and hat, 35in (89cm) $225-250
    2001, blue brocade gown, 16in (41cm) $120-125
Royal Britannia Collection, 1997 reissue of 1982 doll. Wedding gown, **12in (31cm) boxed** $25
Peggy Nisbet, 1982.
    Wedding gown $30-35
    Engagement dress $30-35

Raleigh

History Jessie McCutcheon Raleigh, Chicago, IL, U.S.A. 1916-1920. Designed by Jessie McCutcheon Raleigh.
Comment Mrs. Raleigh came from an artistic family and always stressed the beauty and quality of her American-made dolls. She employed students from the Art Institute of Chicago to paint the faces of her dolls.
Mark None.

Raleigh Doll

All heavy composition, appropriate clothes; all in good condition.
    Child
        11in (25cm) wigged $450-500
        13in (33cm)
           molded hair $600-650
        18in (46cm)
           molded hair $950-1,050
        22-24in (56-61cm) shoulder head on cloth body, composition arms . . .$350-450
    Baby
        12in (30cm) $400
        18in (46cm) $600

12in (30cm) Raleigh baby. Howard & Jan Foulke.

Ravca

Bernard Ravca Doll

Paris, France, 1924-1939; New York, NY, U.S.A. 1939-on. Stockinette face individually needle-sculpted; cloth body and limbs; original clothes; all in excellent condition. **MARK:** Paper label, "Original Ravca Fabrication Française."

10in (25cm) French peasants . . .**$65**
16in (41cm) **$135-150**
21in (53cm) **$275-300**
American Historical Figures; George Washington, Betsy Ross, Ben Franklin and others. 9in (23cm) . . .**$100-125**
Circus Figures **$50-60**
Composition heads, bendable bodies, 7½in (19cm) **$35-45**
Crepe paper figures, 6in (15cm) **$15-25**

19in (48cm) Ravca-type peasant lady. *Howard & Jan Foulke.*

Ravca-type

Fine quality peasant man or lady.
17in (43cm) **$160-185**

Frances Diecks Ravca Doll

New York, 1935-on.

Queen Elizabeth II and others, 1952. 36in (91cm) **$330-440**
"Easter Sunday", 1973. 12in (30cm) black child **$250**
Little Women, 12-13in (31-33cm), each **$100-125**
Ballerinas, each **$100**

Reliable Toy Co.

History Reliable Toy Co., Toronto, Canada. 1920-on.
Mark "RELIABLE//MADE IN//CANADA."

Marked Reliable Doll

All-composition or composition shoulder head and lower arms, cloth torso and legs, sometimes composition legs; painted features; original clothes; all in good condition; some light crazing acceptable.

Barbara Ann Scott (Ice Skater),
15in (38cm) **$400-500**
Canadian Mountie,
17in (43cm) **$150-175**
Clicquot Club Soda Eskimo,
14in (36cm) **$125-150**
Her Highness, 15in (38cm) **$350-375**
Hiawatha or Indian Maiden,
13in (33cm) **$35-55**
Military Man, 14in (36cm) **$125-150**
Scots Girl or Boy, 14in (36cm) **$35-55**
Shirley Temple, 22in (56cm) **$1,200**
Maggie Muggins, 15in (38cm) **$165**

13in (33cm) *Highland Laddie,* all original. *Howard & Jan Foulke.*

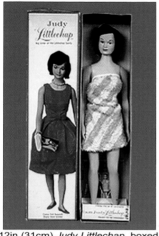

12in (31cm) *Judy Littlechap*, boxed.
Sidney Jeffrey Collection.

12in (31cm) Santon, all original.
Howard & Jan Foulke.

Remco Industries

Littlechap Family
1963. Basic doll, unplayed-with, in original box. Deduct 50 percent for out-of-box dolls.

Dr. John, 14½in (37cm) $50-60
Lisa, 13½in (34cm) $50-60
Judy, 12in (3 1cm) $50-60
Libby, 10½in (27cm) $50-60
Rooms $150-250
Office $200-300
Tagged clothes (packaged outfits) $30-75
Trunk $75

Television Programs & Personalities
All prices are for dolls that are mint, in original box.

Addams Family, 5½in (14cm), each $100-125
I Dream of Jeannie
   6in (15cm) $40-50
   Bottle Playset $85-95
Laurie Partridge (Susan Dey), 1973. 19in (48cm) $110-135
Orphan Annie, 1967. 15in (38cm) $35-45
Beatles, 1964. 4½in (11cm) set of four with guitars $350-400
Mimi Sings, 1970s. 20in (51cm) boxed $75

Santons

> History Simone Jouglas, J.P. Marinacei, Syndicat de Satonniers de Provence and others. Provence, France. 1930s to present.

Santons
Figures representing the elderly people of Provence. Clay character heads, clay hands and legs, wire armature bodies; authentic costumes, many representing various occupations and activities; all original, excellent condition.

7in (18cm) $35-45
10-12in (25-31cm) $75-100

Sandra Sue

History Richwood Toys, Inc., Annapolis, MD, U.S.A. 1952-on.
Designed by Ida H. Wood.

Sandra Sue

1952 on. All-hard plastic, slender; Saran wig, molded eyelashes; unmarked.

8in (20cm)
**Basic doll (camisole, panties, half-slip, shoes
     and socks)** $110-125
Boxed $225-250
In street dresses $125-150
In gowns $175-200
Little Women $200-225
Outfits, packaged $50-100
Bridal gown $125
Communion dress $110
Shoes $25

Cindy Lou

1951. All-hard plastic walker; Saran wig. Many outfits matched Sandra Sue's.

14in (36cm)
**Basic doll (camisole, panties, half-slip, shoes
     and socks)** $250-300
In street dresses $375-425

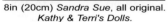

8in (20cm) *Sandra Sue*, all original.
Kathy & Terri's Dolls.

Studio Model *Sasha* dolls, late 1950s.
Annelise Norhudi.

Sasha

History Commercial production by Puppenfabrik Hans Götz, Rödenthal, Germany, 1964-1970, 1995-2001; Frido Ltd./Trendon Toys, Ltd., Reddish Stockport, England, 1965-1986. Designed by artist Sasha Morgenthaler, Zurich, Switzerland.

Comment Sasha dolls are very high quality and have an avid following of collectors who love their childlike faces and simple clothing and particularly their rooted hair. All early dolls and all brunette dolls sometimes experience hair loss, so gently pull on a few strands in numerous places on the head to check for tightness. Values are for dolls with no falling hair. If there is moderately falling hair, reduce the value by about 50%.

Sasha Course Doll, all original. *Howard & Jan Foulke.*

Studio Model

1940-1975. Handmade by Sasha in her studio. 4 face models with gypsum heads, gypsum or cloth bodies. Signed on foot.

20-21in (51-53cm) **$4,000-6,000**

Course Doll

Made by students in Sasha's studio classes. **Cloth over molded gypsum face, hand-painted features, cloth body.** **$1,500-2,000**

Götz Serie Sasha

1964-1970. All vinyl, long rooted hair, painted features; original clothing, wrist tag; excellent condition. **MARK:** Serie Sasha on head and torso.

16in (41cm) **$850-950**
"No Nose" **$1,000-1,100**
Naked or later clothes **$600-700**

Frido/Trendon

1965-1986. Unmarked. Original clothing, excellent condition. Allow 20-25% additional for box or tube.

Frido dolls, 16in (41cm) blonde or brunette
  1966-1968
    no philtrum **$3,500-4,500**
  1968 girl, hand-painted eyes,
    thin fringe bangs **$2500**
  1968 boy, jet black hair . . .**$950-1,250**
Sasha, 16in (41cm) blonde or brunette
  1968-1971 blonde
    or brunette **$450-500**
  1968-1969 blonde
    with side part **$950-1,150**
  1968-1970 dungarees,
    red braids **$1,400-1,500**
  1968-1969 ballet,
    red pony tail **$1,600-1,800**
  1968-1970 blue cord dress **$950**
  1968-1969 brown cord dress **$1,000**
  1969-1970 side part, pink dress **$1,000-1,200**
  1969-1970 kilt, 2 pony tails **$1,250**
  1970 London, brown "leather" **$800-850**
  1972-1974 . . . .**$250-350**
  1972-1973, in picture tube **$400-500**
Gregor, 16in (41cm) blonde or brunette
  1968-1969 in shorts **$1,400-1,650**
  1968-1971 all models **$250**
  1972-1974 denims **$175-200**
Sasha & Gregor, 1975-1986 . . . .**$175-275**
  Boxed **$200-300**
Cora or Caleb (black), 1972-1986 . . . .**$175-225**
  Boxed **$225-275**
Sexed Babies, 1970-1978 . . . .**$150-175**
  Boxed **$200-275**
Unsexed Babies, 1979-1986 . . . .**$100-115**
  Boxed **$125-150**

Götz *Serie Sasha,* all original. *Howard & Jan Foulke.*

1986 *Sasha Sari*, all original.
Howard & Jan Foulke.

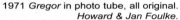

1971 *Gregor* in photo tube, all original.
Howard & Jan Foulke.

Limited Edition Dolls
Boxed

1981 Velvet	$350-375
1982 Pintucks	$225-250
1983 Kiltie	$300-350
1984 Harlequin	$300-325
1985 Prince Gregor	$250-300
1986 Princess	$1400-1600
1986 Sari	$700-800

Götz

1995-2001 .... $175-225

Dating Sashas

1966-1967	Large gold wrist tag, plain back
1968-1971	Large gold wrist tag, printed back
1971-1974	Large silver wrist tag
1975-1986	Small silver wrist tag
1969	Arms and legs with striped elastic
1970	Arms and legs with white elastic
1971-1974	Arms with white, legs with brown, tan or orange elastic
1975-1986	Arms with white, legs with brown elastic
1969-1971	Tube with colorful writing
1971	Photo tube
1972-1974	Plain box
1980-1986	Photo box

Shirley Temple

History Ideal Novelty & Toy Co., New York, NY, U.S.A. 1934-on. Designed by Bernard Lipfert.

Comment It's amazing to realize *Shirley Temple* dolls have been in production for over 70 years. Although prices have dropped for dolls in ordinary condition, examples in outstanding condition are bringing prices higher than ever.

All-Composition Child

1934 through late 1930s. Marked head and body, jointed composition body, all original including wig and clothes, entire doll in excellent condition. Sizes: 11-27in (28-69cm).

Marks	On cloth label:
On body: SHIRLEY TEMPLE 18 On head: 18 SHIRLEY TEMPLE	GENUINE SHIRLEY TEMPLE DOLL REGISTERED U.S. PAT. OFF. IDEAL NOVELTY & TOY Co. MADE IN U.S.A.

11in (28cm) $800-900*
13in (33cm) $650-700*
15-16in (38-41cm) $700-750*
18in (46cm) $750-800*
20-22in (51-56cm) $850-900*
25in (64cm) $950-1,050*
27in (69cm) $1,150-1,500*
Button $90-100
Dress, tagged . . . .$225 up
Shoes $75-125
Trunk $150-200
Carriage $400-500
Hawaiian Shirley, 18in (46cm) $900-1,000
Baby Shirley, composition/cloth; original clothing; good
condition, 16-18in (41-46cm) $1,250-1,500
Shirley at Organ, mechanical, at auction $3,500-4,000

12in (30cm) 1957 vinyl
Shirley Temple, all original.
Howard & Jan Foulke.

13in (33cm)
composition *Shirley
Temple*,
all original.
Howard & Jan Foulke.

17in (43cm) composition
Shirley Temple, all original.
Howard & Jan Foulke.

18in (46cm) composition
Shirley Temple, all original.
Howard & Jan Foulke.

*Allow 50 to 100 percent more for mint-in-box doll. Allow extra for Texas Ranger, Captain
January and other unusual outfits.

Other Composition Shirley Temples
Made in Japan, 7½in (19cm) $125-175
Reliable (Canada), all original and boxed,
   18-22in (46-56cm) $1,200

Celluloid
Japan $150-175

Cloth
Blossom Doll Co., 25in (63cm) $500

Vinyl and Plastic
Excellent condition, original clothes.
   1957
      12in (30cm) $150-165
         Boxed $225-275
         Boxed with trousseau $450-550
      15in (38cm) $225-250
      17in (43cm) $250-300
      19in (48cm) $325-350
      36in (91cm) $1,000-1,200
         Heidi Outfit $2,250
      Script name pin $40-45
      Name purse $25
      Tagged or boxed dress ....$65 up
      Black Plastic Curler Box $80
   1973
      16in (41cm) size only $50
         Boxed $100
         Boxed dress $35
   1972, Montgomery Ward, 14in (36cm) $125-150
   1982, 1983
      8in (20cm) $15-20
      12in (30cm) $20-30
   1984, Dolls, Dreams & Love, 36in (91cm) $150-175
   Porcelain, all original and boxed, Danbury Mint,
      Various models $40-60

Skookum Indians

History Created and designed by Mary McAboy, Missoula, MT and Denver, CO. U.S.A. Dolls made by various companies including Arrow Novelty Co., New York and H.H. Tammen Co., New York, Denver and Los Angeles. 1913-on.
Mark Sometimes a paper label on the sole of the foot.
Trademark Skookum (Bully Good)

13in (33cm) squaw with papoose, all original.
Howard & Jan Foulke.

Skookum Indian Doll

Composition character face, black mohair wig; Indian blanket folded to represent arms; cotton print dress or shirt and felt trousers, headband with feathers; beads; suede hoots; all very colorful; excellent unplayed-with condition.

Mailer **$20-30**
6in (15cm) **$35-45**
9-10in (23-25cm) **$75-85**
14in (36cm) **$125-175**
16in (41cm) **$200-250**
20in (51cm) **$350-450**
36in (91cm) **$1,200-1,600**

10in (25cm) black Sun Rubber dolls.
Kiefer Collection.

Sun Rubber Co.

History Sun Rubber Co., Barberton, OH, U.S.A. 1930s-on.
Marks "Sun Rubber Co." with various numbers. names and dates.

Silly and Popo

1937. Comic characters with molded clothes.
10in (25cm) . . . .**$55-65°**

Minnie Mouse

1937. In red-and-white polka dot sundress.
10½in (27cm) . . . .**$125-150°**

Bonnie Bear, Wiggy Wags, Happy Kappy, Rompy

1940s. One-piece squeeze dolls with molded clothes and hats. Designed by Ruth E. Newton.
6-8in (15-20cm) **$20-30**

So-Wee

1941. Designed by Ruth E. Newton with painted or sleep eyes. molded hair; excellent.
10-12in (25-31cm) **$65-75**

°Few price samples available.

Sunbabe

1950. Drink-and-wet baby with painted eyes and molded hair; excellent.

11-13in (28-33cm)	**$45-55**
In original box	**$110-125**
Sewing set, boxed	**$150-175**

Amosandra

1940s. From "Amos & Andy" radio show. **MARK:** "Amosandra© Columbia Broadcasting System, Inc. Designed by Ruth E. Newton."

10in (25cm) naked	**$95-125**
Boxed with accessories	**$300-400**

Baby Bannister

1954. All-vinyl drink-and-wet doll based on the famous baby photographs by Constance Bannister; excellent.

12in (31cm) naked	**$50-60**
In original box	**$100-135**

Gerber Baby

1955. All-rubber with inset eyes and molded hair, open/closed mouth; excellent.

11-13in (28-33cm)	**$100-125**
In original box	**$275-325**

Terri Lee

History TERRI LEE Sales Corp., V. Gradwohl, Pres. 1946-Lincoln NE then Apple Valley, CA, U.S.A., from 1952-Ca. 1962.

Comment Terri Lee has a large and avid following of collectors who appreciate her cute face, chubby child-like body, and extensive wardrobe of clothing, ranging from pjs to evening gowns.

Marks First dolls, "TERRI LEE PAT. PENDING" raised letters. Later dolls, "TERRI LEE."

Terri Lee Child Doll

Original wig, painted eyes; jointed at neck, shoulders and hips; all original tagged clothing and accessories; very good condition. 16in (41cm).

Composition, stiff hair	**$500-600°**
Hard Plastic	
Pat. Pending	**$525-675**
Terri Lee only	**$375-525**
Mint-in-box	**$650-750**
Talking Terri, boxed	**$600-700**
Push walker, at auction	**$975**
Vinyl head	**$600°**
Patty-Jo (black)	**$900-1,100**
Bonnie Lou (black)	**$1,300**
Jerri Lee, 16in (41cm)	**$400-500**
Benji (black)	**$700-800°**
Clothing	
School dress	**$125-150**
Party dress	**$150-175**
Gown	**$150-200**
Shoes	**$30-50**
Majorette outfit with boots	**$225**
Cowgirl outfit with hat, boxed	**$475**
Fur coat	**$125-150**
Clothes rack	**$125**
Trunk	**$150**

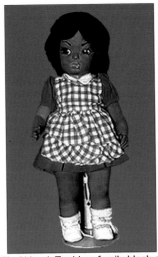

16in (41cm) *Terri Lee*, all original. *George & Kathleen Bassett.*

16in (41cm) *Terri Lee* family black girl. *Gidget Donnelly.*

Tiny Terri Lee **or** Jerri Lee, **inset eyes, 10in (25cm)** $165-185
  Boxed $250-300
Tiny Terri & Jerri Lee, **matching pair** $460
Connie Lynn $375-425
Gene Autry $1,800-2,000
Linda Baby, **10in (25cm)** $150-165
Ginger Girl Scout, **8in (20cm)** $175-200

Tiny Town Dolls

History Alma LeBlanc dba Lenna Lee's Tiny Town Dolls, San Francisco, CA, U.S.A. Trademark registered January 11, 1949.
Mark Some have a gold octagonal wrist tag with "Tiny Town Dolls" on one side and name of doll on the other.

Tiny Town Dolls

Molded felt faces with painted eyes and mouths, mohair wigs of various styles and colors; wrapped cloth bodies over wire armatures, felt hands, weighted white metal shoes, original clothes, excellent condition.
  4in (10cm)* $75-100
  Boxed $125-165

4in (10cm) Tiny Town *China Boy.* *Howard & Jan Foulke.*

*Other known sizes are 5in (13cm) and 7¼ (19cm) but no prices are available.

Tonner Doll Company

History Robert Tonner, designer and owner. 1991 on.
Comment Robert Tonner is one of the foremost designers and manufacturers of modern dolls. Production is very high quality. Collectors eagerly look for limited designs especially made for doll events. All prices are for dolls mint-in-box.
Mark on Head Tonner
Mark on Body Robert Tonner Doll Co., Inc.

American Models
1993. 19in (48cm) all vinyl.
Nude $125

Tyler Wentworth
2000. 16in (41cm) all vinyl.
C'est Magnifique Blanc, Limited Edition of 100 ....$200-225
Vienna Waltz, CU 2001 ....$200-225
Romance, 10th Anniversary, Limited Edition of 500 .....$200-225

Kitty Collier
2000. 18in (46cm) all vinyl.
Sapphire Sashay, dealers exclusive $100-150

Mei Li
2001, 16in (41cm) all vinyl. $250
Embassy Dinner, 2003. ....$430

Sydney Chase
2001. 16in (41cm) all vinyl.
Winter Nocturne, CU $260-275
Spellbinding Sydney, Halloween Convention, 2005 .....$185-195
Cinderella, 2005 Modern Doll Convention $350
Cocktails at the Plaza, CU 2005 ....$500
Focus on Fashion, 2001 UFDC $450

Regina Wentworth
2005 UFDC Souvenir.
16in (41cm) all vinyl. $200-225
Roaring 20's Outfit, UFDC Luncheon $190-200

Wicked Witch of the West Trunk Set
2005.
16in (41cm) FAO Schwarz exclusive $400-500

18in (46cm) *Kitty Collier, Sapphire Sashay,* dealer's exclusive display doll. *Sidney Jeffrey Collection.*

17in (43cm) rare-size *Pollyana*, all original. *Sidney Jeffrey Collection.*

Uneeda Doll Co.

History Uneeda Doll Co., New York, NY, U.S.A. 1917-on.

Composition Dolls

Lucky Lindy (Charles Lindbergh), **1927.**
Composition/cloth; brown aviator
suit; good condition;
14in (36cm) ....$350-$450°
Rita Hayworth as Carmen, 1948. All-
composition; red mohair wig, all
original clothes, excellent,
14in (36cm) $300-400
Toddler, Ca. 1940. All-composition, all
original clothes, very good
condition;
13in (33cm) $125-150

Hard Plastic and Vinyl Dolls

Excellent, unplayed-with condition with original clothes, perfect hair, rosy cheeks.

Dollikin, 1957. Fully-jointed hard plastic.
8in (20cm) mint-in-box $45-50
11in (28cm) mint-in-box $75-80
19in (48cm) $250-300
Boxed $350-400
Baby Dollikin, 1958. Jointed elbows and knees,
21in (53cm) $175-185
Saranade, 1962. With phonograph and record,
21in (53cm) $175-185
Pollyanna, 1960. Hayley Mills in pink-and-white checked outfit.
10½in (27cm) $35-40
17in (43cm) $125
31in (79cm) $125-175
Wee Three; Mother, daughter and baby brother.
Set $125
Boxed set $200
Suzette, 1960. 12in (31cm) $75-85
Bob, 1962. 12in (31cm) boxed $70-90
Annette Funicello, Ca. 1960. 10in (26cm) $75-85
Blue Fairy, 1959. 10½ in (25cm) $65-75
Miss Deb, 1972. 16in (41cm) growing hair, boxed $100
Tiny Teen, 1967. 5in (12cm), mint-in-bubble package $65

14in (36cm) *Bonnie Miss* with layette by Allied Grand. $295.
Rosemary Kanizer.

Vinyl Dolls

All dolls must be in excellent condition with perfect hair, excellent coloring, no discoloration and crisp original clothes.

14R Fashion Dolls
1957-1965. All-vinyl, excellent quality ladies.
19-20in (48-51cm) $40-60
Boxed $90-100

James Bond, Secret Agent 007
1965. Gilbert Toys, movie character.
12½in (31cm) boxed $100-125

Angela Cartwright
1961. Natural Doll Co., featured as Linda Williams on "The Danny Thomas Show."
14in (36cm) smiling character lace $20-25

Betty Bride
1959. Eeegee.
32in (81cm) all original $100

Ballerina
1958. Valentine.
19in (48cm) jointed ankles $90-110

Dick Clark
1958-1959. Juro Novelty Co.. personality portrait doll, original clothes.
26in (66cm) at auction $125-150

Debutante
Ca. 1960. Goldberger. high-heeled fashion doll, vinyl and hard plastic.
29in (74cm) $90-110

Flagg Flexible Play Doll
Boxed $50
Unboxed, but all original $25-30

16½in (42cm) *Judy Garland*,
World Doll Co., boxed.
Sidney Jeffrey Collection.

Grandmother
1960s. Royal Doll Co.
19in (48cm) **$85**

Hello, Dolly
1961. Kaysam. all-vinyl.
**21in (53cm), costume
from musical** **$50-75**

Honey West
1965. Gilbert Toys, hard plastic and vinyl,
painted eyes.
11½in (29cm) boxed **$125**
**Packaged #16261
Secret Agent Outfit** **$90**
Boxed #16263 gold gown **$65**
Package #16264 Pet Set **$100**

Judy Garland
1980s. World Doll Co.
16½in (42cm) **$50-60**

Lonely Lisa
1964. Royal Doll Co., vinyl and cloth, large painted eyes.
20in (51cm) **$70-90**

Man from U.N.C.L.E.
1965. Gilbert Toys, characters from television series.
12½in (31cm) boxed **$75-100**

Miss America
1957-1959. Sayco Doll Co., vinyl fashion doll.
10in (25cm) **$75-85**
18in (46cm) **$90-110**

Marilyn Monroe
1983. World Doll Co.
18in (46cm) boxed, red dress **$50-60**

Moni
1979, Uranium, Baar, Switzerland.
7½in (19cm) boxed **$50-65**

Puppetrina
1963. Goldberger. vinyl head, cloth body. hand puppet doll.
22½in (57cm) **$40-50**

Queen for a Day
1957. Valentine, vinyl fashion doll.
20in (51cm) in taffeta gown and velvet cape **$90-110**

Ginger Rogers
1983. World Doll Co.
18in (46cm) boxed **$50-60**

I Dream of Jeannie
1966, Libby Majorette Doll Corp.
All original, 19in (48cm) $200
      Boxed $300

Roxanne, Beat the Clock
1953. Valentine.
16in (41cm) boxed $250-300

Sally Starr
1960s. Philadelphia television personality.
10½in (26cm) cowgirl outfit $35-40

Lili
1955. *Bild* (German Newspaper) promotional doll, BARBIE-type.
11½in (29cm) $1,400-1,800
    In container $3,000-4,000

19in (48cm) *I Dream of Jeannie*,
Libby Majorette Doll Co., all original.
Sidney Jeffrey Collection.

Vogue

History Vogue Dolls, Inc., Medford, MA, USA. Created by Jennie Graves; clothes designed by Virginia Graves Carlson.
Clothes Label "Vogue," "Vogue Dolls" or "VOGUE DOLLS, INC. MEDFORD, MASS. USA ® REG U.S. PAT OFF"
Comment The hot Vogue doll is the early strung *Ginny*. Not only is she sweet, she has an outstanding wardrobe. Collectors avidly vie for examples in outstanding condition, which can easily sell for over $1,000. For mint-in-box dolls or especially desirable outfits such as *Tiny Miss* and *Kindergarten* series, allow 25-50% extra.

All-composition Girl
1940s. Original clothes, all in good condition, with perfect hair. **MARK:** None on doll; round silver sticker on front of outfit. May have name stamped on sole of shoe.
    7in (18cm) Valerie $265-285
    11in (28cm) Dora Lee $300-350
    13in (33cm) Betty Jane $350-400
    14in (36cm) Sandra Lee $400-450
    19in (48cm) $475-525

All-composition Toddles
1937-1948. Painted eyes looking to side, original clothes, all in good condition.
MARK: "VOGUE" on head; "DOLL CO." on back; "TODDLES" stamped on sole of shoe.
    7-8in (18-20cm) $275-325
    Boxed $400-500
  Sunshine Baby,
    molded hair $250-300

13in (33cm) *My Sisters & Me*,
all original.
Howard & Jan Foulke.

8in (20cm) strung *Ginny*, all original.
Kathy & Terri's Dolls.

8in (20cm) composition Toddles
Little Miss Muffet, all original.
Howard & Jan Foulke.

Hard Plastic Ginny

Original wig and tagged clothes, all in excellent condition with perfect hair and pretty coloring. 7-8in (18-20cm). **MARK:** On strung dolls, "VOGUE DOLLS;" On walking dolls, "GINNY//VOGUE DOLLS."

1948-1949
  Painted eyes $375-425
  Half-Century Series $1,000
  Crib Crowd Baby $800-900
  Easter Bunny Baby $1,200-1,400
1950-1953
  Painted eyelashes. strung, excellent and crisp $500-600
    Very good $250-350
  Caracul wig, poodle cut excellent $500-600
  Beryl, Cheryl, Tiny Miss, Kindergarten, Debutante,
    boxed, like new $1,200-1,500
  Queen Elizabeth II $900-1,000
  Black Ginny $2,000
  Hawaiian, boxed $950
1954, painted eyelashes, walks $300-350
1955-1957
  Molded eyelashes, walks $225-275
  Davy Crockett $350-400
  Girl Scout or Brownie $275-325
  Bon Bon, boxed $400
  Tiny Miss, Debs, boxed $350-400
  Nun $200-250
1957-1962, Molded eyelashes, walks, jointed knees $150-200
1962-on, Vinyl head, hard plastic body with
    jointed knees $80-90

Accessories

All in excellent condition.
  Ginny's Pup $200-225
  Cardboard suitcase with contents $50
  Parasol $35-40
  Gym set $350-450

Dresser, bed, rocking chair, wardrobe, vanity, each $55-65
Trousseau Tree $150-175
School bag $75-85
"Hi I'm Ginny" pin $75
Ginny's First Secret book $100-125
Swag bag, hatbox, auto bag and garment bag, each $25-35
Roller skates in cylinder $35
Hats $25-50
Headband $8-10
Dress and panties, tagged $50-75
Glasses $4-5
Shoes, center snap $40-60
Shoes, plastic $10-15
    Boxed $30-35
Locket & chain $65
Purse (Ginny) $6
Boxed Clothing, 1950-1954 . . . .$150-225
Socks, 4 pair in cylinder $55
Matching shoes, purse, necklace, bracelet, packaged $35

Vinyl Ginny
1972
    Children and internationals $10-15
    Gift Set $25
1977-on
    8in (20cm) children $10-15
    International costumes $5-10
    Sasson $5-10
    Black Ginnette $8-10

Other Dolls
All must be in excellent condition with perfect hair, excellent coloring and original clothes.
Jill, 1957. All-hard plastic, adult body.
    10in (25cm) $175-225
    Boxed outfits $75-105
Jeff, 1957. Vinyl head.
    10in (25cm) $50-75
        Boxed $100-125
Jan, 1958.
    All-vinyl $125-150
        Boxed $150-175
Ginnette, 1957. All-vinyl baby.
    8in (20cm) . . . .$125-$150
    Nursing bottle $30-40
    Baby Tender $40-50
    Crib $40-50
    Boxed outfits $50-85
Jimmy, 1958.
    8in (20cm) painted eyes $135-150
        Boxed $175-200
Lil Imp, 1959-1960. Vinyl head, hard plastic body with bent knees.
    11in (28cm) $150-200
        Boxed $250-300
Wee Imp, 1960. All-hard plastic, red hair,
    8in (20cm) $200-225
Baby Dear, 1960-1964. Designed by Eloise Wilken. Vinyl head and limbs, cloth body.
    12in (31cm) $125-150
    18in (46cm) $250-300
Baby Dear One, 1962-1963. 25in (63cm) $275-325

11in (28cm) *Lil Imp*,
all original and boxed.
Kathy & Terri's Dolls.

10in (25cm) *Jan*,
all original and boxed.
Mary Jane's Dolls.

Baby Dear Two (toddler), 1963.
 17in (43cm) $175-225
 23in (59cm) $275-325
Miss Ginny, 1962. 16in (41cm) $20-30
Ginny, 1960. 36in (91cm) $300-500
Brikette, 1961
 16in (41cm) $100-125
 22in (56cm) $150
Love Me Linda, 1965. All-vinyl, 16in (41cm) $65-75

Wright, R. John

History R. John Wright Dolls, Bennington, Vt. 1977 on
Comment R. John Wright is the leading American doll artist, creating dolls and figures of exceptional charm produced to exacting standards from only the finest materials.
Description Molded felt, hand-painted features, mohair wigs, jointed neck, shoulders and hips. All prices for are dolls in excellent, unplayed with condition with certificates and boxes, if issued.

Early Characters, 1977-1981.
 17in (43cm) Seth, Emma, Guido, Rosa, Guiseppe, MacTavish, Jenny, Maria, Bernard, Karl, Mario, Emma, Gretchen, Erica, St. Nicholas $1,000-1,300
Children, 1980 on. 16-18in (41-46cm) $800-1,200
Christopher Robin & Pooh
 Series I, 1985. 18in (46cm) $1,250-1,650
 Bedtime, 1999. 18in (46cm) $1,100-1,300
 Pocket Collection, 1998. Set of 12in (31cm) C.R., Pooh, and all friends, 8 pieces in all $3,000-3,500
  Matching numbered set, at auction $5,400

Winnie the Pooh & Piglet
- Lifesize Pooh, 1987. 18in (46cm) $800-1,000
- Lifesize Piglet, 1987. 9in (23cm) $275
- Pooh with Bee, 1988. 14in (36cm) $450
- Pooh with Honeypot, 1988. 14in (36cm) $600
- Piglet with Violets, 1988. 8in (20cm) $350

Pinocchio Series (Disney)
- 18in (46cm) Geppetto
  - & 9in (23cm) wood Pinocchio $3,700-4,000
- Geppetto Searches for Pinocchio $1,700
- 9in (23cm) Pinocchio Pleasure Island, 1992 ....$3,200
- 16in (41cm) wood Pinocchio, 2000 ....$1,500-2,000

Snow White & Seven Dwarfs, 1989-1994. Complete set $3,750
Little Prince, Centenary, 2000. 15in (38cm) $750
Kewpies, 1999 on. 6in (15cm) $500-600
Scootles, 2003. 6½in (17cm) $525-575
Golli & Miss Golli, 1996. 11in (28cm) each $400-500
Gollibaby Boy & Girl, 2000. 6in (15cm) pair $400-500
Teddy Roosevelt, 2002. 15in (38cm) $2,300

Raggedy Ann Collection
- Raggedy Ann, 2004. 18in (46cm) $900
- Raggedy Andy, 2004. 18in (46cm) $700
- Raggedy Ann, The Magical Hour, UFDC 2004.
  - 9in (23cm) $450
  - Wood bed with bedding, boxed $300

Mickey Mouse (Disney), 2005. 12in (30cm) $2,300
Musette, Candy Container, UFDC 2003 ....$350-400

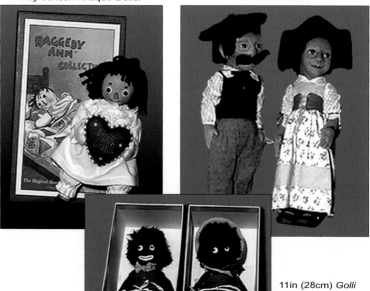

UFDC 2004 Luncheon Souvenir
Raggedy Ann, The Magical Hour.
Kay Jensen Antique Dolls.

Early characters, all original.
Diane Costa.

11in (28cm) *Golli
and Miss Golli,*
all original.
Keifer Collection.

Bibliography

Anderton, Johana
Twentieth Century Dolls. North Kansas City. Missouri: Trojan Press. 1971.
More Twentieth Century Dolls. North Kansas City, Missouri: Athena Publishing Co. 1974.

Angione, Genevieve
All-Bisque & Half-Bisque Dolls. Exton. Pennsylvania: Schiffer Publishing Ltd.1969.

Borger, Mona
China, Dolls for Study and Admiration. San Francisco: Borger Publications, 1983.

Cieslik, Jürgen and Marianne
German Doll Encyclopedia 1800-1939. Cumberland, Maryland: Hobby House Press, Inc. 1985.

Coleman, Dorothy S., Elizabeth Ann and Evelyn Jane
The Collector's Book of Doll Clothes. New York: Crown Publishers, Inc., 1975.
The Collectors Encyclopedia of Dolls, Volumes I& II. New York: Crown Publishers, Inc., 1968 & 1986

Corson, Carol
Schoenhut Dolls, A Collector's Encrclopedia. Cumberland, Maryland: Hobby House Press, Inc., 1993. .

Foulke, Jan
Blue Books of Dolls & Values, Volumes I-XVI. Cumberland, Maryland: Hobby House Press, Inc. 1974-1997.
Doll Classics. Cumberland, Maryland: Hobby House Press, Inc. 1987.
Focusing on Effanbee Composition Dolls. Riverdale, Maryland: Hobby House Press, 1978.
Focusing on Gebrüder Heubach Dolls. Cumberland, Maryland: Hobby House Press, Inc. 1980.
Kestner, King of Dollmakers. Cumberland, Maryland: Hobby House Press, Inc., 1982.
Simon & Halbig Dolls, The Artful Aspect. Cumberland, Maryland: Hobby House Press, Inc., 1984.
Treasury of Madame Alexander Dolls. Riverdale, Maryland: Hobby House Press. 1979.
China Doll Collecting. Grantsville, Maryland: Hobby House Press, Inc., 1995.
German 'Dolly' Collecting. Grantsville, Maryland: Hobby House Press, Inc. 1995.
Doll Buying & Selling. Grantsville, Maryland: Hobby House Press, Inc., 1995.

Gerken, Jo Elizabeth
Wonderful Dolls of Papier-Mâché, Lincoln. Nebraska: Doll Research Associates. 1970.

Hillier, Mary
Dolls and Dollmakers. New York: G. P. Putnam's Sons, 1968.
The History of Wax Dolls. Cumberland, Maryland: Hobby House Press, Inc.; London: Justin Knowles, 1985.

Izen, Judith
Collector's Guide to Ideal Dolls. Paducah, Kentucky: Collector Books. I999.

Izen, Judith and Carol Stover
Collectors Encyclopedia of Vogue Dolls. Paducah. Kentucky: Collector Books. 1999.

Jensen, Don
Collector's Guide to Horsman Dolls. Paducah, Kentucky: Collector Books. 2002.

Judd, Polly and Pam
Hard Plastic Dolls. Cumberland, Maryland: Hobby House Press, Inc., 1985.
Hard Plastic Dolls II. Cumberland, Maryland: Hobby House Press, Inc., 1989.
Glamour Dolls of the 1950s & 1960s. Cumberland, Maryland: Hobby House Press, Inc., 1988.
Compo Dolls 1928-1955. Cumberland, Maryland: Hobby House Press, Inc., 1991
Compo Dolls, Volume II. Cumberland, Maryland: Hobby House Press, Inc., 1994.

Krombholz, Mary Gorham
The Story of German Doll Making 1530-2000. Grantsville, Maryland: Hobby House Press, Inc., 2001.
German Porcelain Dolls 1836-2002. Grantsville, Maryland: Hobby House Press, Inc., 2002.
Identifying German Chinas 1840-1930. Grantsville, Maryland: Hobby House Press, Inc., 2005

Mathes, Ruth F. and Robert C.
Dolls, Toys and Childhood. Cumberland, Maryland: Hobby House Press, Inc., 1987.

McGonagle, Dorothy A.
The Dolls of Jules Nicolas Steiner. Cumberland, Maryland: Hobby House Press, Inc., 1988.

Merrill, Madeline 0.
The Art of Dolls, 1700-1940. Cumberland, Maryland: Hobby House Press, Inc., 1985.

Mertz, Ursula R.
Collector's Encylopedia of American Composition Dolls, 1900-1950. Paducah, Kentucky: Collector Books. 1999.

Osborn, Dorisanne
Sasha Dolls Through the Years. Annapolis, Maryland: Gold Horse Publishing, 1999.

Pardee, Elaine and Jackie Robinson
Encyclopedia of Bisque Nancy Ann Storybook Dolls, 1936-1947. Paducah, Kentucky: Collector Books, 2003.

Pardella, Edward R.
Shirley Temple Dolls and Fashions. West Chester, Pennsylvania: Schiffer Publishing, Ltd., 1992.

Richter, Lydia
Heubach Character Dolls and Figurines. Cumberland, Maryland: Hobby House Press, Inc., 1992.

Schoonmaker, Patricia N.
Effanbee Dolls: The Formative Years. Cumberland. Maryland: Hobby House Press, Inc., 1984.
Patsy Doll Family Enyclopedia. Volumes I & II. Cumberland, Maryland: Hobby House Press. Inc., 1992.

Tabbat, Andrew
Collector's World of Raggedy Ann & Andy. Volumes I & II. Annapolis, Maryland: Gold Horse Publishing, 1997.

Tarnowska, Maree
Fashion Dolls. Cumberland, Maryland: Hobby House Press, Inc., 1986.

About the Author

The name Jan Foulke is synonymous with accurate information. As the author of numerous books on dolls, including 16 editions of the *Blue Book of Dolls & Values*®, she is the most quoted source on doll information and the most respected and recognized authority on dolls and doll prices in the world.

Born in Burlington, New Jersey, Jan Foulke has always had a fondness for dolls. She recalls, "Many happy hours of my childhood were spent with dolls as companions, since we lived on a quiet country road, and until I was nine, I was an only child. My bedroom was filled with dolls and their accessories, and my mother sewed doll clothes for me."

Jan received a B.A. from Columbia Union College, where she was named to *Who's Who in American Colleges and Universities* and was graduated with high honors. Jan taught for 12 years in the Montgomery County, Maryland, school system, and also supervised student teachers in English for the University of Maryland, where she did graduate work in Education and English.

Jan and her husband, Howard, who photographs the dolls for her books, both antiqued for a hobby, and in 1972, they decided to open a small antique shop of their own. Their daughter, Elizabeth, was quite interested in dolls, and that sparked Jan's curiosity about the history of old dolls. Gradually, the stock in their antique shop evolved into an antique doll shop. At this point, they realized the need for more accurate and reliable doll information, and their writing career began.

Jan and Howard Foulke now dedicate all of their professional time to the world of dolls: writing and illustrating books and articles, appraising collections and individual dolls, lecturing on antique dolls, acting as consultants to museums, auction houses and major collectors, and selling dolls by mail order, the internet and exhibits at major shows throughout the United States. They are members of the United Federation of Doll Clubs, Doll Collectors of America and past officers of the National Antique Doll Dealers Association. Jan has appeared on numerous television and radio talk shows and is often quoted in newspaper and magazine articles as the ultimate source for doll pricing, identification and trends in collecting. They can be contacted via their web site at www.janfoulke.com.

Jan Foulke has written and Howard Foulke has done the photography for the following books: *Kestner, King of Dollmakers; Simon & Halbig Dolls, Doll Classics, Focusing on Dolls, Effanbee Composition Dolls, Treasury of Madame Alexander Dolls, Gebruder Heubach Dolls, China Doll Collecting, German "Dolly" Collecting* and *Doll Buying and Selling*. Jan has been a regular contributor to *Doll Reader*® magazine for 33 years. Her current column is the popular "Antique Q&A."

Howard and Jan Foulke.

Glossary

Applied Ears: Ears molded independently and affixed to the head. (On most dolls the ear is included as part of the head mold.)

Bald Head: Head with no crown opening, could be covered by a wig or have painted hair.

Ball-jointed Body: Usually a body of composition or papier-mâché with wooden balls at knees, elbows, hips and shoulders to make swivel joints; some parts of the limbs may be wood.

Bébé: French child doll with "dolly face."

Belton-type: A bald bisque head with one, two or three small holes for attaching a wig or stringing the body.

Bent-limb Baby Body: Composition body of five pieces with chubby torso and curved arms and legs.

Biscaloid: Ceramic or composition substance for making dolls; also called imitation bisque.

Biskoline: Celluloid-type substance for making dolls.

Bisque: Unglazed porcelain, usually flesh tinted, used for dolls' heads or all-bisque dolls.

Breather: Doll with an actual opening in each nostril, also called open nostrils.

Breveté (or Bté): Used on French dolls to indicate that the patent is registered.

Character Doll: Dolls with bisque or composition heads, modeled to look life-like, such as infants, young or older children, young ladies, adults and so on.

China: Glazed porcelain used for dolls' heads and Frozen Charlottes.

Child Dolls: Dolls with a typical "dolly face," which represents a child.

Composition: A material used for dolls' heads and bodies, consisting of such items as wood pulp, glue, sawdust, flour, rags and sundry other substances.

Contemporary Clothes: Clothes not original to the doll, but dating from the same period when the doll would have been a plaything.

Crown Opening: The cut-away part of a doll head.

DEP: Abbreviation used on German and French dolls claiming registration.

D.R.G.M.: Abbreviation used on German dolls indicating a registered design or patent.

Dolly Face: Typical face used on bisque dolls before 1910 when the character face was developed; "dolly faces" were used also after 1910.

Embossed Mark: Raised letters, numbers or names on the backs of heads or bodies.

Feathered Eyebrows: Eyebrows composed of many tiny painted brush strokes to give a realistic look.

Fixed Eyes: Glass eyes that do not move or sleep.

Flange Neck: A doll's head with a ridge at the base of the neck which contains holes for sewing the head to a cloth body.

Flapper Dolls: Dolls of the 1920s period with bobbed wig or molded hair and slender arms and legs.

Flirting Eyes: Eyes which move from side to side as doll's head is tilted.

Frozen Charlotte: Doll molded all in one piece including arms and legs.

Ges. (Gesch.): Used on German dolls to indicate design is registered or patented.

Googly Eyes: Large, often round eyes looking to the side; also called roguish or goo goo eyes.

Hard Plastic: Hard material used for making dolls after 1948.

Ichimatsu: Japanese play doll. See *Oriental Doll Section* for full description.

Incised Mark: Letters, numbers or names impressed into the bisque on the back of the head or on the shoulder plate.

Intaglio Eyes: Painted eyes with sunken pupil and iris.

JCB: Jointed composition body. See *ball-jointed body*.

Kid Body: Body of white or pink leather.

Lady Dolls: Dolls with an adult face and a body with adult proportions.

Mama Doll: American composition and cloth doll of the 1920s to 1940s with "mama" voice box.

Mignonnette: Term used in France for small dolls, but usually applied by collectors to French all-bisque dolls with swivel necks and slender limbs. When used with a capital M, it refers to the small all-bisque doll Mignonette from the French child's magazine *La Poupée Modèle*.

Mohair: Goat's hair widely used in making doll wigs.

Molded Hair: Curls, waves and comb marks which are actually part of the mold and not merely painted onto the head.

Motschmann-type Body: Doll body with cloth midsection and upper limbs with floating joints; hard lower torso and lower limbs.

Open-Mouth: Lips parted with an actual opening in the bisque, usually has teeth either molded in the bisque or set in separately and sometimes a tongue.

Open/Closed Mouth: A mouth molded to appear open, but having no actual slit in the bisque.

Original Clothes: Clothes belonging to a doll during the childhood of the original owner, either commercial or homemade.

Painted Bisque: Bisque covered with a layer of flesh-colored paint which has not been baked in, so will easily rub or wash off.

Paperweight Eyes: Blown glass eyes which have depth and look real, usually found in French dolls.

Papier-mâché: A material used for dolls' heads and bodies, consisting of paper pulp, sizing, glue, clay or flour.

Parian: Very fine quality white bisque with no complexion tint, usually used to make molded hair dolls.

S.G.D.G.: Used on French dolls to indicate that the patent is registered "without guarantee of the government."

Shoulder Head: A doll's head and shoulders all in one piece.

Shoulder Plate: The actual shoulder portion sometimes molded in one with the head, sometimes a separate piece with a socket in which a head is inserted.

Socket Head: Head and neck which fit into an opening in the shoulder plate or the body.

Solid-dome Head: Head with no crown opening, could have painted hair or be covered by wig.

Stationary Eyes: Glass eyes which do not move or sleep.

Stone Bisque: Coarse white bisque of a lesser quality.

Toddler Body: Usually a chubby ball-jointed composition body with chunky, shorter thighs and a diagonal hip joint; sometimes has curved instead of jointed arms; sometimes is of five pieces with straight chubby legs.

Topsy Turvy: Doll with two heads, one usually concealed beneath a skirt.

Turned Shoulder Head: Head and shoulders are one piece, but the head is molded at an angle so that the doll is not looking straight ahead.

Vinyl: Soft plastic material used for making dolls after 1950s.

Watermelon Mouth: Closed line-type mouth curved up at each side in an impish expression.

Wax-Over: A doll with head and/or limbs of papier-mâché or composition covered with a layer of wax to give a natural lifelike finish.

Weighted Eyes: Eyes which can be made to sleep by means of a weight which is attached to the eyes.

Wire Eyes: Eyes that can be made to sleep by means of a wire which protrudes from doll's head.

Index

Mold Number Index

Mold Number Index

343

SELECT TITLES FROM BANGZOOM

TV Guide:
The Official Collectors Guide
Celebrating an Icon

The book covers the complete run of American icon from the first, regional, te listing guides which Walter Annenberg cre n order to form the magazine in 1953, to last issue in guide format on October 9, 2 . The book includes full color reproductions of every *TV Guide* cover ever printed. It is both a collectors guide with a pricing supplement included, as well as a retrospective view of the medium.
List Price: $29.95

The Birth of Christmas
by Clifford F. Boyle

This perfect holiday gift book by author, Clifford Boyle, uses lyrical expression and spiritual imagery to educate readers on the birth of Christ. This book is illustrated with hauntingly beautiful 19th century photographs of children posing as angels. At a time when many seek to remove elements of religion from modern-day life, *The Birth of Christmas* helps its readers discover the true meaning of Christmas.
List Price: $19.95

Hallmark Keepsake Ornaments
Value Guide — 2nd Edition

Contains over 7,500 full-color photos and includes the 2006 ornaments as well as additional items collectors have requested such as Kiddie Car Classics, Legends in Flight, and Merry Miniatures. Editorials cover the history of ornaments and everything Hallmark has done to promote ornament collectability, plus "The Ornaments that Never Were," and "Collecting Hallmark With Passion" which profiles 3 prominent collectors.
List Price: $24.95

Available at www.bangzoom.com or call 1-800-589-7333.